BALZACIAN MONTAGE:

BALZACIAN MONTAGE

Configuring *La Comédie humaine*

Allan H. Pasco

UNIVERSITY OF TORONTO PRESS
Toronto Buffalo London

© University of Toronto Press 1991
Toronto Buffalo London
Printed in Canada
ISBN 0-8020-2776-8

University of Toronto Romance Series 65

Printed on acid-free paper

Canadian Cataloguing in Publication Data

Pasco, Allan H.
   Balzacian montage

   (University of Toronto romance series ; 65)
   Includes bibliographical references and index.
   ISBN 0-8020-2776-8
   1. Balzac, Honoré de, 1799–1850. Comédie humaine.
   I. Title. II. Series.
   PQ2159.C72P38 1991   843'.7   C90-095812-X

This book has been published with the generous assistance of a grant from
The Hall Family Foundations and The Kansas University Endowment
Association.

For Berdelle

Contents

1   *Disjecta membra poetæ*   3

Widespread claims that Balzac's *La Comédie humaine* is fragmented should be considered in the light of the novelist's conventions. For him, a fragment was an indication of a whole, requiring interpretation; on both small and large scales, he depended on readers to grasp the sense of these parts and to tie them together with others. Precise principles guided the novelist's claim that his work was unified. Readers who sense these guidelines will perceive Balzac's perhaps flawed and certainly incomplete cycle as a unit of exceptional rigor and consistency.

2   Image Structure   122

The continuing controversy around *Le Père Goriot*, where established critics disagree on whether Goriot or Rastignac resides at the center of the novel, provides an incentive to consider the degree of Balzac's commitment to plot as an organizing device. In fact, a study of his theoretical writings and, more important, such creations as the already mentioned *Le Père Goriot* and *Les Secrets de la princesse de Cadignan* indicate that Balzac's narration is subordinated to description, though description is usually illustrated by one or more narrations. Description, moreover, is keyed by central images which are subordinate to what Balzac called 'the generative idea [*l'idée mère*].'

Balzac's images are linked to each other and to the whole by repetition, which is played out through parallels, opposition, development, and systematic variation. This principle can be seen at work in the creations studied in the preceding chapter but perhaps more easily by observing the way Balzac brought together fragments of his previous publications to create the units titled *Splendeurs et misères des courtisanes*, *La Femme de trente ans*, and 'La Fille aux yeux d'or.' The novelist deploys details, characters, motifs, images, symbols, and repeated plots in ways that weave these writings into a tapestry of incredible density and strength.

Balzac's weak commitment to plot grew more obvious in the 1840s, as his ideas about his magnum opus clarified in his own mind, but the orientation can be seen very early in his career. Collections like *Autre étude de femme*, *Jésus-Christ en Flandre*, and *Histoire des Treize* show him successfully putting together works which earlier seemed marginally related, at best, but which gain considerable luster in their new arrangements. His skill in repeating elements continues in evidence, though it is perhaps more interesting to realize that his limited use of chronology and his important use of arrangement point to significant devices responsible for bringing the entire *Comédie humaine* into a coherent pattern.

Balzac's narrative frames are particularly skillful. In *Sarrasine, La*

Maison Nucingen, 'Facino Cane,' 'Z. Marcas,' 'Un Prince de la Bohème,' and 'Le Chef-d'uvre inconnu' his frames serve not only to highlight through parallels, but also to emphasize oppositions and to cast light outward both onto the incorporating *Comédie humaine* and onto reality itself. Balzac was acutely aware of context, which he used to frame and, also, to suggest that other visions could be conceived (if not perceived) in the interstices of his works.

La Comédie humaine reveals Balzac's intuition of a non-Aristotelian world, where causal and chronological sequences are subordinated to the entire configuration or image. As the novelist said repeatedly, he relied primarily upon 'idea' and 'image' to unify his individual and corporate works. While readers are generally agreed about the consistent philosophy undergirding the cycle, it is perhaps now possible to see how the philosophical position is reflected in the techniques bringing the carefully arranged, constituent units of the *Comédie* into a whole. Balzac was the master, not of collage – the construction of a whole from isolated pieces – but of montage... he regularly constructed wholes from other wholes, which he then cast into the magnificent vision of *La Comédie humaine*.

Acknowledgments

Years ago, as a young, inexperienced professor, I was asked to teach the courses of a colleague who had left in mid-term. It was a survey of nineteenth-century French literature, which should have presented little problem. To my dismay, however, my former colleague's syllabus was full of Balzac, a writer about whom I was sadly unprepared. While in graduate school, I had rapidly perused a novel or two, and I had absorbed enough critical commentary to get through doctoral examinations, but I found myself standing in front of a particularly bright class of undergraduates at the University of Chicago. I remember that class vividly. Sure that their favorite game was 'get the prof,' to say that I was frightened understates the case. I immersed myself in *La Comédie humaine*, reading night and day, and, strangely, what began as a burden rapidly became a joy, indeed, a life-long passion. I am grateful to those intelligent, curious, aggressive students and to the circumstances that put me with them.

Working on Balzac has tremendous advantages, for he has had many intelligent exegets. I have never been alone. Not only have I called on generous colleagues like Wayne Connor, Alexander Fischler, Anthony Pugh, and David Rubin, but excellent editions are easily available, and fine scholars and critics have solved what in less widely read writers presents annoying problems and dangerous traps. I could not have written what follows without the help of my predecessors.

Portions were previously published. An early version on *Le Père*

Goriot appeared in *French Forum* 7 (1982): 224–34, one on *Les Secrets de la princesse de Cadignan* in *Romance Quarterly* 34 (1987): 425–33, and one on *Splendeurs et misères des courtisanes* in *L'Esprit créateur* 22 (1982): 72–81. I am grateful for permission to reprint.

Abbreviations

Unless otherwise mentioned, all references to Balzac's work are to Pierre-Georges Castex's edition of *La Comédie humaine*, 12 vols, Bibliothèque de la Pléiade (Paris: Gallimard 1976–81). I shall refer to it without any attribution other than volume and page. When I call on other editions, usually to refer to the comments of editors, I precede the volume and page numbers with the following abbreviations:

HH: *Œuvres complètes de Balzac*. Ed. Maurice Bardèche. 24 vols. Paris: Club de l'Honnête Homme 1968–71.

FR: *L'Œuvre de Balzac, publiée dans un ordre nouveau par des écrivains d'aujourd'hui*. Ed. Albert Béguin and Jean A. Ducourneau. 16 vols. Paris: Formes et Reflets / Club Français du Livre 1949–55.

CI: *La Comédie humaine*. Ed. Pierre Citron. 7 vols. Collection l'Intégrale. Paris: Seuil 1965–6.

BALZACIAN MONTAGE

CHAPTER ONE

Disjecta membra poetæ

As the post-structuralists have insisted on the separation between the sign and its referent, so they have also stressed discontinuity. 'Fragmentary,' 'dismembered,' 'cut up,' 'parceled,' 'disintegrated,' 'deconstructed'... these words and synonyms fill recent criticism. Whether the critics have merely chosen works exemplifying such traits – concentrating on Joyce in preference to Proust, on Thomas Pynchon rather than García Márquez – or whether they follow Roland Barthes's advice and break up the text themselves,[1] or whether, finally, a disintegrating civilization is reflected in both works and their readers, there can be no question of the vision offered in today's criticism. Nor are readings of fragmentation limited to contemporary art. Through a conscious misprision, even the most stable productions are destabilized. Pascal's God is ignored, for example, and the *Pensées* shatter. Zola's referential conventions are denied their referents, and the edifice of his world collapses. I am reminded of Balzac's vivid portrayal of the beauty's post-ball dismemberment in 'Ferragus.'

> Most women, returning from a ball, impatient to go to bed, let drop their dresses, their wilted flowers, their bouquets whose odor has faded. They leave their little slippers under a chair, . . . taking out their combs, carelessly unrolling their tresses. It matters little to them that their husbands see the hooks, safety pins, artificial fasteners which hold up the elegant edifices of their hairdos or finery. No more mystery, everything is revealed to the husband, no more makeup for the

husband. The corset most often lies where it falls, if the sleepy maid forgets to take it away. Finally, the whalebone stays, the armholes lined with gummed taffeta, padding, false hair sold by the hairdresser, all the artificial woman is scattered there. *Disjecta membra poetæ*, the sham poetry so admired by those for whom it was conceived and elaborated, the pretty woman clutters the whole room. (V.839)

Although Balzac seldom allowed readers into the 'dressing room' of his masterpiece, *La Comédie humaine*, it would be amazing if his patchwork had passed unnoticed, for the patently fragmented nature of his universe cannot be denied. There is in fact nothing new in recent recognitions of his 'discontinuous style' or, on a larger scale, of 'a very modern discontinuity.'[2] Not everyone views the Balzacian fragmentation favorably, of course. Herbert Hunt mentions 'a certain disparateness in the ingredients' of 'La Fille aux yeux d'or' (1834–5), remarking that the story's introduction might have better served as 'a preface to the *Scènes de la vie parisienne* in their entirety, than as a prelude to a very strange story.'[3] Pierre Macherey mentions the frequent 'gaps' in the novelist's 'disparate text.'[4] Pierre Barbéris thoughtfully proposes that as an overview, 'perhaps it is very simply more useful here to accept the notion of a disparate text.'[5] Often the transitions between narrative blocks remain absent or so cursory that, as in *Splendeurs et misères des courtisanes* (1838–47), what might have been a masterpiece seems on first perusal so flawed as to be scarcely worth reading. In the typical Balzacian novel, Gaëton Picon says, 'The unity of action . . . is rather doubtful' (FR III.10). Seldom is there much of anything tying the various novels together and to the whole of the *Comédie humaine*. Early on, Sainte-Beuve said flatly that in Balzac's 'numerous productions . . . there is a frightful jumble.'[6] Indeed, on considering the way the expository opening of 'La Fille aux yeux d'or' fits with the subsequent story of Henri de Marsay and Paquita Valdès even the most charitable might come to the conclusion that the 'stones' of Balzac's 'edifice' have very little mortar and are occasionally separated by discomfiting gaps. S. de Sacy observes wryly, '[W]hen [Balzac] wants to put his novels in order, he renounces the resources of chronology, he breaks the destinies and links, he isolates *Goriot* from the *Illusions*, the *Illusions* from *Splendeurs et misères*, he smashes his own construction to bits, and he disperses the pieces to the four corners of the *Etudes* and *Scènes*; perhaps he has an old account to settle with time?' (FR VI.930–1). Balzac seldom explains the lacunæ. When he does, his explanations not infrequently are only slightly less cavalier than Stendhal's frequent protestations of haste. In one instance Balzac even claims that it is up to the reader to complete a character by putting several traits and their causes together (V.119). Confronted by apparently total fragmentation, some critical essays invite us to marvel at the shambles; others encourage us to script our own text.

Lucien Dällenbach provides examples of both attitudes when he considers *La Muse du département,* a work which recommends itself, he suggests, because it reflects reading activity across the fictive reception of 'a dilapidated text'[7] and thus permits 'a modern reading accorded to the fragmentary' (ibid.). Dällenbach's intelligent articles constitute an attempt to salvage (*récupérer*) *La Comédie humaine* into the ken of post-structuralist criticism. Dällenbach concentrates on the novelist's claims of unity, the narrator's hints of coherence, and the textual reality of fragments separated by gaping blank spaces, and he points to the conflicts between fragment and whole. Having accepted one current orthodoxy, which holds as a canon of faith that modern readers reject texts considered 'readable' (*lisibles*), he is struck by the fact that they continue to enjoy Balzac. And they do.[8] By 'readable' works, he means those that attempt to explain everything chronologically or logically, that flee the contradictory and the unresolved, that encourage the reader, not to script his own text, but to accept passively the one presented – *read* rather than *write* – and thus imagine the text within well determined limits. If one may believe Balzac's prefaces and pseudonymous apologies, *La Comédie humaine* leaves the reader little or none of the liberty that many recent critics believe essential to modern enjoyment.[9] Faced with the seemingly irreconcilable opposition between readers' manifest pleasure in Balzac's masterpiece, despite its problematic qualities, Dällenbach returns to Balzac's apparently asystematic junctures separating presumably unified scenes, novels, and parts. He then argues that these empty, 'blank' spaces reveal the fragmentary nature of Balzac's monumental work.[10] The 'completude,' that is, 'exhaustiveness,' for which Balzac putatively strove is thus 'mythical,' by which Dällenbach means that it does not exist though it serves as an enticement. Far from dismayed by his conclusion, he sees the evidence of Balzac's 'failure' to achieve unity as the very reason modern readers return repeatedly to the nineteenth-century novelist.[11]

Dällenbach's argument that readers enjoy fragmentary works, which allow them the unrestricted freedom to create something of their own, highlights certain problems with recent critical theory. We get so involved in the steps of the theory that we forget to question the axioms. Simply put, the fact that Balzac designed his system to prevent the reader from creating in ways that would deviate from his design does not mean that the reader cannot read, create, enjoy. All creation is structured, and indeed human pleasure demands structure. Lack of structure is chaotic and frightening, unstructured creation senseless. Balzac said that the 'empty spaces' (blancs) permit the reader to create, and they do, but the creation involved is carefully constrained by the surrounding context, whether fictional or societal. Furthermore, we forget that Balzac was working with different conventions. No one – neither Balzac nor his readers – doubted that reality was unified. It never occurred to authors that readers might not seek the principles that give order, coherence, unity to their works. One of Realism's more powerful devices for increasing verisimilitude was, for example, to concentrate on the way representative parts operated. Writers like Flaubert assumed that the reader would automatically move metonymically from part to part with a vision of the whole. Though they did not explicitly state that readers should show such good will, the implicit exigency is clear. On both small and large scales, Balzac knew and depended on the fact that people reading his work would seek to tie things together.[12] They are implicitly invited to interpret according to the context, to 'close' the parts according to the design implied by the text or texts. In short, while nineteenth-century readers lived within the convention of wholeness and unity, certain modern critics with different socially imposed conventions resist closure and seek fragmentation and chaos.

In the following pages, I hope to come to grips with the way Balzac's *Comédie humaine* is organized.[13] It seems to me that precise principles guided his claim and assumption of unity. By concentrating on the Balzacian text itself, I think one can understand the empty spaces, the gaps interrupting certain stories, the incompletions, and the absences as they occur across the length and breadth of his oeuvre, for one perceives why Balzac did not feel them to be a problem. On several occasions he explained the plans he held for the entire work, though for a detailed explanation his 'Avant-propos' directs readers to the explanations given by Félix Davin. Balzac meant his cycle to be broken into three parts or *études* (studies). The *Etudes de mœurs* would consider particular social 'effects,' with a view to universals and types. Then the *Etudes philosophiques* would focus on the causes. Finally the *Etudes analytiques* would present the principles. As he explained to Mme Hanska, '[A]s the work spirals up to the heights of thought, it grows close together and is condensed. If 24 volumes are necessary for the *Etudes de mœurs*, only 15 will be necessary for the *Et[udes] phil[oso-phiques]*; only 9 are necessary for the *Etudes analytiques*.'[14]

The *Etudes de mœurs* were to be broken into six *scènes* (in the 'Avant-propos' he calls them 'six books' – I.18): *Les Scènes de la vie privée, de Province, parisienne, politique, militaire,* and *de campagne*. He saw the first section on private life as representing infancy and adolescence. Davin explains, 'There, principally emotions, unconsidered sensations; there, sins less willful than as the result of inexperience with customs and through ignorance of the world's ways' (I.1146). These episodes are not limited geographically; they come from the countryside, from the provinces, and from Paris. However, not only are the *Scènes de la vie de Province* limited in subject matter – '[they] are destined to represent this phase of human life where passions, calculations, and ideas take the place of sensations, thoughtless impulses, images accepted as realities' (ibid.) – but in setting as well. Though not neglecting the inescapable relationships to Paris, they are centered on provincial life: 'the daily clash of moral and financial interests that elicits drama and sometimes crime in the midst of what in appearance is the calmest of families' (ibid.).

The *Scènes de la vie parisienne* are of course set in the capital city and in what Davin, using Balzac's vocabulary, calls 'the age bordering on decrepitude' (I.1147). In Paris 'true feelings are exceptions and are quelled by the play of selfish interest, crushed between the cogs of this mechanical world; virtue is maligned; innocence is sold, passions give way to ruinous tastes, to vices' (ibid.). Everything and everyone is for sale. Davin tells us that Balzac's interest in individuals ends here. The *Scènes de la vie politique* take up the interests of groups, as do the *Scènes de la vie militaire*. In the *Scènes de la vie de campagne*, however, we find 'in a way, the evening of this long day' (I.19).

For the *Etudes philosophiques*, the author says, 'Life itself is painted at grips with Desire, the origin of every Passion' (ibid.). He leaves the *Etudes analytiques* with little comment, however; the latter were, as he says, largely incomplete (ibid.). In short, Balzac discussed the outline of *La Comédie humaine* at length, allowing us to be quite certain of the contour, if not the detail, of the whole. His direction is clear.

I am not the first to look at the organization of Balzac's massive work. Though only a few studies attempt to elicit the principles organizing *La Comédie humaine*,[15] everyone who has approached an aspect of the entire cycle cannot fail to have dealt with the whole and wholeness to some degree. Most obviously, given the importance of reappearing characters, Ethel Preston's early and Anthony Pugh's recent studies were actively involved in an essential feature of the work's unity. In other instances, though perhaps less obviously, when someone like Martin Kanes approaches Balzac's oeuvre thematically and considers Balzac's theory of language, he is effectively providing a helpful overview.[16] Nonetheless, while I make no claims for discovering the problem of Balzac's theory of unity, I can perhaps shed a brighter light on how he hoped to achieve it.

I have come to believe that certain principles governed placement and conjunction within Balzac's *La Comédie humaine*. It would be possible to study the chronology of Balzac's conceptualization of those principles, just as many scholars have been interested in the sequence of Balzac's creation. Some of the necessary dates are easily available; most others can be deduced. That is not, however, my purpose. Likewise, while I can say with no hesitation that, though the principles I shall detail came to the novelist at different times and, often, over time, he was conscious of them by the early 1840s (and in some cases long before). Balzac's relatively early understanding of what gave his work unity explains why, despite his many attempts to resolve discrepancies in his characters' lives, his revisions show little concern for coordinating the plots of contiguous texts by either chronological or causal means. But neither is that my purpose. I come instead to the definitive text, which I take to be – with some exceptions – the corrected Furne edition as published in the Pléiade volumes from 1976 to 1981.[17] In short, I am interested in Balzac's final optic, the lens that allows today's reader to view *La Comédie humaine* as a magnificently unified monument (though with a few disturbing gouges), rather than as a collection of bits and pieces that the author jumbled together here and there through the years. In no way do I deny the interest of Balzac's creative process. I merely wish here to limit my efforts to considering the principles operative for us as we plunge into Balzac's marvelous world. The most important are the following:

1. *Narration is subordinated to description, though description is usually illustrated by one or more narrations.*

Because reading for plot has caused considerable confusion, I shall spend a fair amount of time on this point. Balzac's descriptions are extraordinarily well organized and focused.

2. *Description is keyed by one or more central images, which are subordinated to what Balzac called* l'idée mère *(generative idea). Whether as concept or image, Balzac consistently sought some sort of principle that would unify all aspects of his works.*

In general, these major images are symbols which can be fleshed out in several ways. Occasionally the image is revealed in the title, as Balzac does with fatherhood in *Le Père Goriot*;[18] elsewhere, readers are introduced to the central symbol in long introductions, as in the case of the masks of *Splendeurs et misères des courtisanes*. Balzac may have been inspired by the image itself, being led, for example, from the masks of the first pages of *Splendeurs* to the disguises of the spies or the pseudonyms of criminals. To this degree, it is appropriate to recall that images are complexes composed of elements which may generate other images. Although we seldom know whether the generative image came first or subsequently, the high incidence of, say, orphans in the *Scènes de la vie parisienne* is tantalizing to consider. Did the extraordinary selfishness of a series of characters lead the author to construct the orphan image, or did Balzac's synthetic overview of a society where individuals were cut off from the institutional restraints of Family, Church, and King elicit this image, which then spawned characters as diverse as Montriveau or Xavier Rambourdin? It may not matter, of course. Whether as a character type like a miser, or as the incarnation in M. Grandet, or in Gobseck, they are important in the conceptual unity of the whole.

It would be a mistake to neglect the didactic side of Balzac – 'He is taken for a novelist, but he is also a student of the human condition [*un moraliste*],' Bardèche reminds us.[19] The author of *La Comédie humaine* had a clear conception of society as a whole and of humanity's place in it. As he says in the 'Avant-propos,' taking off from Voltaire: 'Man is basically neither good nor evil, though he is born with instincts and aptitudes; Society, far from corrupting him, as Rousseau claimed, perfects him, improves him, but self-interest then significantly encourages his bad propensities' (I.12). Behind every novel and short story, behind the cycle as a whole, was a system of expository thought which summarized Balzac's view of society and the steps necessary for its amelioration. Eventually it becomes possible to state, 'The unity of *La Comédie humaine* results especially from the organic unity of the society Balzac created.'[20] In *Louis Lambert* we see the interplay of pure ideas: 'Vision expresses itself through the mysterious phenomenon of the Word. Everything in the universe is indicative of an hierarchical order. Over and above the three realms of nature is the world of ideas. Ideas are living creatures, active and activating, like flowers.'[21] Although there might not always be an image, inclusive ideas always undergird the novels and short stories of *La Comédie humaine*.

In the largely positive essay where Balzac discussed *La Chartreuse de Parme*, he did however criticize Stendhal on the basis of what he considers 'the fundamental principles of Art. The dominant law is Unity of composition; whether you place this unity in the generative idea [*idée mère*] or in the framework, if it is lacking there is nothing but confusion.'[22] Balzac saw himself as a 'historian of customs' (e.g., IV.962) whose task was to find adequate syntheses which would then serve as his work's unity: 'Consequently, the author's business is for the most part to come to synthesis through analysis, to depict and assemble the elements of our life, to posit the themes and to prove them all together, to paint finally the enormous physiognomy of a century while picturing the principal characters' (II.267–8).

On the level of the detail, which Balzac emphasized continually – he said, for example, '[T]he author firmly believes that details alone will from now on make up the merit of works improperly termed *Novels* [*Romans*]' (I.1175) – he was clearly conscious of the unity provided by repetition.

3. *Images are linked to each other and to the whole by repetition, which is played out through parallels, opposition, development, and systematic variation.*

The repeated elements may be something as important as the author's concern that the youth of France was being wasted in the July Monarchy's gerontocracy, or they may be nothing more than details, motifs that make up larger images, for example, the red of Paquita's bedroom repeated in her blood as it is later spilled. Occasionally, the repetition is extremely subtle and intricate imagery, for example, in Paquita's love nest shaped like a shell and her mother's name, Concha (shell). It may be in terms like 'a "genteel" lady [*une femme comme il faut*],' which Balzac dealt with at length in *Autre étude de femme*, or it may be the anecdotal tone which gives this work considerable unity. One might also wish to empty certain plots of specific actors, leaving an empty form which I label a 'plot system' or a 'narrative armature.' Balzac was very skillful at using such abstract narrations to unify. I think of the penetration plots of the stories in *Histoire des Treize* or the filial disobedience theme in *La Femme de trente ans*. It may seem strange to consider a plot as an abstract form into which various materials can be set up, but such a concept was clearly in Balzac's mind. As he said in the 'Avant-propos,' 'It is not just men but also the principal events of life which are expressed as types. There are situations, typical phases, which arise in everyone's existence, and that is what I have most sought to represent accurately' (I.18). As he repeats these events and movements in different lives, he emphasizes their analogous nature and points to the underlying armature.

Varying stories that are in fact from the same plot system make the reader conscious of how the global structure is brought together and unified.[23] The same may be said of the images, as I mentioned previously. When such complexes are manifested in different ways, through repetition of the central image, albeit with variations – for example, the monsters of *Histoire des Treize* – the analogous representations serve to unify. The secret leagues in *Un Curé de Tours* and *La Rabouilleuse* help link the two works to each other and to *Les Célibataires*. It is also worth noting that such factions are not absolutely out of control in the family-dominated realm of the provinces, but nothing restrains them in the egocentric world of Paris and the *Histoire des Treize*. Characters, as well, tie various episodes of a work together when they appear repeatedly, but they also serve as links joining specific works to others and to the incorporating *scènes*. Viewed as types – mentor,[24] master, victim, violator, villain – they permit more complex forms of variation. One thinks of the ways the plebeian, bourgeois, and aristocratic classes of the victims are varied paradigmatically in *Histoire des Treize*, or the increasing penetration revealed in the three stories that make up the work. Similarly, though perhaps more subtly, when the female guide of *Jésus-Christ en Flandre* tells the author, 'You are my son,' the allusion suggests that the author may become a savior, analogically relating him to the Savior of the collection's legendary first panel. One understands how Balzac can say, 'It is not enough to be a man, one must be a system' (I.1151).

In fact, whether motifs or characters, such details never stand alone. They join with others to create larger entities and, finally, are an important part of the unity of *La Comédie humaine*. For this reason, while not denying the importance of detail, Balzac can say without contradiction, 'The work which the author is creating will one day be recommended much more for its range than for the value of its details'

(III.37). In all cases, as Félix Davin expressed it, '[T]he distinctive task of art is to choose the scattered parts of nature, the details of truth, in order to create of them a homogeneous whole' (I.1164).

In the process of finding just the right arrangements, Balzac shifted the position of specific works regularly. Occasionally, he did so because he needed a piece to fill out a volume. At other times, he had changed his mind. Accordingly some critics have felt they could legitimately reorganize *La Comédie humaine*. The best-known example of radical disregard for the author's expressed arrangement is, of course, the Formes et Reflets edition, where Albert Béguin and Jean A. Ducourneau organized the cycle in the chronological order of the fictional setting, but this is not the only case.[25] I suggest that we should respect our best understanding of Balzac's last wishes regarding the arrangement of *La Comédie humaine*.

4. *The unchronological arrangement of* La Comédie humaine *can be explained by the consistent esthetic vision of the entire work.*

The number of times that specific texts changed position within the cycle does not indicate Balzac's lack of interest in the order his novels and short stories finally took. There can to the contrary be no doubt of his perhaps exaggerated efforts to place each work exactly right. Since, in general, we accept the Furne edition, which Balzac corrected as the definitive edition of individual creations, we should do likewise for the organization of the entire oeuvre.

I am reminded of Balzac's pathetic complaint to Mme Hanska on 27 March 1836: 'The month of May '36 approaches, and I will be 37; I am still a nobody, I have finished nothing, and not done anything grand, I have only amassed stones.' It was not the only time he was to use this image. Earlier, he openly discussed the fact that his works had appeared in seemingly random order. He explained it as a result of changing fashion, his need for variation to renew his inspiration during the gargantuan labors, and so on. 'Consequently, a given fragment had nothing philosophical and suited the *Scènes de la vie privée*, while another scene was an *étude philosophique*, but the fatal exigencies of commerce, the needs of the moment transposed them' (X.1202). Nonetheless, '[t]he author no more worried about these transpositions than an architect inquires about the place on the building site where the stones with which he is to make a monument have been brought' (ibid.). It is only after the structure has been erected that the position of the building materials matters. During the building process, each window, door, lintel, and door knob can be appreciated in itself and compared with similar items, but total appreciation can only be achieved when the edifice is standing complete and ready for habitation. 'But it is not with these supposedly little things exactly as with stone blocks, scattered capitals destined for columns . . . which, seen at the building site, . . . seem insignificant and which the architect destined in his plans to decorate some rich entablature . . . and to run along the big intersections of his cathedral's rib vaults' (X.1206). The order of their creation, the order of their publication, the way the rocks were piled, none of these factors makes a difference to the final order of the monumental *Comédie humaine*. It is only after the stones have taken their appropriate place – whatever that may be and however often the builder/author may have changed his mind – that position and order matter.

Certainly, though no one would insist that every reader begin with the cycle's 'Avant-propos' and end with the final *Pathologie de la vie sociale*, there are special pleasures for those who read (or consider) each of the 'stones' of *La Comédie humaine* in its appointed place. The multiple points of view on probity in *Histoire de la grandeur et de la décadence de César Birotteau* gain more than a little, for example, when seen in the context of *La Maison Nucingen*. César Birotteau is honest; we are told so repeatedly. But some have wondered about the integrity of a man who will claim that his product is superior to the competition because he uses hazelnut oil, when in fact any oil would have the same effect. It never even occurs to César to question the ethics of his advertising campaign, any more than would one of today's pharmaceutical firms claiming superiority for their aspirin over the competitors' chemically identical pill. No one would doubt the dishonesty of claiming virtues that a product lacks, of course, but César's *Huile céphalique* apparently has beneficial effects for the balding, and the novelist's silence would indicate that the ads are perfectly ethical for his day. Still, incomplete truth is not up to the highest of standards, and one might be justified in summarizing César's behavior as, if not dishonest, at least somewhat tainted honesty. When held up in comparison with Nucingen, however, he shines with virtue. Though Nucingen apparently breaks no laws, he knows full well that he is defrauding others. In this case, he is cheating not just a ruffian like Philippe Bridau, as he does in *La Rabouilleuse*, but friends, widows and orphans. Few would fail to view Nucingen with serious reservation. It might be possible, however, to mention his clearly immoral, though perhaps legal, dishonesty. Whatever the case may be, our appreciation for both César and Nucingen are enhanced by reading the two works together.

Balzac always thought of his works as a part of a whole. Occasionally he frames his creations explicitly. Such frames are skillfully constructed. Like any good frame, they limit, define, intensify, but Balzac almost always succeeds in making them do more. The incorporating fiction usually sets up a parallel or an opposition with the enclosed story which operates rather like a tuning fork that begins at some point to reverberate. The reader becomes increasingly conscious of the resonances as he proceeds through the fiction. The author did not stop there. He envisaged every single one of his works as being within the compass of its *Scène*, its *Etude*, and indeed of the whole of *La Comédie humaine*. One might call this its context, whether in the entire cycle or in the reality that served Balzac as a backdrop. In the 'Avant-propos,' he mentions that the enormous number of lives included in his work 'required frames and, if I may be excused this expression, galleries' (1.18). Readers of his prefaces might be surprised by the apology, since his analogy is by no means new. Félix Davin, for example, compares the *Etudes de mœurs* to 'a gallery of paintings cleverly divided into rooms each of which has its purpose' (X.1204). Even more interesting, Balzac's spokesperson says that 'the big rooms' of this particular gallery 'are infinitely extended' (X.1207). For Balzac there were no gaps. He merely chose and framed the segment to be shared with his readers. Then he created the gallery in which he carefully arranged the show. Although there were spaces between the various 'paintings' (X.1205), he could have inserted something in every single space. For him the lives in *La Comédie humaine* were continuous and flowed into the reality of his day. Balzac carefully chose the appropriate gallery, setting each work with its own lighting and context. In addition, the gallery was in the world, with doors opening onto the street. Balzac's frames enclose, but they also open to give additional definition, intensity, and meaning.

5. *Balzac's works, often placed within an explicit frame, are always set within an implicit context, which is essential to the creation.*

Certain of Balzac's terms, particularly those denoting small parts, cause modern readers significant confusion. There is, indeed, no doubt that we misinterpret some of his vocabulary, particularly words referring to the microcosm: 'fragments,' 'pieces,' 'details,' and 'small stones.' When, for example, Balzac calls his works 'fragments' of the whole, we tend to construe the fragment as a broken, isolated piece, empty of significance, which is put into what Balzac called a 'mosaic' that gave the piece its only significance. We might incorrectly imagine that he wished to suggest that each individual novel, novella, short story (or fragment) was an incomplete bit which was meaningful only in relation to the whole, a torn piece of paper in the midst of a gigantic collage of more or less successfully integrated parallels, oppositions, continua, and interruptions.

By fragment Balzac meant something very different. For him all 'fragments' trail clouds of glory. They imply the whole from which they come and through which the genius, seer, magus can grasp the previous whole as well as the present one into which the fragment has been inserted – just as Cuvier could take a random bone and conceive an entire prehistoric animal (X.75). One might say that Balzac's fragments resemble molecular structures. Each fragment is whole, as is a molecule. When two molecules adhere, the individuality of each remains, as does the newly created whole. We do not understand precisely why molecules adhere to each other. Yet when inserted into another whole, each continues as part of two wholes. Balzac had a vision of the entirety of his work, and, though he frequently announced (and received advances for) future creations, to the annoyance of his editors he often failed to write them. Other ideas distracted him. Still, whether merely announced, cursorily sketched, or actually completed, all fit into the whole. The 'blank spaces' are rendered less noticeable by reappearing characters and a common epoch, by a similar vision of society, and by analogy. But there are other mechanisms at work. I think, for example, of the many announced but never completed *études*. The fact that he did not actually write some of these works does not negate their importance in *La Comédie humaine*. In a particular sense, they do exist. They suggest an unseen backdrop teeming with life and import.

Some of Balzac's fragments and fragmentations have been accepted, even praised, through the years. In the case of the widely acclaimed reappearing characters, however, there have been dissenting voices. Proust, for example, felt there was too little room in the midst of auctorial explanations and judgments for the reader to create, as in life, a whole person from disparate visions.[26] Certainly, as Jean-Yves Tadié has demonstrated conclusively in his *Proust et le roman* (Paris:

Gallimard 1971), Proust's characters do encourage the reader's creation and have much to do with the structure of *A la recherche du temps perdu*. One might wonder whether Proust's perhaps valid reservations should be tempered by the realization that the brilliant improvements he wrought on the device in *A la recherche du temps perdu* would not have been possible without Balzac's seminal work in *La Comédie humaine*. One might even conclude that Proust should have been more generous with his great predecessor. His debt was enormous – some day, a courageous person will study the subject in detail. But this point aside, on balance few would dispute that Balzac's pride in his construction of characters' lives across numerous volumes has been largely vindicated.

There are, of course, other ways of viewing Balzac's patchwork. While some modern critics find pleasure in Balzac's fragmentation – for, as pointed out previously, they view it as an opportunity to ignore the author's intention and indulge in their own unrestrained creation (or so they say) – others would simply explain the gaps away, in essence ignoring them and continuing to create according to their view of Balzac's design. Though the results would undoubtedly be different, the theoretical implications of free composition are precisely the same as those of composition according to a design that is wrong or at least different from the one implied by the text.

Some of the more troubling interstices in *La Comédie humaine* probably had nothing to do with design. One might suspect occasionally that there were moments when Balzac's manic intensity broke and left flaws. Perhaps he was unable to envision a pre-existent order – Proust felt that his predecessor only saw 'a *Comédie humaine* in his novel after the fact.'[27] Balzac stated explicitly that his vision of the whole *Illusions perdues* came gradually and, at that, piecemeal, with numerous unproductive detours (V.119). He makes a similar comment in respect to the entire *Comédie humaine* (III.37–8). Moreover, the author's inability to leave well enough alone contributed to the current state of the text. Time after time, he would return to add a phrase or a whole section – I think of the 1835 coda to *Gobseck*. Such examples are reasonably easy to live with, however, even when they cause apparent defects, since we can justify both his constant retouching by the obsessiveness of a great but all too human genius and the flawed articulations by haste or sickness.

As persuasive and as common as such explanations may be, I want to suggest that in some cases it may be ill advised to accept them. I have come to suspect that many of the apparent disjunctions derive not from the author but from the reader, in particular from the latter's lack of a unified field theory which could help him both span the Balzacian universe and integrate its component parts. Careful consideration of the spaces between various elements, large and small, gives reason for believing that they are governed by surprisingly consistent mechanisms of transition and framing, of pairing, opposing, and grouping. Even when the design is not intentional, a significant number of the empty spaces between elements easily fit within systematic patterns of Balzac's fictional coordination.

I suggest that *La Comédie humaine* reveals Balzac's intuition of a non-Aristotelian world, where causal and chronological sequences are subordinated to the entire configuration or Gestalt. Like the creative person Arthur Koestler described in *The Act of Creation*, readers with the requisite capabilities seek the kind of creation that might better be described as discovery. Not offended by the thought that the text in hand may refer to an objectively verifiable though imaginary world, he seeks to discover its conventions, which permits 'decoding' its truth and enjoying its esthetic reality. If Jacques Derrida is correct in seeing two kinds of interpretation – one that seeks to decipher a truth or an origin and one that affirms play and attempts to go beyond humanism – what follows is of the former variety: a humanistic endeavor, an attempt to discover, a quest for what Koestler calls 'Eureka!'[28] The resultant configuration of Balzac's monumental cycle, as it exists in the reader's mind, suggests the actual context of Horace's phrase, 'disjecti membra poetæ,' which Balzac cavalierly burlesques in the passage previously quoted from 'Ferragus.' Horace is distinguishing poets from those of lesser gifts. 'Take from the verses which I am writing now, or which Lucilius wrote in former days, their regular beat and rhythm – change the order of the words, transposing the first and the last – and it would not be like breaking up: "When foul Discord's din / War's posts and gates of bronze had broken in," where, even when he is dismembered, you would find the limbs of a poet [*disjecti membra poetæ*].'[29] Behind the fragmentary *Comédie humaine*, I believe one may find a unifying configuration worthy of the master's genius.

No one can doubt that Balzac was conscious of some, if not all, of this discontinuity. Indeed, he presented it as a virtue. In regard to certain characters, like Félix de Vandenesse and Lady Dudley, he explains that while readers would be amused by their situation if they knew their whole story at first acquaintance, the necessary insight is gained only farther on in a completely different work. As in life, he generalizes in the 'Préface' to *Une Fille d'Eve* (1839), 'Often this scandalous or honorable, beautiful or ugly story will be told you the next day or a month later, sometimes in parts. Nothing is of a piece in the world; everything is a mosaic. A story of something in the past is the only kind you can tell chronologically. Chronology is a system which is inapplicable to a forward moving present. The author has the nineteenth century in front of him for a model, but it is a restless model, difficult to keep still' (II.265). Elsewhere, he begs for indulgence. After all, 'When a writer has undertaken a complete description of society, seen from all angles, grasped in all its phases. . . . might he not be granted the benefit accorded science, which is permitted delay when its monographs are written in line with the importance of its undertaking. May the author not be allowed to go forward step by step in his work, without being required to explain at each new stage that the work is one of the edifice's stones and that all the stones will one day fit together and form an enormous edifice?' (V.109–10).

However sympathetic we may be to the above plea, other explanations are more interesting, at least from the standpoint of the notably fragmentary nature of *La Comédie humaine*. I think in particular of the preface to *Même histoire*, which Balzac published in 1834. He was responding to those who have sensed that the central characters of the stories making up the volume are in fact one and the same person, after which he gathered together the significant portions from the version of 1832, added several sketches, and gave them the common title, *Même histoire*. He justified the collection by claiming, 'The character who crosses so to speak the six pictures [*tableaux*] which make up *Même histoire* is not a figure, but rather a thought. The more this thought dons dissimilar costumes, the better it renders the author's intentions. His ambition is to communicate to the reader's soul the vagueness of revery and awaken in women a few of the vivid impressions that they have conserved, reviving life's scattered memories, so as to bring forth a few lessons. . . . Female readers will doubtless complete the imperfect transitions' (II.1037). The passage is, I believe, significant for the whole of Balzac's work. While it is true that the 1842 version, renamed *La Femme de trente ans*, eventually brought these six disparate narrations into one more or less coherent vision around Julie d'Aiglement, the tone of the explanation makes one realize how very little Balzac found the lack of narrative transition disturbing. True, he did recognize 'too great a gap in this sketch between *Le Rendezvous* and *La Femme de trente ans*,' but he merely filled it with 'a new fragment titled *Souffrances inconnues*' (ibid.). On considering the fragmentary state of the 1834 version of *Même histoire*, however, there may be an indication of why he later worked to smooth these particular seams, while he never bothered to do so for numerous other examples of narrative asyndeton. The key to whether or not he worked to integrate fragments does not, I suspect, lie in degree of fragmentation. One cannot say that because *Même histoire* was just too fragmentary, he molded it into *La Femme de trente ans*. The works *Jésus-Christ en Flandre*, *Histoire des Treize*, 'La Fille aux yeux d'or' are neither more nor less broken up than *Même histoire*. The difference lies in function. By bringing the pieces of the latter work together into *La Femme de trente ans* – a task he accomplished primarily by turning the reappearing idea into a reappearing character with the same name and thus creating a mother whose destructive behavior affects several generations of her family – he extended and deepened the meaning of the whole. Increased coherence, in short, served a purpose beyond mere narrative linking. Balzac's allegiance to plot was weak.

From these observations (and the developments of the following chapters), I am then led to the next principle of Balzac's unity:

6. *Balzac was the master, not of collage – the construction of a whole from isolated pieces – but of montage: he regularly constructed wholes from other wholes.*

Especially on the larger scale of his entire cycle, Balzac consciously cultivated montage. Though the concepts suggested by collage and montage are appropriate to Balzac's thoughts on structure, the terms, as I use them, are anachronistic, for they were applied specifically to works of art only in the twentieth century. Still, they are helpful in understanding how Balzac proceeded.

Unfortunately, the meaning of the term 'montage' has lost its precision. Consecrated by the fine arts where it formed an opposition to collage, it had the misfortune to become a rallying cry and a point of contention. For Eisenstein montage was 'everything.'[30] It was 'any two pieces of a film stuck together [which] inevitably combine to create a new concept, a new quality born of that juxtaposition' ('1938,' 63), in short it was the syntagmatic contiguity of any two elements. Eisenstein's montage was most often formed from bits and pieces rather than from complete units, but the unity of his films also depended on the paradigmatic elements within each of the juxtaposed pieces, whether light, sound, or the connotations of such images as the religious idols in his film, *October*. Or, for another example, my wife, Dallas, reminds me that when she worked at CBS in 1960, the crews entertained themselves at lunch with composites of material deemed too explicit for TV and censored from movies. Of course, an hour of cleavage and bikinis differed significantly in both effect and meaning from the films in which the brief segments first occurred.

In a consideration of Balzac, it seems productive to reestablish the distinction between collage's composition of fragmentary elements and montage's creation from potentially independent unities. Among its chief virtues when viewed in this light, montage focuses not on disintegration but on integration, on the conventions accepted by the artists which, when accepted by readers, permit the perception of unity.

Just as post-structuralism might be viewed as a necessary transition into a post-Aristotelian world view, so Balzac seems to have intuited something approaching the world modern science suggests, a world where sequences may become orbits joining beginning to end, where opposing or parallel entities are integrated into the subsuming whole, where order may grow from real (following Prigogine) or apparent chaos.[31] As is so often the case with great artists, his vision went far beyond the science of his day, perhaps even of our own. He saw his world as a whole, but he also was firmly convinced that it bore the seeds of its own destruction. Through the radical changes taking place in his society because of the industrial revolution, the stabilizing institutions of Family, Church, and State were being weakened to the point where eventually they would fall. Balzac developed a means of portraying disintegration, fragmention, and destruction within a whole, a process within a picture.

The principles I have been outlining suggest that a detail – whether quality, concept, thing, character, theme, or episode – may, as it is repeated, become a motif or be incorporated into a more complex plot or image. Images are always subsumed to ideas but are joined to each other by various kinds of repetition. In all cases, Balzac was interested in wholes, which he then brought into larger, more global unities.[32] The artist's 'task,' as Balzac put it, 'consists in merging analogous facts into a single picture' (IV.962). Our job is now to consider some representative stories, not as they first appeared in the rock pile, but as they now function with Balzac's monumental edifice, *La Comédie humaine*. It is not enough to see what he wrote in his prefaces, most of which were expressly deleted from *La Comédie humaine* (I.14); though they are a more or less trustworthy indication of his intention at the point of their writing, only the definitive, fictional text can provide any assurance of what he actually did.

The following chapters do not center on these six factors, since the second, third, and fourth principles, in particular, are too inter-dependent to break up and treat chapter by chapter. The logic of my study is nonetheless clear. While discussing the way Balzac unified particular works in chapter two, I shall quite naturally focus on how his plots are subordinated to the description that almost without exception organizes the whole. I shall deal in some detail in chapters two and three with the second principle, the way image and idea key individual novels and short stories. Chapter three, however, is particularly involved with works in which the novelist allows us into his workshop and gives us insight into the coordination of *Splendeurs et misères des courtisanes, La Femme de trente ans,* and 'La Fille aux yeux d'or.' Although it is generally believed that the organization of these three works remains seriously disarticulated and thus flawed, they provide access to Balzac's esthetics of unification. Principle four, concerned with the author's weak commitment to chronological organization, becomes particularly important whenever two or more creations are brought into a larger unit; it is then highlighted in chapters four, five, and six. Chapter four concentrates on three works that bring several stories together into something more than a mere collection. Since neither plot nor character, as normally defined, is especially involved in a compre-hensive view of *Autre étude de femme, Jésus-Christ en Flandre,* and *Histoire des Treize,* these works are particularly helpful in the study of the mechanisms of both coherence and unity. Chapter five considers the way fictional frames are related to the incorporated work and to both the entire *Comédie humaine* and the non-fictional society in which Balzac's masterpiece is set. And, finally, the last chapter reviews the first five principles while emphasizing how all six work with the montage of the entire *Comédie humaine.*

CHAPTER TWO

Image Structure

We understand how expert critics can provide impeccable readings according to their particular methods and arrive at conclusions diametrically opposed to one another. When we look closely, it is usually possible to discover that the various readers have differed in goals, definitions, methods, or data, not to mention conflicting attitudes toward the validity of subject or object, thus accounting for diverging conclusions. It is easy, for example, to see why Lukács's view of a novel would differ from that of, say, Emile Faguet, for they share almost nothing in their basic view of literature. The divergence among like-minded critics that occurs through the length and breadth of *Le Père Goriot's* (1834–5) secondary literature is puzzling, however, since the participants have almost without exception come to the novel with the same critical tools consecrated within the traditions of literary analysis. With minor differences, they share assumptions, approaches, and procedures. They work with the same text, and they have an identical desire to explain the unity of the whole. They also accord equal stature to those aspects of *Le Père Goriot* that they consider important. They have paid particular attention to the real and imagined setting, the characters, and, especially, to the element of plot, and they have split into two distinct camps.

Even scholars as compatible as Castex and Surer have diverged on the question of the novel's unity. Castex and many others insist that '[f]or anyone who holds to the novel's text, the true hero is the victim, Goriot.'[1] The most convincing evidence advanced to support his opinion is the novel's title itself. Unfortunately, the story of Goriot's decline, despair, and death fails to integrate several important factors. I think, for example, of the magnificent creation, the criminal Vautrin. While a major portion of the novel is dedicated to the development of this personage, he has no impact at all on Goriot. Were it not for the title, one might be tempted to join Paul Surer and legions of like-minded when he states with an assurance rivaling that of Castex, 'In fact, an attentive reading of the novel reveals that only Rastignac is at no time lost from view and that the central subject is the story of this young student.'[2] But the title is not easily dismissed. Though there can be no doubt that the story of Rastignac's education and conversion from aspiring law student to student socialite touches almost every page, Père Goriot remains so massive and powerful that the young man, for all his charm, can scarcely compete. In short, one might be confused by the almost universal agreement that Le Père Goriot constitutes a masterwork. Pulled in two or – thinking of Vautrin – three directions, it seems to lack coherence and unity.[3] Certainly without further insights one would be forced to conclude that the novel fails to satisfy Balzac's own 'capital obligation': 'Whatever the number of the accessories and the multiplicity of the figures, a modern novelist must . . . group them according to their importance, subordinate them to the sun of his system, an interest, or a hero, and conduct them like a brilliant constellation in a certain order.'[4]

The criticism, in short, points to an apparent lack of cohesion, and one might then be tempted to conclude that Le Père Goriot constitutes a failed novel. One should, though, be given pause by the fact that generation after generation has returned to this work with esthetic pleasure and profit. I have taken a different tack and wondered whether an approach at variance from the others might succeed in explaining how the work achieves unity. Careful consideration of the analyses of those who have sought to understand the unity of Le Père Goriot reveals a common denominator. Without exception, they have come to Balzac's novel expecting to find plot as the central organizing device; that is, they counted on having all the constituent elements integrated into an action and an agent. It is understandable that they would do so. Few indeed are those who would not subscribe to the view expressed by Philip Stevick: '[T]he history of the genre ever since [*Pamela, Clarissa, Joseph Andrews*, and *Tom Jones*] has tended to confirm the idea that a novel is a novel insofar as it is an action and as it ceases to be an action it becomes not a novel but something else.'[5]

But what if Balzac's novel is not primarily a plot? Perhaps in their search for an inclusive action which does not exist critics have succumbed to the temptation of elevating one or another subordinate plots to positions of unjustified and unjustifiable importance. No one will be surprised if I suggest that we tend to find what we look for... even if it is not there. As Montaigne put it in the 'Apologie de Raimond Sebond,' 'We willingly grasp the sense of another's writings according to the opinions that we previously established.'[6] Therein, I suspect, lies the problem. While looking for an overriding action, critics have paid insufficient attention to the feature that serves as the novel's nucleus. Like Jacques Cartier, who found it difficult to appreciate the St Lawrence River fully when he was seeking a new route to China, so it has not been easy for scholars seeking a significant plot to evaluate appropriately the ramifications of the figure, Père Goriot.

Let me give an example of what I think is happening in this novel. Imagine a sculpture entitled *Chemistry Today* at Chicago's Art Institute. In one corner there is a portable laboratory where crack is being 'cooked up.' Though a chemical process is taking place, most would be willing to view the activity as an image, reflecting one of the tragedies of our society. Spectators will know something of the system that brings cocaine into the country and something of the problems arising when the processed drug is distributed, but the sculpture includes only the working laboratory. The plot turning around Goriot resembles this laboratory. The character goes to see Gobseck, he gestures, moves, cries. Still, none of these particular actions is of great significance, certainly no more than what we learn of his past, and what we divine of the future he will leave after his story is over. In another corner of the sculpture a television set shows the Indianapolis 500. While an action is being presented, from the start of the race to the end, the significance of the competition is not at all in the particular driver who wins, but rather in the cars, the power, the noise, and, of course, the television set itself. My sculpture is rather like the tale of Rastignac. It has a beginning and an end. Both he and the cars deteriorate significantly in the course of the adventure. Still, neither Rastignac's story nor the video of the race have importance beyond the degree to which they represent their age. The 'plot' in the laboratory or on the television has no more significance than other 'objects' making up the sculpture, for example, a plastic mannequin configuring a female weight lifter, a photograph of a man suffering from emphysema, etc. While the work uses 'action,' the total effect is to present the sculptor's idea of society today. And this, I think, is what Balzac is about, though for his day rather than ours.

If *Le Père Goriot* is not predominantly process, but image, not narration, but description, the various plots would then take a secondary, subordinate role to the vision described. This pattern is fairly common in Balzacian novels. We remember from the 1842 'Avant-Propos' to the *Comédie humaine* how Balzac claimed to be a historian of his day and how often in his novels he insists that the reader is to be treated to a study of society. He explained what he meant by that on numerous occasions. This 'historian' is a 'historian of manners: his task consists of bringing analogous facts together into a single picture' (IV.962). Rather than being involved in creating a narration, he is 'a writer [who] has undertaken a complete description of society, seen from all angles, grasped in all its phases' (V.109). It is worth recalling that in 'Etudes sur M. Beyle,' when he provided categories for all of literature, plot is subordinated to other, less changeable concepts. He sees the *Literature of Images* as incorporating 'lyricism, the epic, and everything that depends on this manner of looking at things.' *The Literature of Ideas*, on the other hand, draws those writers who love 'rapidity, movement, concision, shocks, action, drama, who avoid discussion, who have little taste for reverie and are pleased by results.' Balzac, however, includes himself in the third category, *Literary Eclecticism* or 'a total view of things. . . . which . . . requires representation of the world as it is: images and idea, an idea in an image or an image in an idea, in movement, and in reverie' (HH XXIV.214). Everything is subordinated to the central image or the idea. In the opening pages of *Le Père Goriot,* the narrator points to the Maison Vauquer and states, 'Such a gathering should and did offer a microcosm of a complete society' (III.62). Here and, with few exceptions, elsewhere, the emphasis rests not on a chronological development, but on a view of some situation at a point in time.

Once one understands the importance of description, in opposition to narration, a completely different light shines on numerous passages. Take, for example, the well-known passages where Daniel d'Arthez criticizes Lucien de Rubempré's work: 'If you do not wish to ape Walter Scott, you must create a different manner, but you have imitated him. Like him, you begin with long conversations in order to set out your characters; when they have talked, description and action come into play. . . . Reverse the terms of the problem. Replace these diffuse talks, magnificent in Scott but colorless in your work, by descriptions to which our language is so well adapted. In your writing let dialogue be the expected consequence crowning your preparations' (V.312–13). While Balzac's insights into Scott and dialogue are no doubt interesting, the barely noticeable comments on narration and description indicate a revolutionary principle of fictional construction. The opposition and interplay of description and action occur in all such works where, in general, description is subordinated to narration. Balzac does not take Lucien, or even d'Arthez, to the logical end of his thought. Here he considers making dialogue grow from narration and description. As his work demonstrates, however, he fully understood the possibilities of reversing the dominance of narration and description, of posing a creation where narration is submitted to the needs of description.

In *Le Père Goriot*, the overture provides both a symbol to help the reader focus and a reason why the Rue Neuve-Sainte-Geneviève is 'like a bronze frame, the only one suitable for this account' (III.51). The symbol is 'a statue representing Love.' In expanding on it, Balzac points to the reason for the setting: 'To see the scaly varnish covering it, lovers of symbols would perhaps uncover a myth of Parisian love which is healed a few steps from there' (ibid.). Whenever Balzac's narrator calls on 'lovers' of anything at all, it usually means the reader should pay particular attention. In this case the narrator highlights the 'symbol' even more emphatically by suggesting that the scaly statue of Cupid recalls the venereal diseases that were treated at the nearby hôpital des Capucins. As though that were not enough, he gives the statue an inscription by Voltaire which insists on love's sway: 'Whoever you may be, here is your master: / Love it is, was, and is to be' (ibid.).

The book title itself says much the same thing as the statue, at least if one perceives its resonances. *Père* (Father) serves to signal the all-important theme of paternity.[7] The concept of father, however, must not be diluted. Père should be understood not merely as one member of a family, but as the representative of Family. Clearly, for Balzac and for this novel, an attack on fatherhood was an attack on the whole familial institution. As he said in the preface he added to the second edition in May of 1835, '[F]ather Goriot's sentiments imply maternity' (III.46). Likewise, the father's relationship in his family implied that of God with the world, and, in Goriot's words, 'A father is for his children as God is for us' (III.160). Indeed, the family represents one of the essential pillars of society. Goriot is not far from the truth when he raves, 'The fatherland will perish if fathers are trampled on. That is clear. Society, the world runs on paternity, everything collapses if children do not love their fathers' (III.275). Fatherhood has been attacked – the title suggests as much, since Père Goriot can mean either 'Father' Goriot or, a term of disdain, 'Old' Goriot.

Love of father and family has been corrupted, as has love in all its forms. 'In this country. . . . love especially is in essence boastful, impudent, wasteful, delusive, and wastefully extravagant' (III.236). Such a state of affairs is, of course, to be expected. 'How could great sentiments be allied in fact to a small, superficial, petty society?' (III.270).

Balzac seems to have had the three classic forms of love in mind; for there are examples of *eros*, *philia*, and *agape* in significantly degraded forms. The tainted, venal nature of eros, or sexual desire, perhaps comes through most clearly in the disfigured statue of Love decorating the Maison Vauquer's little garden, coupled with a reference to venereal diseases. When Vautrin predicts, 'You [i.e., Rastignac] will go to show yourself off at some pretty woman's house, and you will take money. . . . for how will you succeed if you do not capitalize on your love?' he goes on to comment with heavy irony that this kind of behavior is by no means honorable (III.145). It is, however, common. Mme de Beauséant tells him,

> [T]reat this world as it deserves to be. . . . You will probe the depths of feminine corruption, you will estimate the breadth of men's miserable vanity. . . . The more coldly you calculate, the further you will go. Strike without pity. . . . Do not accept men and women as anything but post horses that you leave exhausted at each relay station, and you will thus arrive at the pinnacle of your desires. Understand that you will be nothing here if you do not have a woman interested in you. She must be young, rich, elegant. But if you have a sincere feeling, hide it like a treasure; never allow anyone to suspect it, or you will be lost. . . . If you ever fall in love, be certain to keep it a secret. Learn to distrust this world. (III.115–16)

Rastignac then not surprisingly subordinates eros to the power it produces. ' "Having a mistress is a quasi-royal position," he said to himself. "It is the sign of power!" ' (III.154). After all, in the twisted morality of this society, an adulterous relationship arranged by a father serving as his daughter's procurer seems downright virtuous. Rastignac observes, 'In this liaison there is neither crime nor anything which might bring a frown from the severest virtue. Many well-bred people contract similar unions!' (III.216).

Philia, or brotherly love, appears in equally degraded form. Vautrin, a criminal who 'does not love women' (III.192), announces that 'only one real sentiment exists: the friendship of one man for another' (III.186). He offers a venal relationship where, in exchange for a murder, Rastignac will extort 200,000 francs from his promised wife. When arrested, he brags of his 'more than 10,000 [criminal] brothers ready to do anything for [him]' (III.220). We are far from the worlds of Daman and Pythias or of David and Jonathan.

Agape is also debased. This, a self-sacrificing, perfect love, is expressly elicited when Goriot is termed 'this Christ of Paternity' (III.231). We know, however, that his priorities are out of order on learning that he would sell 'the Father, the Son, and the Holy Ghost in order to prevent either one [of his daughters] from shedding a single tear!' (III.177). As the narrator says, '[T]he sentiment of paternity developed to the point of unreasonableness in Goriot' (III.124). Furthermore, Goriot's love is by no means selfless. He never forgets what he has given, and, worse, his love is unquestionably destructive. In the end he rightly recognizes that 'I alone caused my daughters' disordered lives; I spoiled them' (III.276). Still, in a society that had not sold its birthright, Goriot's aberrations would not have resulted in such absolute misery. Here, however, because of the very excess of his love and the fact that he has revealed it, thus breaking the cardinal rule Mme de Beauséant exposed to Rastignac, he has become a victim, the object of his daughters' exploitation.

To show the social contamination that affects the institution of family, the author linked 'Le Père' to a name that suggests the ultimate corruption of love: Goriot. Balzac probably was acquainted with one or more Goriots. The name was rather common, and he may well have known one either in his Parisian neighborhood or during his vacations when he was a young man in L'Isle-Adam.[8] But whether he did or did not, it is inconceivable, given his deep love of Rabelais, that he would not have made the connection between Goriot and Rabelais's *la grande Guorre*, or syphilis, whom Raminagrobis married *'en secondes nopces'* (noce can mean either wedding or binge). As J. Wayne Conner has written, '[I]t is important to remember that Balzac was not only an amateur etymologist but also an avid reader of Renaissance literature, where *gorre* (with its adjective *gorrier*) is commonly found in two senses:

"elegance, luxury in dress," and "venereal disease." [9] To Père, Balzac has joined Goriot, that is, the love of luxury and perhaps not unrelated physical contamination. The novel's title then suggests self-indulgence, the illicit, and disease. Fatherhood and family have been infected.

It is consequently a mistake to view Goriot as nothing but a character. In this novel, 'ideas are beings,' as Balzac wrote elsewhere (XII.775). Père Goriot is an idea in the guise of an image. 'Every image,' the author once said, 'corresponds to an idea, or more exactly to a sentiment, which is a collection of ideas' (HH XXIV.214). Goriot should be seen as the incarnation of a society where the values have gone awry, where a debauched, profligate people have perverted the family, one of the basic institutions of civilization. Rastignac merely illustrates the theme. Beginning as a young man with high ideals, he quickly learns the lessons of his day. As he himself sees, he has no right to condemn Anastasie. He muses, '[F]or your own self-centered future, you have just imitated what she did for her lover!' (III.127–8). He has exploited his mother, his aunt, and his sisters in precisely the same way as Anastasie and Delphine do their father. Beizer correctly concludes that in going secretly to the female members of his family, Eugène is in fact committing a crime against his father and thus acts analogously to Delphine and Anastasie (130–2). He does so for money. From the time that '[t]he demon of luxury bit him at the core, the fever of gain caught him, the thirst for gold dried his throat' (III.107), Rastignac finds it easier and easier to compromise with the world. It is finally to be expected that the young man 'was ready to sacrifice his conscience for his mistress' (III.262). His mistress herself indicates how far he has descended: he knows that 'she was capable of trampling her father's body in order to go dancing' (ibid.), knowledge that makes his concluding and celebrated 'first act of defiance against society' (III.290) all the more pathetic. In his decision to 'dine at madame de Nucingen's house' (ibid.), he has accepted and thus shares his mistress's 'elegant parricide' (III.261). His love serves his ambitions: 'He loved selfishly' (III.262). Through it all, the young man's story serves effectively to provide fuller insight into his society, though it by no means integrates all the loose ends.

Goriot remains the best symbol of this world and everything it represents. He is the only character who has manifested all three of 'the three great manifestations of society: Obedience, Struggle, and Revolt; the Family, the World, and Vautrin' (ibid.). It is true that the unforgettably powerful Vautrin epitomizes revolt – 'His expression was that of the fallen archangel who always seeks to go to war' (III.219). Vautrin explains that he is 'a man who is less cowardly than others, and who protests against the profound deceptions of the social contract, as Jean-Jacques [Rousseau] – whose pupil I glory in being – called it. Finally, I am alone against the government with its pile of courts, police, budgets, and I play them for suckers' (III.220). Nevertheless, Goriot also has functioned in this role: '[T]his old Ninety-Three' not only 'sold grain to the head choppers,' he was 'section president during the Revolution' (III.114). His involvement in the Revolution gave birth to his fortune, but it was his activity, his effort, that solidified his position. For a while he was the living example of 'struggle.' 'If it was a question of grains, of flour, of seed, of recognizing their quality, their provenances, of looking after their preservation, of foreseeing the market, of prophesying abundant or poor harvests, of procuring food grains at a good price, of stocking up in Sicily, in the Ukraine, Goriot had no second. . . . Patient, active, energetic, persistent, quick to get his trips behind him; he had an eagle's eye, he preceded everything, foresaw everything, knew everything, kept everything secret; he was a diplomat in his conceptions, a soldier in his actions' (III.123). When he tries to buy his daughters' love, he merely takes the 'struggle' of a merchant to an extreme. Finally, as we know, he gives flesh to the concepts of Family and Obedience. '[F]or Eugène,' and for us, Goriot 'represented Paternity' (III.287).

Family still exists in this world of 1819, but it is in a very precarious state. Marriage no longer extends family, it divides it. When a son-in-law takes one's lovely and lovable daughter, 'he will begin by taking up her love as though it were an axe, so as to cut to this angel's palpitating heart and excise all the sentiments attaching her to her family. Yesterday, our daughter was everything for us; we were everything for her; the next day, she is our enemy' (III.113). Some maintain a modicum of family loyalty. Rastignac, we learn in *L'Interdiction*, provides the dowry so that his sisters might be married off. The fact that he does not do so until he is comfortably wealthy should not cover over the generous nature of the act. Victorine Taillefer continues to love her father and brother, though she has been sacrificed on the slenderest of excuses in order to pass a superb fortune on to the brother. And we know how Goriot suffered for having committed 'the foolishness of abdicating my rights' (III.276). In this society, a father dare not give up his fortune. 'Money gives us everything, even daughters. . . . If I had treasures to leave, they would bandage me, they would care for me. . . . A father must always be rich; he must keep his children on a tight leash like treacherous horses' (III.273–4).

In the world of *Le Père Goriot* blood-related families are primarily means to be used unscrupulously for success. Rastignac plays on his family's love for him to extract the money for his entrance to society. M. Taillefer would have cheated his daughter out of her rightful inheritance if Vautrin had not arranged to do away with the son. Goriot's daughters took him for everything he had: 'The lemon squeezed dry, the daughters discarded the peel on the street' (III.115). As for families formed by marriage, Anastasie steals from her husband to pay her lover's debts. Nucingen is more interested in having unlimited use of Delphine's money than in having a true marriage. In short, in the whole of *Le Père Goriot* there is not a single example of a family that is not exploited for selfish ends. One wonders whether Victorine and Rastignac's sisters will not learn to do likewise. Certainly, this society encourages 'jokers who would sell their families to climb up a notch' (III.138).

With the exception of Rastignac's family, which seems more or less normal, traditional families are conspicuous by their absence from the pages of *Le Père Goriot*. Instead, we are thrust into a world where virtually everyone is in the process of creating unnatural, if not illicit, 'families.' One thinks of Mme de Beauséant's 'morganatic' liaison with Ajuda-Pinto, which leaves her husband free for his own pleasures, Mme de Nucingen's affair with Rastignac, which releases Nucingen for his mistress, or Mme de Restaud's passion for Maxime de Trailles, which, as Mme de Beauséant predicts, will ruin her. Such affairs can become a veritable prison, as is suggested by the allusion to Telemachus and Calypso in the novel's overture.[10]

Mme Couture's relationship to Victorine Taillefer, 'for whom she serves as a mother' (III.55), is more acceptable, given the facts that they are related and the girl's mother has died. But other references to 'families' cannot fail to astonish. Mme Vauquer presides over her boarding-house where 'the gathering for breakfast looked like a family meal' (III.56). Vautrin, if no one else, calls her 'mama.'[11] Vautrin himself yearns to be a father, though without the assistance of the female of the species. I have already noted the bargain he offers Rastignac. His reasons for wanting an additional 200,000 francs are also worth mentioning: 'My idea is to go live the life of a patriarch in the middle of a large domain' (III.141). For this 'patriarchal' life, of course, he does not wish sons; he wants slaves: 'I want two hundred negroes, so as to satisfy my taste for a patriarchal life. Negroes, you understand, are ready-made children with whom you do as you wish, without some nosey king's prosecutor coming and asking for an accounting' (ibid.). He looks at Rastignac 'with a paternal and contemptuous air' (III.118). He knows him 'as though I had made you' (III.135). Sylvie refers to him as the 'big papa Vautrin' (III.80), and he calls himself 'papa' repeatedly.[12] One can even comprehend, in the topsy-turvy world of *Le Père Goriot*, why, 'If ever you search the hearts of Parisian women, you will find the usurer before the lover' (III.86). After all, the usurer in question is 'papa' Gobseck (III.86, 259). Given the above, readers will not be astonished by Rastignac's delight on finding a tailor 'who had understood the paternity of his trade' (III.130). Balzac everywhere calls attention to the degradation of fatherhood and family. One more example will serve to summarize the rest: he compares the sorrowing Mme de Beauséant, 'one of the heights of aristocratic society' (III.76), to Niobe (III.264), though he leaves it for the reader to recognize the ludicrousness of the analogy. Their grief may be similar, but the causes make any serious comparison impossible. Niobe has lost her children, thus her world. Mme de Beauséant has lost – not even her husband – but the young man of whom she is enamored.

This is a society where, if women 'did not know how to sell themselves they would eviscerate their mothers to get what they need to shine' (III.87), where it is normal for wives to be 'at war with their husbands over everything' (III.140). Its tainted love is best exemplified by Père Goriot. His excessive passion ably sets it off, for he actively encourages the irregular relationships that Paris has accepted in the stead of family and fatherhood. Moreover, he has taken part in all aspects of this society. He has been a rebel, he has struggled, and he has obediently submitted to the whims of his daughters. The price he pays for the latter failing is awesome. Fatherhood as represented by Goriot has worth in this world only to the degree that it has financial value, the one value that has subsumed all others. Familial, fatherly love has indeed been corrupted. One might even say it is diseased, for it has been polluted by the all-consuming desire for luxurious self-gratification. Paternity has become a boarding house, a tailor, adulterous relationships, a venal bargain. In order for a father to be near his daughter, he sets her lover up in an apartment and promises him, 'I will be more than a father for you, I want to be a family' (III.252).

The problems that have arisen in the criticism of *Le Père Goriot* grow from the expectations we have of nineteenth-century novels, expectations summarized by Frank Kermode's belief 'that a novel is a fictional prose narrative of a certain length.'[13] This has also been the guiding concept of those critics who have come to this novel with varying results. They have sought the novel's unifying principle in an action that would pervade the novel and, because of its essential nature, would draw together all the constituent parts. Their expectations are doomed to frustration, despite the fact that they are widely shared. Critics since Lessing's *Laocoön* – I think most notably of Apollinaire – have used time to distinguish between poetry and prose. Poetry, it is argued, is atemporal, for it describes, while narrative prose is dominated by time and chronology.[14]

In a fine study, first published in 1945, Joseph Frank pointed to another fictional structure. He traces 'the evolution of form in modern poetry and, more particularly, in the novel. For modern literature, as exemplified by such writers as T.S. Eliot, Ezra Pound, Marcel Proust, and James Joyce, is moving in the direction of spatial form; and this tendency receives an original development in Djuna Barnes's remarkable book *Nightwood*. All these writers ideally intend the reader to apprehend their work spatially, in a moment of time, rather than as a sequence.'[15] Spatial form, or what I would call image structure, may be compared to what others term descriptive (rather than narrational) or metaphoric (rather than metonymic) or paradigmatic (rather than syntagmatic) structure. I prefer to concentrate on image, since it calls up widely understood psychological realities which correspond directly to the kinds of patterns I see in many fictions. For psychologists, an image is a sensorial, emotional, or intellectual complex of data represented in the mind. Though the complex may include process (or movement), its emphasis is on its wholeness. It incorporates a number of elements, each of which is related to the others and to the whole. Molecular structure provides a good example of such a complex, though mental images are far more complicated than most of the models we see in chemistry laboratories. Within the image, each of the constituent elements is capable of forming a link to another analogous or identical element serving as a part of another image. The image of the whole may then incorporate numerous constituent images, each composed of multitudes of elements tied to the senses, the emotions, or the intelligence. Elder Olson calls this sort of thing 'descriptive plot,' by which he means an 'action' that is 'complete when it has adequately described its object.' As Olson recognizes, such structures are present through the ages in 'documentaries, chronicle plays, and many historical, biographical, and pageant pieces.'[16] Image structure is by no means original with twentieth-century literature, though there has been renewed interest in its novelistic possibilities.

Balzac, in particular, organized a number of his novels in a pattern that subordinates chronological experience to a momentary comprehension of the whole. The basis for the central image may be a type, for example the usurer Gobseck (1835),[17] or a symbol, such as the chimera in 'La Fille aux yeux d'or' (1834–5), or a concept, such as the courtesan in *Splendeurs et misères des courtisanes* (1838–47), or the image of corrupted paternity. At the end of *Le Père Goriot* the plots of a dying father and of a young man determined to rise in society on his mistress's back are subordinated to a vision of Paris in the early years of the industrial revolution. Both plots exemplify that tableau, as do the novel's other images, relationships, and events. The picture Balzac leaves us is not a pretty one. We see a society where 'a fortune is virtue!' (III.118), where '[m]oney is life. Currency accomplishes anything' (III.242). Still, as a work of art, it is unquestionably a masterpiece, since Balzac succeeded in unifying the extremely complex ramifications of his theme of a degraded society where familial love has no more value than it will bring in cold cash.

The kind of structure I see in *Le Père Goriot* requires us to focus on elements that may seem trivial to most *aficionados* of fiction. Just as readers of much recent poetry must be aware of conflicting rhythms, so readers of most novels must be sensitive to plot and character. Balzac's work, however, differs. Those who come to *La Comédie humaine* must be particularly sensitive to detail and to the possibility that his details produce images that key the whole and are thus essential. It may be a name, a particular term, a comparison, in short, an element that elsewhere would seem minor indeed. One then understands why he insisted on the importance of detail (e.g., I.1175; V.118; VIII.1681). Commonly, alert readers will find a word or formula that encapsulates the work. In emblems it would be called a *mot* or a motto. Balzac called it a 'generative idea [*idée mère*]' (HH XXIV.253). It may be in the title, as in *Le Père Goriot*, or it may appear in the text itself, as I shall suggest is the case with *Les Secrets de la princesse de Cadignan*. In addition, there is always some sort of an image, which symbolically illuminates the central idea or theme. I think of the scaly statue of Love, which, when found in the courtyard peopled by

Madame Vauquer and her little 'family,' might well be viewed as an expansion, a more detailed illustration, if not an explanation, of the book's title.

Near the beginning of *Les Secrets de la princesse de Cadignan*, Balzac made two comparisons to 'Antinous.' The first is at least an acceptable use of a tired cliché – Georges de Maufrigneuse is 'as handsome as Antinous' (VI.951) – but when the analogy is repeated within a few pages – Lucien de Rubempré is 'an Antinous and a great poet' (VI.956) – the seemingly poorly motivated repetition poses a problem, especially since it was one of those late corrections penned into the margin of the author's copy of the Furne edition. Either it should be included in the litany of Balzac's stylistic infelicities or it is an attempt to focus the reader's attention on an image that is central to the story. Past experience would indicate that one should at least consider the latter possibility. I think of Gobseck's *'lunar* face,' which, though it elicited Faguet's wrath, is in fact the story's central image.[18] There is no doubt that the author of *Les Secrets de la princesse de Cadignan* was thinking of the emperor Hadrian's companion known for his extraordinary beauty. Both the young duc de Maufrigneuse and Lucien de Rubempré were uncommonly handsome young men. But the repetition of comparisons to Antinous, especially in such narrow confines, draws attention to the name itself, suggesting that Balzac may have had more in mind. Some may think of other personages who bore the name – for example, the selfish, cruel, and treacherous leader of Penelope's unwelcome suitors, but there is little in the story to encourage such an association. Others will remember the name's etyma: *anti* (against) and *nous* (reason) I have come to suspect that the story exploits these etymological meanings, that the image is made unspecific by its repeated use. Whether or not the suspicion is correct, it encourages us to take another look at the story and to discover that from start to finish the account of the lovely princess focuses our attention on an environment where the limits of reason will be manifest. Balzac, rightly known as a transitional writer between Romanticism and Realism, was well aware of the direction of his increasingly rationalistic, soon to be positivistic culture. *Les Secrets de la princesse de Cadignan*, first published in 1839, bears a warning about the limitations of reason and an insistence on the importance of *esprit*, which I have variously translated as 'wit,' 'sensitivity,' 'ingenuity,' 'cleverness.'

Not the least of the problems posed by the story arises from Balzac's commentary in a letter to Mme Hanska: 'I have gone through *Une Princesse parisienne* for the last time; it is the most wonderful comedy of manners. It concerns the pile of lies with which the duchesse de Maufrigneuse, having become princesse de Cadignan through succession, succeeds in having herself taken for a saintly, virtuous, chaste girl, by her fourteenth adorer. It is the ultimate in the depravation of sentiments; as Mme Girardin would say, it is *Célimène in love*. The subject is of all countries and all ages. The master stroke is to have shown the lies as just, necessary, and to justify them by love.'[19] In the story the narrator leaves no doubt that the princess is a beautiful but depraved woman who succeeds in hoodwinking her latest (and last) lover. Nonetheless, despite her mendacity, deceitfulness, and unsavory past, the criticism makes it clear that Balzac succeeds in arousing sympathy for the princess.[20]

In 1844, *Une Princesse parisienne* joined the Furne edition of *La Comédie humaine*. In the process it also gained two important additions: a new title, *Les Secrets de la princesse de Cadignan*, which stresses the importance of the hidden side of the princess's life, and a coda, which announces a conclusion open only to 'people of wit [*les gens d'esprit*].'[21] The story tells of the last metamorphosis of the protean Diane, once the innocent d'Uxelles, then the wildly profligate duchesse de Maufrigneuse, and now the retiring princesse de Cadignan. Diana Festa-McCormick aptly terms these incarnations, and the concepts others have of her, as 'frames stand[ing] side by side as in a portrait gallery' ('Deception,' 217). As the names change, so, seemingly, does the person.

Here, the still beautiful Diane decides to add to her string of conquests one Daniel d'Arthez, writer, conservative deputy, authentic genius. Diane's name is surely purposeful, for it recalls 'Diana, the Huntress,'[22] who in her corrupted Roman form, had affairs with a series of runaway slave 'kings.' Though perhaps not a king, d'Arthez 'bears per bend *gules* and *or*, a besant and a torteau counterchanged' (VI.965), a heraldic description which in Balzac's curious world reveals an aristocrat with impressive credentials, and he is Diane's 'slave' (VI.985). The latter's given name, Daniel, also has significance, for, as Alexander Fischler has mentioned, it recalls the apocryphal story of Daniel's judging Susanna innocent despite the accusations of the two perfidious accusers.[23] Balzac's 'Daniel' at first seems to operate as a negative allusion, for he apparently lacks the unerring judgment of the biblical prophet. '[T]his great man' (VI.986) 'was the dupe' (VI.973, cf.

979). But Madame d'Espard correctly recognizes that his 'completely retrospective penetration operates after the fact and disrupts all calculations. You surprise him today; tomorrow he will no longer be fooled by anything' (VI.967). As the reader with the qualities Balzac demanded eventually learns, Daniel's apparent inability to appreciate Diane correctly in *Les Secrets de la princesse de Cadignan* hides surprising depths.

When Balzac's Daniel accepts the image Diane creates and projects, we are encouraged to explain his seeming misperception as an outgrowth of his inexperience in society. He had a long, slow, difficult apprenticeship; he experienced true poverty; and, through it all, he managed to keep those admirable traits that mark him as a true genius. The narrator describes him as 'Daniel d'Arthez, one of these rare men who in our day unite a beautiful character to a beautiful talent' (VI.962). When fame finally arrives, a fortune does as well. A lesser man might have become undisciplined, dissipating both his talent and his genius. The narrator tells us Daniel is no ordinary person: 'This sudden change did not change Daniel d'Arthez. He continued his work with the simplicity of antiquity' (ibid.). This may indeed be the trait that raises him above the failed geniuses of *La Comédie humaine*. As Besser demonstrates, 'The outstanding genius is not only destined to govern society, manipulate other men, and understand the deepest secrets of their hearts; he is expected to penetrate those areas of experience which have always been considered to lie beyond the domain of science and reason' (*Genius*, 161). D'Arthez provides an example for Besser. 'His diligence, perseverance, and endless exhausting labor set him up as an example of what the true creative artist must be, in opposition to Lucien and his second-rate friends' (*Genius*, 222). Indeed, d'Arthez is 'this superior man that all women desire' (VI.977), and, even better, he is seemingly unaware of his attractiveness: 'To this noble simplicity, which decorated his imperial head, d'Arthez joined a naive expression, the naturalness of a child, and a touching benevolence' (VI.978). An innocent (VI.977), he has 'a new and fresh soul' (VI.996).

As the opposite number for this 'child' (VI.963, 985), we have an aging woman 'still deliciously beautiful, thirty-six years old, but justified in only admitting to thirty' (VI.951). Because we are in the narrator's confidence, we know that she is a master of disguise. 'The princess . . . can make herself into anything she wishes: playful, childish, despairingly innocent, or astute, serious, and so profound as to be disquieting'

(VI.969). To find out what she really is, one should perhaps turn to 'these two corrupters' (VI.965), Rastignac and Blondet, who encourage d'Arthez to discover 'the exquisite pleasures of a noble and delicate passion that certain well-born and well-brought up women inspire or feel,' in short, to discover '*a woman* there where Nature made a female' (VI.964). Rastignac and Blondet know Diane well. They describe her at length for the benefit of their innocent friend, and we see her clearly. 'These two clever men [*hommes d'esprit*] . . . had finally turned Diane d'Uxelles into the most monstrous of Parisian women, the most gifted of flirts, the most intoxicating courtesan in the world' (VI.967). We are not left to wonder whether she is being slandered. The narrator advances to evaluate the portrait: Rastignac and Blondet are correct. 'Although they were right, the woman they treated so lightly was saintly and sacred for d'Arthez' (ibid.).

From start to finish, the story praises Diane's wit, cleverness, beauty, acting ability, lineage. Simultaneously, it paints her character in the darkest colors, and attributes her virtues to necessity. It is only, for example, after she has wasted her inheritance in riotous living that she accepts her responsibilities as a mother: 'Misfortune had turned this woman into a good mother. For the fifteen years of the Restoration, she was having too much fun to think of her son, but in taking refuge in obscurity, it occurred to this illustrious egotist that maternal feelings pushed to an extreme absolve her of her past with sensitive people who forgive an excellent mother anything' (VI.952–3). Diane later comments about the appalling portrait she paints of her mother (which she fabricates), '[W]hat is bad for one woman to another becomes horrible for a mother to her daughter' (VI.990). And from daughter to mother? As the narrator's irony flays Diane, the reader cannot fail to be suitably impressed by the princess's further 'sacrifice.' She permitted her long-ignored but now 'beloved' son to dabble in the conspiracies after the revolution of 1830: 'There was nobility and greatness in thus risking her only son and the heir to a historic family' (VI.955). Finally, in a few deft lines, the narrator sums her up: 'She had passed her life amusing herself. She was a true, female Don Juan, with the single difference that she would not have invited the stone statue to dinner and would certainly have won out over the statue' (VI.982).

D'Arthez is subjected to 'a novel prepared well in advance' (VI.989), or, better – at least if the quantity of comparisons represents an index of truth – he becomes the unwitting participant in a comedy starring 'the greatest actress of the day' (ibid.). 'Here begins one of those secret dramas played out deep within the consciousnesses of two people, one of whom is the other's dupe, and which pushes back the boundaries of human perversity. It is one of those black comedies, in comparison to which *Tartuffe* is trivial' (VI.979). The very first sentence shows the princesse de Cadignan in a lie; the rest of the story details a life where every appearance is mendacious. She has withdrawn from the world, having 'so to speak taken the veil and cloistering herself in her own home' (VI.951). She hopes to be forgotten. 'In 1832, three years had thrown piles of snow on the adventures of the duchesse de Maufrigneuse and had so thoroughly whitened her that it required great effort of memory to recall the grave circumstances of her previous life' (ibid.). Rastignac, Blondet, and others are of course more than willing to make the effort necessary to recall everything.

The game of mirrors continues. All appearance is false. Diane seems twenty (VI.977, 989); in reality she is thirty-six (VI.951). Everything results from her studied efforts to deceive: 'She visited the marquise with the intention of being a simple, sweet woman who had known only disappointments, a spirited though maligned and resigned woman, in short a wounded angel' (VI.969). '[I]t was her opportunity to pose as a misunderstood, maligned woman' (VI.974). Unfortunately, the supposed calumnies are, in fact, the pure, unadulterated truth. Clever actress that she remains to the end, Diane plays on '[t]hese clever dissonances' (VI.972), she 'poses' (VI.974), she resorts to one 'ploy' (VI.985) after another; she carries out the 'game' (ibid.) with masterful control. As the narrator phrases it in one instance, it is a 'coldly worked out but divinely acted ploy' (ibid.). But the true masterpiece is played the day d'Arthez works up his courage and asks her to tell him of her life of supposed trials. She hesitates prettily: 'Only a monster could have imagined any hypocrisy in the gracious undulation with which the malicious princess raised her pretty little head in order to gaze once again into the avid eyes of the great man' (VI.986). We already know he is not a monster, she is. And d'Arthez drinks in this 'false confidence' (VI.987).

Should the reader lose perspective, the author sprinkles the bewitching princess's long story with reminders of the reality. This is a 'comic lie' (VI.989); she is a marvelous actress (ibid.); she entwines him in inextricable creepers (ibid.). '"What an angel!" d'Arthez thought.' In the midst of this charade, she maligns her mother (VI.990). Finally, after hearing similar slander about her husband, 'D'Arthez once again kissed this saintly woman's hand, which, after having served him a mother hacked to pieces, had made of the prince de Cadignan . . . a particularly horrible Othello. Now she began to acknowledge her own faults, scourging herself, in order to assume in the eyes of this ingenuous man of letters that virgin freshness which the simplest woman tries at all cost to offer her lover' (VI.994).

However much one must admire the creation Diane presents to the avid audience, it becomes difficult to view the woman behind the mask indulgently as the author bathes her in an unsparing searchlight. We have seen the princess bemoaning the fact that she has never had 'a man of wit [*un homme d'esprit*] to play with. I have only had partners and never adversaries. Love was a game rather than a combat' (VI.967). Then, after a few introductory parries, she complains that d'Arthez 'is an adorable child. He is just out of swaddling clothes. Truly, as always, there will be another victory without a struggle' (VI.975). When d'Arthez's sympathy grows so great that tears moisten his eyes, 'Diane devoured the tears with a sideways glance that made neither her eye nor its lid quiver. It was nimble and neat as the movement of a cat catching a mouse' (VI.988). And, finally, at the moment it seems clear that the innocent writer has been completely taken in, he drops his head, and 'Mme de Cadignan could allow a malicious smile of triumph steal across her lips, a smile one might see on a monkey as it played a particularly successful trick, if monkeys laugh. "Ah! I have him," she thought' (VI.995–6). The comparison makes it difficult to admire the much admired princess. This portrait, and the understanding one forms from it, is what Balzac called 'the ultimate in the depravation of sentiments' in his previously cited letter to Madame Hanska.

There is an author in heaven, however, and Balzac does not let off unscathed the villain of the piece. Lucienne Frappier-Mazur points the way. To keep Daniel, Diane must continue to play the role she has created. 'A precarious position for the princesse de Cadignan, for she could not relax. The unending act she is condemned to perform in order to be true is the working out of Diderot's *Paradoxe sur le comédien*, a work which had profound influence on Balzac.'[24] If Diane is to play the role effectively, she must keep true love at a distance, for she must have firm control, thus emotional distance. And at the end, we find her caught in the web of her own making. 'She had woven the tissue of such cruel lies because she longed to know true love. She felt that love was starting to grow within her, she loved d'Arthez. She was condemned to deceive him, since she needed for him to continue to see her in the sublime role she had played in this comedy' (VI.1004). By whatever means she must prevent her love from getting out of hand. To keep the man she is beginning to love she must play a lie.

While some readers would surely continue to forgive the beautiful Diane for the sake of 'gaiety or fantasy,' as the indulgent Rose Fortassier phrases it,[25] I suspect this is all that one could reasonably expect of readers prior to the reworkings of 1844. One can readily agree that it is 'the most wonderful comedy of manners,' as Balzac told Mme Hanska, but one would probably never suspect that he had wanted us to see 'the lies as just, necessary, and to justify them by love.' Perhaps Balzac realized on rereading the story for republication in the Furne edition that he had asked too much of his readers. We know only that he added 'Les Secrets' to the title and a goad to the conclusion: 'Is it a conclusion? Yes, for people of wit [gens d'esprit]; not for those who need to have everything spelled out' (VI.1005).

Few would not like to consider themselves among these elite 'gens d'esprit,' since, if Voltaire is to be believed, esprit is 'logical ingenuity' and, elsewhere, at more length: 'What people call wit [esprit] is sometimes a new comparison, sometimes a clever allusion; occasionally it is the misuse of a word in order to suggest another or the subtle connection between two unusual ideas; it is a singular metaphor; it is looking for what an object does not let us see at first but which is in fact a part of it; it is art, or bringing together several distant things, or dividing things which seem joined, or opposing them to each other; it is only suggesting one's thought so as to allow others to divine it.'[26] Balzac is inviting us, 'people of wit [gens d'esprit],' to read or reread the story with full use of the mental and spiritual qualities that characterize his geniuses.

It has to be admitted that there is considerable reason for frustration in the story's last paragraph. D'Arthez has returned victorious from Mme d'Espard's gathering. Diane announces that she loves him 'madly,' and the narrator breaks in: 'From that day, there was no question of either the princesse de Cadignan or of d'Arthez. The princess received something of an inheritance from her mother, she spends her summers in a villa in Geneva with the great writer, and returns to Paris for a few months during the winter. D'Arthez is only seen in the Chamber of Deputies. Finally, his publications have become very rare. Is it a conclusion? Yes, for people of wit...' (VI.1005). We gather that the affair has been remarkably durable and that furthermore the great writer has been sufficiently enamored of Diane to have remained away from other occupations. Remembering that his earlier liaison with a vulgar woman had finally become unbearable (VI.965), and that the narrator has left us no illusions about the princess, one may be excused for being surprised to find him and Diane still together. Page after page, we have watched the princess struggle to keep her former life hidden from d'Arthez, and we have understood her fears that he would turn away should he learn the truth. One by one, the reader has watched her secrets revealed to him. Still, contrary to expectations, he has become more attached. The princess was wrong.

Diane does not realize, and the reader may forget, that from the beginning Daniel was fully apprised of her previous adventures. Even after the malicious Rastignac and Blondet have taken it upon themselves to enlighten him, thus encouraging him to make her acquaintance, the narrator tells the reader: 'D'Arthez told them that he had learned more than they could tell him about her through their poor friend, Michel Chrestien, who had adored her in secret for four years' (VI.966). He repeats the claim farther on, 'I know everything' (VI.987). What his friends have apparently added is something more mysterious: 'After this conversation, the princess had the depth of an abyss, the grace of a queen, the corruption of a diplomat, the mystery of an initiation, the danger of a siren. These two clever men [hommes d'esprit], incapable of predicting the conclusion of this pleasantry, had finally turned Diane d'Uxelles into the most monstrous of Parisians, the cleverest of coquettes, the most intoxicating of courtesans' (VI.967). We recall the first explanation proposed for d'Arthez's 'vulgar . . . relationship with a woman who was beautiful enough but who belonged to an inferior class, had no education, no manners, and was kept carefully out of sight' (VI.963–4): '[P]erhaps he had at first despaired of ever meeting a woman who would correspond to the delightful ideal that every man of wit [homme d'esprit] dreams of hopefully?' (VI.964). Thanks to Rastignac and Blondet, he sees his chimera. True, on several occasions d'Arthez is led astray. Still, his performance at the d'Espard gathering makes it clear that he knows all. When confronting the character assassins, he does not deny Diane's promiscuity. He takes a different and much more effective tack. As Nathan sees, 'It is as clever as it is difficult to get revenge for a woman without defending her' (VI.1003).

This Daniel, this 'judge' (VI.988), this man gifted with 'second sight in regard to character' (VI.973), with 'completely retrospective insight which operates after the fact and upsets all plans' (VI.967), sees the princess as 'saintly and sacred' (ibid.). He has discovered the ultimate, 'unbelievable secret' that Diane had shared with Mme d'Espard: 'I have had a good time, but I have not known love' (VI.957). 'My heart has grown old, but I sense an untouched innocence in it. Yes, beneath all that experience there lies a first love that someone could take advantage of' (ibid.). Because she has never had the joy of loving someone who loves her, she joins Mme d'Espard in being 'innocent as two little boarding school girls' (VI.958). But she is wrong to believe that no one will ever be able to find 'the undiscovered woman in me' (VI.971) and recognize her 'innocence' and 'virtue' (VI.959). D'Arthez has the gifts that allow him to see her as she truly is: elegant and experienced, though fresh and innocent. She loves him (VI.977, 979, 1004); he loves her: 'Bianchon and Rastignac are right: when a man merges the heights of the ideal with the delights of desire, in loving an elegant, witty [*pleine d'esprit*], delicate woman... that has to be the ultimate in happiness' (VI.997–8). '[P]eople of wit [*gens d'esprit*]' will remember that *L'Envers de l'histoire contemporaine* [*The Underside of Contemporary History*], a title that suggests a hidden life of debauchery and misery, is a brotherhood devoted to welldoing, the 'Ordre des Frères de la Consolation.' Such readers will enjoy Balzac's little joke on recognizing that what the narrator of *Les Secrets* calls 'a horrible drama that would have to be named the underside of vice' (VI.979), in fact, reveals as virtue the far from seamy depths of the princess's vice.

Besser may be right to regret d'Arthez's lack of productivity – 'A woman's pernicious influence causes the . . . ultimate indolence of d'Arthez'[27] – but Balzac recognized the importance of one man's and one woman's right to the joy of mutual love. His unrepentant Romanticism, dedicated to the individual rather than to the mass, is perhaps revealed in the future he grants his creation. D'Arthez has already made his contribution (cf., VI.962). He has earned his reward. In a society that is progressively choosing 'head' over 'heart,' Balzac creates d'Arthez, 'one of these privileged beings in whom ingenuity [*finesse de l'esprit*] and mental capacity exclude neither the strength nor the grandeur of sentiment' (VI.963). D'Arthez is able to discover a truth that would have brought guffaws from the hardened rakes gathered around Mme d'Espard, because it is unreasonable: the princesse de Cadignan is innocent, ready for a first love. He could see beyond the limits of reason and recognize the real Diane de Cadignan – an astonishing combination of wit and elegance, of intelligence and sensitivity, of experience and innocence. (In Balzac's lexicon, she, like all who integrate such opposites, is a monster.) As Daniel knows her, so she knows him, since when he returns from visiting Mme d'Espard, she knows he did not defend her: '[T]hey slandered me and you got even for me.'[28] With two such unusual and outstanding people, one can hope that Diane will eventually understand that she may stop the pretense and open the way, so that they may love each other for who they are. To say that the story presents a world which is *anti-nous* is too strong. One should understand, rather, that total dependence on reason and logic will fail to uncover the truth. Because Diane and Daniel can bring the other powers of 'heart' and *esprit* into action, they are able to go beyond reason and find a surer grasp of reality and of each other. They then enter that paradise of completely absorbing love. Those *gens d'esprit* capable of devoting similar qualities to the story will perceive this conclusion, though it will remain forever beyond the capacities of 'those who need to have everything spelled out.' It is for good reason that Diane's and Daniel's given names – the more intimate and individual of their names – are virtual anagrams of each other.

Once again Jacques Cartier and the St Lawrence River come to mind. What had seemed a disappointing geographical feature, because it turned out to be a river rather than a new path to Asia, became the lifeline to an enormous new land Cartier was claiming for France and, to some degree at least, settling. Likewise, rather than a mere character, 'Père Goriot' provides the focus that allows *Le Père Goriot's* system of related themes to coalesce, and a seemingly clumsy repetition may mark the major theme of *Les Secrets de la princesse de Cadignan*.

I do not wish to exaggerate the importance of detail, however; it always takes second place to the entire work. In one way or another, Balzac repeatedly insisted on the importance of wholes. As his spokesman, Félix Davin, put it: '[T]he distinctive task of art is to choose nature's scattered parts, the details of truth, in order to make of them a homogeneous whole' (I.1164). Readers want to be sensitive to details, but only as a means to grasping the specific work, whether *Le Père Goriot* or *Les Secrets de la princesse de Cadignan*. It does not matter that the work is called a 'fragment' (e.g., VII.879), or a 'picture' (e.g. I.1175), or a 'painting' (X.1205), or a 'mosaic' (II.265), or even a 'chapter in the great novel of society' (V.110); readers must come to terms with Balzac's novels and short stories as independent units. To do so requires both sensitivity to the particular details and, as well, the ability to see how various details relate to each other within the context of the entire work. Such elements set up relationships, thus patterns, which illustrate and explain the central theme but are also interesting because of the way they relate to each other.

As is often the case in Balzac's fiction, *Les Secrets de la princesse de Cadignan* is constructed on a paradox. Diane represents innocent depravity, virtuous vice. To evaluate her justly readers must surpass mere reason with qualities of 'heart' and *esprit*. Balzac clearly adored such 'monsters' as Diane de Cadignan, since paradoxical characters are a constant in his fiction. *Le Père Goriot,* as well, sets up the paradoxically unnatural family, which governs the entire novel. On another level, however, Goriot fits into a paradigm. He has been inflected as the three possibilities of his society: rebellion, struggle, and slavery. The entire cast of characters inflect another societal paradigm – *eros, philia,* and *agape.* Here, I move away from the stories, so that the themes lose their texture, and I attempt to delineate the models that allow us to perceive the basic patterns. Paradox is doubtless the most common figure of relationship, but paradigms, similes, and other 'figures of construction' are by no means rare. Such relational devices are important, since they can be perceived in isolated novels and stories, but they also serve as structuring principles linking parts to the whole of *La Comédie humaine.*

CHAPTER THREE

Unifying Units

The transitions between the narrative blocks of *La Comédie humaine* are often either absent or so cursory that some skepticism is justified when one is confronted by Balzac's repeated claims of having created an 'edifice' (V.110). If he has succeeded in making coherent wholes in some of his works, as I argued in the preceding chapter, there are others that include shocking inconsistencies and disconcerting gaps. The complaints about Balzac's structure began rather early, as shown by the essays of Félix Davin, Balzac's spokesman. Although Davin called for patience, surely the grace period has passed. The time has come when it should be possible to 'unveil his plan to the public . . . in order to clear the edifice of the scaffolding and its enclosure of planks' (X.1202). Of course, Balzac's comparison of his opus to a building is nothing but an analogy. Because its walls will not fall and crush anyone, we might then be tolerant of many of the empty spaces between the 'stones' of the master's 'monument' (VII.883). Still, it is not unreasonable to expect to understand the placement and articulation of particular novels and short stories. Occasionally, however generous one might like to be, what Félix Davin called the 'lacunae of its construction' (X.1202) become a real distraction. Especially when the two parts of a single short story such as 'La Fille aux yeux d'or' seem but cursorily related to each other, the 'edifice' seems all too much like a mere pile of rocks.

In the next few pages I would like to consider Balzacian coordination within individual novels and short stories by looking carefully at several problematic, because seemingly disarticulated, cases. The first example, *Splendeurs et misères des courtisanes* (1834–47), was the object of Balzac's attentions over many years; nonetheless, it continues to have seriously flawed coordination. The second allows us to divine what Balzac had in mind as he turned what he called 'six pictures' into *La Femme de trente ans* (1830–42), and in the last, 'La Fille aux yeux d'or' (1834–5), it is perhaps possible to perceive the author's esthetic logic in the seeming absence of links between the work's two panels. It would not have taken much skill to improve or, occasionally, create the transitions in any of the three works. In the first two, more care with the plot, a willingness to cut ungainly extrusions, and more attention to detail would have made smooth reading of jerky narrations. As for 'La Fille aux yeux d'or,' by introducing Paquita or Henri de Marsay in the first of the two poorly coordinated sections, Balzac could easily have contented most critics. The novelist did none of these things. Instead, he relied on descriptive images to encompass and thus unify the parts.

Because of recent interest in melodrama and the more flagrant examples of Romantic narrations, *Splendeurs et misères des courtisanes* has had some attention from critics. Although one can scarcely say that it escaped attention, it was poorly edited in the past. (The standard edition of *La Comédie humaine* well into the twentieth century did not incorporate part IV into *Splendeurs*.) Most readers preferred *Illusions perdues*, and *Splendeurs* was neglected. The problems begin at the very beginning of the book: with the title. Though I shall suggest that it is in fact brilliantly appropriate, Pierre Citron calls it into question: 'It does not incorporate the entire length of the action: Esther dies at the end of the second part. One single courtesan is in question and not several. . . . But the title's sonorousness is admirable in its sumptuousness . . . it has poetic and not literal value.'[1] Balzac began to compose what was to become *Splendeurs* in 1836, though he had the idea early in 1835.[2] Publication did not begin until *La Torpille* appeared in 1838 and did not end until after the author's death, since it was a handwritten note in his corrected copy of the Furne edition that turned *La Dernière Incarnation de Vautrin* into part IV of the novel.

When critics have considered the novel, they have not been lavish in their praise. René Guise points to 'proof that in setting to work, Balzac did not know exactly where he was going' (IV.1310). Antoine Adam concludes, 'In fact, it is clear that [the novel] was not born of a unique conception, that it is not ordered around a single fact.' He believes the history of composition reveals a series of 'new intentions.'[3] For these and other critics *Splendeurs et misères* is a 'house that Jack built,' with one ungainly structure after another tacked onto a changing core. If the story of Esther is central, one must notice that she kills herself at the end of part II. If the story of Lucien, he commits suicide at the end of part III. Esther's death brings her love affair with Lucien to an end. Vautrin's with Lucien stops when the latter dies. And yet the text continues. For those readers who look to the main character and plot for a novel's focus, this work causes no end of trouble, for it drags on through part IV. And even then there is no conventional conclusion. Given the preceding deaths, a series of characters who die, as they do at the end of Stendhal's *La Chartreuse de Parme*, would have provided closure. It is true that Vautrin has gained a position of authority on the police force at the end, but, since he has neither changed nor stopped his criminal activity, his new role does nothing to give the reader a sense of resolution. Balzac was of course fully capable of solving the terminal irresolution. I believe he did, though by completing the central image rather than by adding other events.

The image at the heart of *Splendeurs et misères des courtisanes* appears prominently in the title, a title that, as Charles Affron has said, 'reveals more than one initially suspects.'[4] Balzac surely had in mind Lucien's prostitution of himself to Vautrin and to the society around him. Readers of *Illusions perdues* will remember that Balzac did not spare Lucien from the basic act of prostitution. Though handled with some delicacy, Lucien became Vautrin's catamite. When, after Vautrin explains 'the depths of this friendship, man to man, which binds Pierre to Jaffier, which . . . changes all the social terms [in Otway's *Venice Preserved*] between them' (V.707), after spelling out the 'pact' he offers – 'We are going to dine in Poitiers. There, if you wish to seal the pact, to give me one sole proof of obedience: it is a big one, but I insist on it' (V.708). After learning that the previously impoverished Lucien subsequently sends David and Eve 15,000 francs, it is not difficult to understand why the young man might write, 'I no longer belong to myself. More than the secretary of a Spanish diplomat, I am his creature. I am starting a terrible existence again. Perhaps it would have been better for me to drown myself.'[5] Throughout *Illusions perdues*, he leaves no doubt of the lengths he would go to succeed in life; his behavior in *Splendeurs et misères des courtisanes* gives even less cause for rejoicing. He has become Vautrin's 'creature': the narrator of *Splendeurs* repeats the evaluation Lucien made previously (VI.488). To rise in this world where he once met ignominious defeat, he will serve and service whomever necessary. As though he died morally and spiritually when he originally decided to commit suicide, no sentiment is sacred. He sold his own body for 15,000 francs – and other considerations – and he offers no objection to Esther's selling hers for a good deal more. Furthermore, as Prendergast points out, his prostitution does not stop with Vautrin: 'If Esther markets her body for money, Lucien uses his body to obtain social protection from the women who count.'[6] Prendergast accurately summarizes: 'Lucien's body thus circulates throughout the social organism like an insidious poison generating corruption, excess, madness and death' (85). 'Effeminate insofar as his caprices were concerned' (VI.477), Lucien was 'half woman' (VI.505), and he has 'a woman's heart' (VI.765). It is hardly surprising when Camusot concludes, 'He is a woman' (VI.768). Balzac could not call him a *courtisane*. French grammar does not easily permit such transformations. Nonetheless, the reality remains clear and the title apt. The title becomes even more marvelously suitable when we see that Esther and Lucien are but exemplars of an entire society of sycophants, ready to pander to any vice whatsoever. With all due apologies to French grammar, it seems extraordinarily appropriate to view this as a world of *courtisanes*.

As *Splendeurs* opens, we see Lucien moving through the crowds of the Opéra ball. 'The handsome young man' (VI.432) finally joins an equally beautiful, but masked, young woman, whom Bixiou recognizes as the notorious courtesan, Esther van Gobseck, 'the Torpedo.' 'At eighteen, this girl had already known regal opulence, base poverty, men at every level of society' (VI.442). She might well be considered the epitome of the courtesan. 'No other woman in Paris can say to the Animal [in men] as she does "Come out!" And the animal leaves his house and rolls in excess' (ibid.). Rastignac feels certain that it must be someone else. 'Esther never looked so much like a genteel lady' (VI.443). But Bixiou tricks her into revealing her identity. Though something has clearly changed (in love's crucible, we soon learn), the mysterious woman is indeed Esther.

Her name, and the fact that through her mother she is Jewish might make one recall another, more famous, Esther. The recollection seems appropriate. Both Balzac's Esther and the biblical one were chosen instruments of a higher power. While the ancient namesake was Mordecai's foster daughter, the nineteenth-century Esther is merely picked up, trained, and controlled by Vautrin. ' [S]he believed herself less the object of solicitude than the necessary part of some plan'

(VI.456). And just as the Hebrew Esther saved her people, so the French version is supposed to be the salvation of Lucien as well as Vautrin and his 'sacred battalion' (VI.912). On reading that Vautrin constitutes a 'somber minister that God would use for nothing but the accomplishment of his vengeance' (VI.471), one might remember the death that Mordecai and his foster-daughter arranged for Haman and the other enemies of the Jews. Esther van Gobseck replaces Delphine de Nucingen as the consort for Balzac's Napoleon of finance, while the other replaces King Ahasuerus's deposed Queen Vashti. Of course, this did not occur without considerable risk. Queen Esther says simply, 'If I perish, I perish' (Esther 4.16). Though Balzac's Esther is considerably more loquacious, not only does she lay her life on the line, she actually sacrifices it.

Such allusions are important means of foreshadowing and emphasis. They become especially interesting when authors seem aware that they are establishing something less than a parallel. In this case Balzac apparently wished to emphasize the differences, differences accentuated by the two stories' lack of congruence. Scripture leaves no doubt, for example, that Mordecai was indeed the instrument chosen by God to act and guide Esther according to His will. And, while the theology of God's relationship to Satan and evil is too complex to examine here, it is surely not just surprising but impossible to consider *godly* a character like Vautrin, who is '[e]ndowed with a genius for corruption' (VI.504), whose kindnesses 'seemed to the poor girl like the entryway to hell' (VI.490), who proposes several 'infernal pacts' (VI.502), and who is consistently compared to hell, demons, and the devil.[7] Vautrin's commitment to God is not even skin deep. It stops with his illegitimately worn priestly garb. One could indeed argue that he attempts to replace God, recreating Esther and turning Lucien into a kind of perverted messiah. It is even more interesting to consider the deeds that were responsible for Mordecai's and Vautrin's elevation to power. In Mordecai's case, because he uncovered treason, he was justly rewarded. Vautrin gains his position through blackmail, and he arranges for another man to bear the punishment for the robbery and murder of a Nanterre widow, which should rightly have fallen to his homosexual friend, Théodore Calvi. In short, on every level, Vautrin's rise to power represents a travesty of civilized (or divine) values. He has not changed. Perhaps he really does not need to, since society's values are no different from his own. Indeed, the very concept of law no longer makes sense.[8]

Balzac's use of the biblical story of Esther becomes an oppositional or ironic allusion. Because of those elements that repeat previously established patterns, the differences are not only noted but highlighted. Queen Esther, by godly means, brings triumph to God's chosen people, while Balzac's 'Madeleine' (VI.449) forsakes the purification she has gained through love to prostitute herself again and bring disaster. She does so to help a weak-willed pretty boy, who, though he had long been little more than the tool of a motley collection of thieves and murderers, thereby becomes a pimp. Furthermore, Esther van Gobseck sacrifices herself to no avail. Indeed, her night with Nucingen ultimately results in Lucien's imprisonment, dishonor, and death. But then, Queen Esther worked for God. Her nineteenth-century reincarnation worked only for Vautrin.

Van der Gun defines a courtesan as a 'woman who is or has been venal, and who seeks to hide or efface her venality,'[9] and it would be wrong to consider Queen Esther a courtesan, at least in these terms. Still, she would not have been so useful to God had she not been female. Balzac frequently stressed the similar necessity of 'Parisian women for every kind of ambitious man' (VI.873). In *Splendeurs,* he returns over and over again to the theme: 'A woman's whims reign over the whole state!' (VI.934). Such passages stress another meaning of courtesan: *a woman of the courts, someone who seeks to please the powerful.* The novel seems to suggest that everyone in this society has taken on such a role. Des Lupeaulx even doubts that people have opinions any more... 'there is no longer anything but self-interest' (VI.435), and, as the narrator points out in a passage I shall quote below, ambitious people tend to be complaisant toward the powerful.

By emphasizing a venal woman's desire to hide or cover up her venality, Van der Gun's definition calls attention to the importance of masks in *Splendeur*'s emblematic overture. Esther was masked at the Opéra ball, and she was brought to the brink of suicide when Bixiou recognized her as the Torpille. The virtuous front she wishes to project is but another mask, and Vautrin will help her learn to attach it more firmly. As masks, disguises, pseudonyms are repeated, they gain additional force. As details repeat and become motifs, then take on further meaning to function as symbols, such images are ideational forms which can be used in different ways and in many different contexts, though in all cases they give shape to the fiction. The symbols are formative and extremely important in the organization of the Balzacian world. In the 'monster' of *Les Secrets de la princesse de*

Cadignan, and in the courtesan of *Splendeurs*, we have seen other examples of symbols. They have significant importance to *Splendeurs et misères* and to *Les Scènes de la vie parisienne* as well.

The names Esther takes on – Mme Van Bogseck (VI.485) and Madame de Champy (VI.621) – are nothing but masks, though of a different sort. In the first scene at the Opéra ball, it is worth noting that Lucien Chardon, 'the son of an apothecary,' not only has 'the air of a prince,' he now has a new name: 'By edict of the king, that of my maternal ancestors, the Rubempré, has been returned to me' (VI.432). He is not alone in having left his old name aside. He maliciously reminds M. de Châtelet that his own title is Napoleonic and that his wife used to bear the negligible Bargeton name. Though the latter change was legitimated by marriage, both husband and wife (not to mention Lucien) would prefer to remain masked.

The sinister figure following Lucien epitomizes the symbolic value of masks, especially as it includes disguises and pseudonyms. The narrator stresses the mask Vautrin wears by pointing out, 'With rare exceptions, men do not wear masks in Paris. A man wearing a domino seems ridiculous' (VI.430). Masks mark the jealous or philandering husband, either one of which strikes the crowd as ridiculous. Though a few do indeed mock the black-garbed figure, 'his build and bearing announced his clear disdain for passing comments' (VI.431), and the reader soon learns that he is anything but laughable. He threatens Rastignac in such a way that the latter, 'who was not a man to swallow an insult, stood stock still as though struck by lightening' (VI.434). Rastignac suspects, and is shortly certain, that he is in the presence of Vautrin. 'The man took off his mask; Rastignac hesitated for a moment, not recognizing anything of the hideous person he had once known at the Maison Vauquer. "The devil allowed you to change everything about you, except for your eyes," he said, "which no one could forget" ' (VI.446). Despite Vautrin's new mask of flesh, Rastignac recognizes him and comes smartly to attention. At the criminal's bidding, he will be Lucien's friend and helper.

Vautrin has changed more than his face. He has assumed a new identity and now passes as a priest. He took the name, papers, role, and life of Carlos Herrera, a priest charged with a secret, political mission for King Ferdinand VII. Of course, this is just one of his many names. 'This Spanish priest's cassock hid Jacques Collin, a celebrity of Prison, and who ten years before was living under the middle class name of Vautrin' (VI.502). He is also known as *Trompe-la-Mort* and

William Baker, and he assumes numerous disguises. His acquaintances do likewise. Paccard is 'called Vieille-Garde, Fameux-Lapin, Bon-là' (VI.547); Fil-de-Soie's real name is Sélérier (VI.827), but he has thirty others and as many passports; Jacqueline Collin goes under the pseudonyms of Asie, Mme de Saint-Estève, Mme de San-Esteban, and Mme Nourrisson. And so it goes. Even the spies, though somewhat more legitimate, change names and disguises so frequently that it is difficult on occasion to keep them straight or to distinguish them from the basest of criminals.

If this were all there were to the mask symbol, one might dismiss *Splendeurs* as popular fiction, and go on to more worthwhile works of art. As always, however, when Balzac takes his devices, themes, or characters from less satisfying creations, he uses them to larger ends.[10] Here, I think the false or varying names, the disguises, and, of course, the generic masks serve to highlight the untrustworthiness of the façades that almost every character presents. Where Esther 'fulfilled the admirable fiction of Arab tales, where there is almost always some sublime creature hidden under a degraded cover' (VI.643), the distinguished and enormously wealthy baron Nucingen hides a despicable character. He owes his wealth to some 'secretly shameful means' (VI.644). As one example, the reader is told of Jacques Falleix who 'had been very helpful in speculation,' who was 'the Nucingen firm's appointed agent for foreign exchange,' and whom Nucingen ruined 'as coldly . . . as if it had been a question of killing a lamb for Easter.' The narrator recognizes that 'asking gratitude of a lynx is like trying to elicit pity from a Ukrainian wolf in winter' (VI.592). Consequently, Esther feels justified in fleecing the financier. '[I]t pleased her to play the role of Ate, goddess of vengeance' (VI.644). While Balzac's mythology is questionable – Ate was in fact the goddess of error[11] – his point is nonetheless patent. Furthermore, Esther is not alone. She and Nucingen represent the type or species: 'Every day a hundred and more passions like Nucingen's are born. . . . On their knees, men offer it to girls who, as Asie would say, like to spend money like water. Without this small detail, good middle-class ladies would not understand how a fortune melts in the hands of these creatures, whose social function, in the Fourierist system is perhaps to counter the evils of Avarice and Greed. These dissipations are doubtless for the body of society what the incision of a lancet is for a plethoric body. In two months Nucingen had watered the economy with more than two hundred thousand francs' (VI.617).

Of course, Nucingen is not the first crooked banker, nor is this his first dishonorable fortune. Perhaps that is why the narrator can remain calm as Vautrin's carefully plotted and well-coordinated plans succeed in plundering the financier. The narrator's horror grows, however, on considering Camusot. He is 'a mediocre man,' and his wife is well aware of his 'incompetence' (VI.881). In fact, he does his job extremely well. He is an excellent interrogator, with a finely attuned sensitivity to crime and criminals. The mediocrity that he reveals in this book, at least, comes from doing his job too well. Without regard to social pressure, he breaks down Lucien and catches out Vautrin, which is, after all, his appointed task. But, in this society, only a fool would have worked so effectively. As a 'courtesan' he is a failure. He has been indiscreet, thus lacking essential qualities for the sycophantic courtier Paris demands.

> Today, when people have turned money into a universal social guarantee, judges have been exempted from having a large fortune, as was previously required. . . . Judges [thus] think of gaining promotions by distinguishing themselves, the way people advance in the army or in government.
>
> This kind of thinking, if it does not affect judges' independence, is too well known and too natural – the effects are too obvious – for the magistracy not to lose its majesty in the opinion of the public. The salary which the state pays turns priests and judges into employees. Ranks to earn develop ambition; ambition engenders indulgence toward the powerful; then modern egalitarianism puts the person on trial and the judge on the same social level. So it is that two of the supports of all social order, Religion and Justice, have been diminished in the nineteenth century, when we are supposedly making progress in everything. (VI.801–2)

We already know what is hidden behind Herrera's cassock; now we learn that the solemn demeanor of an examining magistrate covers helpless terror at the thought of his having carelessly embarrassed some indiscreet society women. Because of the letters Léontine de Sérisy, Diane de Maufrigneuse, and Clotilde de Grandlieu wrote to Lucien, which Vautrin carefully tucked away, they are at the mercy of an 'ignoble convict' (VI.813): 'We are three of Eve's daughters wrapped in the serpent of correspondence' (VI.883). Further, the potential scandal touches three families: 'Three great families in peril!' (VI.892).

Ultimately the king is involved: 'This is no longer a vile criminal proceeding, it is an affair of state' (VI.904). Camusot is quite right to 'shiver' (VI.890), though perhaps for the wrong reasons. When the likes of Vautrin can prostitute the law, the government, and hold great families of the realm in his power, society is in dire straits: 'So it is that diverse interests from top to bottom of society were to meet in the office of the attorney general, brought there through necessity and represented by three men: Justice by Monsieur de Granville, Family by Corentin, in front of this terrible adversary, Jacques Collin, who configured the evils of society' (VI.887).

Everyone involved views the problem of Vautrin's guilt or innocence with absolute indifference. To avert a scandal they are willing to release two 'ferocious animals' (VI.831), and, worse, they are ready to accept Jacques Collin, this 'jailbird Cromwell' (VI.804), as a servant of justice and law. This, I believe, constitutes the most significant of the novel's developments. Those magnificent pages of the overture, which reveal Lucien, Esther, Vautrin, Rastignac, and others within the image of the mask, give depth and luster to Balzac's criminal, and it becomes easy to accept the impact he will have on society. Vautrin is introduced in black, a color he favors because of his role as a priest but also, figuratively, because he is a creature of the night, a leader in 'this underground world' of crime (VI.828). It is not surprising that 'the *Cigogne* [stork],' a slang word for the Palace of Justice, here represented by M. de Granville, 'majestically poured contempt on him in the full light of day' (VI.903). Now, however, what was dark has come into the light; what was hidden deep beneath the earth stands proudly above ground. Vautrin is freed, raised from the underground to the sun, and he is given authority. As Bardèche put it, 'There are moments when. . . . you would say that if you lift a stone the sow-bugs begin to swarm.'[12]

The novel trumpets the lesson. This society lacks acceptable values. Virtue has no standing; only money, glory (VI.761), and success (VI.801) are worth anyone's attention. While the church can be used to hide criminals and train courtesans, France's institution of justice grovels before a common criminal. Church, State, and Family have been perverted. Just as a whole society has turned to the job of pleasing others, at any price, so a whole society has adopted the goals and the sycophantic ways of a courtesan. Paris, like Lucien, like Esther, is little more than a common prostitute. The symbol introduced in Balzac's title prepares the first few pages, where the courtesan, Esther, is followed by a gigolo and a gang leader. The trio draw the crowd's attention, but no one senses the shape of the future suggested in the titular *misères* (misfortunes). The gangster and his friends are man-eating animals, one and all. Just as Vautrin controlled Rastignac by frightening him, so he will rule others by fear. In fact, though Jacques Collin renounces 'the insane struggle that I have continued for twenty years against the whole of society' (VI.922), his values remain the same. He has won. But his victory does not truly derive from his superior abilities. It is simply that society resembles him, and he finally couches his immorality in socially acceptable terms. As he puts it to Corentin, 'You are called the State . . . I want to be named Justice. . . . Let us continue to deal with all the more dignity and propriety, given that we will always be... atrocious scoundrels' (VI.921).

Balzac was so caught up in his melodramatic plot around Vautrin that he considered stringing on another development, 'his subterranean duel with the famous Corentin.'[13] Certainly, he was right to decide against such an extension in an already extravagant narration. With Vautrin's ascension to power, the novel is complete. The plot of this voyage from subterranean worlds to the sun has considerable importance for the novel's structure, but one should not, I think, exaggerate its significance. The narration is overwhelmed once again by the image structure. Vautrin's success has precedent in Bibi-Lupin, a criminal who actually did become chief of police. It has happened before, and, by implication, it will happen again. More significantly, Vautrin's rise serves the purpose of illuminating the picture of a rotten society to which the criminal and his machinations are no longer subordinate. Vautrin's passage highlights the two social systems, which are now co-equal. As the new servant of 'Justice' says, 'The positions people gain in the world are only appearance; reality is idea!' (VI.912). The differences between the criminal mastermind marshaling his forces behind Lucien and the reincarnated policeman are negligible. His governing idea remains. He fits very nicely into a society of courtesans wearing handsome masks hiding the basest of characters. From top to bottom, the system is corrupt, and the lambs, like Lydie Peyrade, will be served to handsome but depraved rapists like Henri de Marsay, soon to be prime minister. The configuration prepared by the title and overture is complete. The 'Madeleine' of the first few pages was pursued through the crowds by a gigolo and a criminal, observed by dandies, suborned journalists, and Rastignac, whom Bory calls 'garbage in butter colored gloves.'[14] When the novel draws to a close, the courtesans, Esther and Lucien, have passed from the scene, but the image and the reality of a monstrous society remain.

Although Paris is termed a monster over and over again in *La Comédie humaine*, it is, I think, in *Splendeurs et misères des courtisanes* that the impact of this epithet gains its full force. As the *Scènes de la vie parisienne* open, the narrator stresses Paris's monstrosity: 'Paris is the most delicious of monsters: here it is a pretty woman; farther on she is old and poor; here everything is as new as the money printed by a new regime; in that corner as pretty as a stylish woman. . . . Paris is always this monstrous marvel, an astonishing conglomeration of machines and thoughts, the city of a hundred thousand novels, the head of the world' (V.794–5). Paris paradoxically carries within its breast saint and criminal, Mme de La Chanterie and Vautrin, innocent and depraved, Lydie Peyrade and that 'living image of the Terror,' Jacqueline Collin (VII.386). In *Splendeurs* we learn that two complete societies exist side by side. In the past evil was kept firmly underfoot by the reigning systems of Family, Church, and King, but that has changed. As Davin says, it is a 'society without ties, without principles, without homogeneity' (I.1169). Society is reflected in its language 'which never has but two rhythms: those based on self-interest and vanity' (VII.1196). Because society no longer has any forces of restraint keeping Vautrin and his legions down, they are rising into the sun. Evil has not yet taken over, but it is tolerated, and the danger is very real, since we know that what one generation tolerates, the next embraces. Paris is a courtesan, prostituted on the altar of self-gratification. As Balzac's Gazonal put it in *Les Comédiens sans le savoir*, 'Paris is an avid, mendacious, show-off prostitute' (VII.1202).

Even if one accepts this reading of *Splendeurs*, the difficulty of the conflicting plots remains. The story centering on Esther and Lucien ends long before the novel concludes and that of Vautrin long after. Readers who have noticed a narrative pattern that is repeated throughout *Les Scènes de la vie parisienne* will not be disturbed by these overlapping plots, however, because they will recognize that as Vautrin moves through the ball following his two minions, he begins a penetration pattern, which ends as he takes his position as chief of police. A character's attempted penetration into a closed circle is the most common type of plot in this portion of *La Comédie humaine*. Like the symbols of mask and monster, such repeated narrative patterns constitute an armature which can be filled with differing material and superficially shaped in a number of different ways. Balzac seems to be thinking of the latter in the unfinished article, 'Théorie du conte [Theory of the Tale].' On returning home, he imagines that he confronts numerous copies of himself. One of them poses the following problem:

> Let there be a husband, his wife, and a lover: derive from this a hundred tales, of which none resembles any other.
>
> In the same way let a cook make a hundred dishes with . . . eggs.
>
> In the same way let a mathematician imagine the possibility of drawing as many circles as he would like and prove that in this circular abyss a man could use up all the chalk in the world.
>
> 'Get lost!' I told him. 'Call in Nodier, that magician of language, that sorcerer whose wand evokes brand new phrases. Call on Etienne Béquet . . . ; ask Eugène Sue. . . .' I was going to call the roll of all our great writers when my own self, who never laughs, smiled [and] showed me the hundred expressions of the algebraic formula represented by the hundred versions of myself. Each of them wanted to get out of their prisons and come recite their formulas, none of which would resemble the others. (HH XXII.661)

Like symbols, narrative armatures reflect Balzac's dominant idea of this society. By focusing on the plot of penetration, as on images of courtesans and masks, one makes no decision about the possibility that Balzac's ideas may have changed while he was writing the novel. It is possible, however, to observe Balzac's intensive use of Esther, Lucien, and Vautrin to establish mutually reflecting penetration plots that loosely stitch together blocks of description, where the reader is presented with an unusually coherent vision of a society with its façade removed. We see a society of pandering courtesans rising through criminal means from the dark, spreading corruption through Church and State, destroying innocent and guilty alike, to luxuriate in the sun. The novel's superstructure consists of an idea: social authority, which should rightly be devoted to the body politic, but which kneels to individual vice. Great aristocratic and powerful financial families are subjected to masks, courtesans, darkness, and corruption. When *Splendeurs et misères des courtisanes* is published with all four parts, the novel seems adequately, if not totally, coherent. Only at the end of the fourth section does Vautrin bow to social exigencies and adopt the sycophantic methods of a courtesan, thus clothing his greed in an acceptable form; only then does the novel achieve the needed closure.

La Femme de trente ans is not as successful as *Splendeurs*. It has many obvious weaknesses, about which Pierre Citron and others have justifiably complained.[15] Unrealistic elements, imprecision, exaggerations, a bothersome diversity of tones, an inconsistent heroine, not to mention an annoying confusion of children and their ages: the flaws are undoubted, though perhaps surprising, for the novel as it stands is the result of a dozen years of revisions. Still, on searching for the elements that tie these often disparate bits and pieces together, the flaws lose their sharp contours, and one understands Balzac's manner of linking somewhat better. Unlike many of his works, the images and allusions help little in this linkage. While Julie d'Aiglemont sings Desdemona's romance in part I (II.1081), for example, and the Parisian's ship is called *Othello* in part V (II.1182), few other details recall the story of Othello. Other apparently promising motifs turn out to be equally unfruitful.

One begins to recognize the Balzacian techniques and indeed skills on noting the way he uses repetition of narrative patterns to emphasize a point. Just as Julie d'Aiglemont disobeyed her father, so her daughters disobey her; and as she breaks her marriage vows, so eventually does one of her daughters. When the pattern repeats in the daughters, thus establishing the armature, the mother is punished terribly. Early in Julie's life, her grief over the death of her passionate companion, Arthur, leads her to regret her physical fidelity to her husband. 'I would like to start a war against this world, so as to renew its laws and customs,' she tells the parish priest of Saint-Lange (II.1116). He understands what her pain and rebellious feelings portend: 'You are lost, madam. . . . You will return to society and you will deceive society. There you will seek and there you will find what you look at as compensation for your problems. Then, some day, you will bear the painful results of your pleasures...' (II.1118). It is anything but an accident that the means of the harshest retribution recalls her own filial disobedience.

When Moïna, Julie's daughter by her lover Charles de Vandenesse, falls in love with Alfred de Vandenesse, Moïna is aware neither that Alfred is 'a man for whom nothing was sacred' (II.1208) nor that he is her half-brother. Nonetheless, despite her ignorance that she commits incest, she knows her mother is distressed, and with the insouciance of youth she serves as a terrible tool of punishment. Balzac explains, 'God who, often, places his vengeance in the midst of families and eternally uses children against mothers, fathers against sons, peoples against kings, princes against nations, everything against everything' (II.1204–5). The passage has considerable importance for *La Comédie humaine* in that it demonstrates once again how Balzac saw individuals in the light of the greater society. Individuals' lives, hopes, dreams, tragedies, joys, charities, and crimes were for him analogous to larger societal realities, as of course were his own stories and his work as a whole. But in the light of *La Femme de trente ans*, its significance is more prophetic and sinister. When Moïna, smitten with her half-brother, answers her mother's veiled warnings by saying, 'Mama, I thought you were only jealous of his father' (II.1213), it wounds her mother severely, and the latter seeks sanctuary in the garden. Unfortunately, rather than peace, she finds the recent prints left by Alfred's boots as he visited Moïna's bed. Julie is devastated and dies shortly thereafter.

Julie's punishment reminds us of the model of her own youth. When she refuses to heed her father's 'prophetic voice' (II.1051) and marries the intellectually and spiritually limited Victor, she begins the pattern that will be repeated in her daughters. Julie's daughter Hélène also ignores her father's voice, which 'was lost in the night like a vain prophesy' (II.1178). Her ravisher (a character in the tradition of the gothic novel) also bears her father's name of Victor, that is, the name of the reason for her mother's earlier disobedience. When a shipwreck finally claims Hélène's pirate husband, she escapes to die with her last child in her mother's arms. Two generations dead as a direct result of the mother's failings. As Hélène says, 'This is all your work! If you had been for me what...' (II.1200) Then, a few moments later, she utters one of the book's lessons: 'Happiness is never found outside the law...' (II.1201).

As always, however, Balzac attempts to illuminate the causes of the social maladies he describes. '[T]his story explains the mechanism and the dangers of love more than it depicts them' (II.1137). The Saint-Lange priest tearfully draws our attention to Julie's 'egotism,' a word that appears repeatedly and a quality demonstrated by both Julie and her illegitimate daughter, Moïna. Julie's father, M. de Chastillonest, points to one of the results of this egotism in children: 'I always see children attributing the sacrifices their parents make for them to personal desire!' (II.1051). While Balzac carefully prepares the more extreme case of Père Goriot and his daughters, the account that directly follows *La Femme de trente ans*, he concentrates here not on the terrible effects that selfishness has on parents but on those resulting in the child herself. The priest of Saint-Lange points directly to the character traits that will eventually destroy Julie: '[T]he way you talk proves that neither family ties nor religious commitment affect you. Consequently, you do not hesitate between the social egotism which hurts you and that human egotism which encourages you to hope for enjoyment' (II.1119). God's voice, he says, has been stifled by 'the great and terrible clamor of egotism' (II.1120).

Many of Balzac's stories have allegorical resonances. This level of meaning strikes modern readers as inconsistent, since allegory is normally antithetical to a realistic portrayal of the world and allegorical overtones then conflict with expectations. In fact, however, Balzac wanted his stories to serve as indices to the social reality of his day. 'In literature,' he said, 'it is not enough to amuse, or to please, you have to connect some meaning to the pleasantry' (HH XXIV.157). The events taking place in the Aiglemont family were occurring in society where the ill effects are multiplied. Balzac studies what he calls the *écorché* (cut-away drawing) of a thirty-year-old woman (II.1137). Julie is 'deaf to the voice of religion, as are all the offspring of this unbelieving century' (II.1120). Given that the French were unwilling or unable to lock up their women – a thought that attracted Balzac, since he mentioned it positively and repeatedly across the *Comédie humaine* (e.g., II.1136) – a thirty-year-old woman is without protection against the love of a young man. Comparing the process to 'the weakest insect walking to his flower with irresistible will, terrified by nothing' (II.1035), he leads his reader to see that society's shields, which formerly protected women, have fallen away. For Balzac, as for Voltaire, when one stripped away the surface, protective layers with which civilization had covered people, one found, not Rousseau's noble savage, but rather a savage beast that wreaked incalculable harm. Where Julie refuses to listen to her father, she is deaf to the voice of the institution of Family, and she seemingly cannot hear that of the priest of Saint-Lange, the representative of the Church. She is consequently 'at an age when marriage is a burden, boring, and tiring, when conjugal affection is no more than lukewarm, if indeed the husband has not abandoned her' (II.1136), and open to the call of natural but self-centered desires. She takes a lover, an act that has unexpected results: it opens Hélène as well as the rest of the family to the assassin, Victor. So that we do not miss the assassin's significance, we are told he has 'the gaze of a serpent' (II.1170), 'something reptilian about him' (II.1174), and 'the appearance of Lucifer picking himself up after the fall' (II.1170). Julie states unequivocally, '[H]e is the devil' (II.1174).

Julie attributes the harvest of little Charles's death, Hélène's disasters, and Moïna's selfishness and incest to 'the designs of Providence, so as to once again be able to love the hand that was striking her' (II.1210). Balzac's narrator, as we have seen, is more precise. He attributes the successive tragedies to 'The Finger of God' (II.1142).

Modern readers have little patience for allegories of divine retribution, but the point here is not to judge the content, rather to understand the technique. Somewhere in the process of creation, Balzac realized that he could make a more complex and interesting use of such disparate pieces as the narrative descriptions of a bored young woman before the Loire valley, a girl watching Napoleon and Victor d'Aiglemont (who benefits from the emperor's reflected glory and her own infatuation), a child causing the death of another. The most obvious technique is the onomastic linkage provided by putting several of the significant characters into the same family and thus giving them the same name. Balzac then calls attention to the familial relationship of the main characters, while emphasizing certain narrative patterns. And as a backdrop he played out a primeval drama, where a woman succumbs to nature and, for the sake of her lover, 'kills an entire family' (II.1129). It is on this allegorical level that one finds an important development. When Julie turns a deaf ear to her father's warning about Victor – '[H]e has no talent and is a spendthrift. God created men like him to eat and digest four meals a day, to sleep, to make love to the first passing woman, and to fight' (II.1050) – it does not seem too serious. It would be neither the first nor the last marriage marked by intellectual and spiritual disparity. But for a woman no longer shielded by vital social institutions, it is only a matter of time until she takes a lover. Here again, while today's reader might not shiver with revulsion, he should note that the adultery is but one more step on the path to destruction. Hélène, the legitimate offspring, is jealous of the love child, Charles, and murders him. It is only a matter of time until she too refuses to heed a parent's warning and brings a killer, an Othello, into the family. The reader observes the crescendo of despair ending when Moïna refuses to heed a parent's warning and goes on to indulge not in 'mere' adultery but in incest, one of the few virtually universal taboos.

When Félix Davin considered the 'scenes' of *Même histoire*, which still lacked the onomastic coordination, he shares the regrets that they 'have no other connection between them but a philosophic thought.' For him, '[I]t was not enough . . . that there was a very logical succession of ideas, a sort of brotherhood of well-chosen principles. Both heart and imagination also insist on being satisfied, as well. It is with difficulty that they renounce the attraction that a character inspires. They grow cold when too many new ones appear. In order to recognize [what that author calls] the "same" heroine in each chapter, you have to have read almost the whole book. While this may create poetry, it also has its dangers: the author runs the risk of not being understood' (I.1164). Balzac did indeed give the figure crossing *Même histoire* the same name when he turned it into *La Femme de trente ans*, but I think he did so not only for the reasons suggested by Davin. Balzac had come to understand that if he integrated all the stories into the same family, the filial disobedience theme could have a meaning that was denied to the less coordinated early collection. At this point the central figure became Julie d'Aiglemont.

Beneath the idea of a society lacking family and religious authority, Balzac configures Julie as a rebellious young woman, who at thirty has no protection against common temptations and thus opens her family to murder and incest. Repeated stories of a child's refusing to obey a parent are made to seem all the more related by involving different offspring of the same family. The sin of the mother destroys only three generations by the end of *La Femme de trente ans*, but the lesson is clear: the virus has no reason to stop spreading in such a society as this. In short, to the dominant idea, images, narrative armatures, and numerous less important motifs operating in *Splendeurs et misères des courtisanes*, Balzac adds family ties, which in *La Femme de trente ans* emphasize the defenselessness of the family by showing the results of Julie's actions, not merely in a series of different thirty-year-old women but in the destruction visited on an entire family.

Another of Balzac's microcosms, 'La Fille aux yeux d'or,' is widely discussed in current criticism because of the violent Romantic drama of conflicting lesbian and heterosexual passions. The pattern created by fitting the long expository introduction with the story of Henri de Marsay and Paquita is typical of much of Balzac's apparently asystematic junctures. It gives a glimpse into the author's fictional morphology, since it reveals how causality joins disjunctive parts to other parts and the parts to the whole. 'La Fille aux yeux d'or' poses the problem of coherence at a level that is at once convenient and appropriate. Certainly, the secondary literature makes clear that its unity is decidedly problematic. After a long, introductory exposition describing Paris and Parisians, suddenly, without apparent preparation, its narrator switches to the apparently unrelated account of one of Henri de Marsay's love affairs.

At first glance, when 'La Fille aux yeux d'or' may seem but one more example of Balzac the egregious Romantic enamored of 'blood and guts,' it has little to recommend it. Rereading raises the interest, however, since one begins to perceive Balzac as Realist-Naturalist in search of man, in his natural habitat. It is well known that Balzac proclaimed himself a 'naturalist,' by which he meant, simply, someone who studied nature in a scientific manner. His prey, however, was the human being in society, and he delighted in emphasizing the parallels between humans and their animal brothers. Father Birotteau is a lamb; Sophie Gamard a spider catching a fly, a bird of prey, a tiger; Gobseck a boa; Vautrin a lion; Nucingen a pig; and poor Goriot a dog. Critics have not missed the metaphor. Nor should they. It is a constant in Balzac's novels, and an important theme in his prefatory apologies.

In the 1842 'Avant-Propos' to the *Comédie humaine*, Balzac made a considerable effort to associate his work with that of 'the greatest geniuses of natural history like Leibniz, Buffon, Charles Bonnet, etc.' (I.8). He wanted us to know that he had no need to wait for the controversy between Cuvier and Geoffroy Saint-Hilaire to understand and use the concept of a single progenitor from which all animals derive. 'Penetrated by this system long before the debates which it elicited, I saw that in this respect Society resembled Nature. Does not society make of man, depending on the milieus where his actions unfold, as many different men as there are varieties in zoology?' (ibid.). Like the scientist who studies wolves, lions, donkeys, crows, sharks, seals, sheep, Balzac has turned his attention to soldiers, workers, administrators, lawyers, idlers, scientists, statesmen, businessmen, sailors, poets, priests (the enumeration of the 'Avant-Propos' recalls a similar catalogue in 'La Fille aux yeux d'or').

Curiously, Balzac's list of attractive research topics neglects monsters, a subject of considerable interest to naturalists. Its absence is particularly conspicuous when we remember that while emphasizing types, Balzac stressed the importance of detail and variations as well. Furthermore, neither he nor other major naturalists of his day neglected genetic sports, and he (perhaps because of his period, perhaps because of his perverse love of the bizarre) was particularly attracted to those abnormal variations that can best be termed monsters. On considering

La Comédie humaine in its entirety, one might wonder whether, instead of a study of types, a detailed analysis of the norm, or a bestiary including only domesticated or well-documented creatures, Balzac has specialized in the deviant and monstrous. One might wonder whether to a substantial degree Balzac was, as Michel Nathan has suggested, a teratologist.[16] Earlier I pointed to the paradoxical quality of many Balzacian 'monsters.' In 'La Fille aux yeux d'or,' we see those fearsome and destructive qualities suggested by the symbol.

'La Fille aux yeux d'or' concentrates on society as a 'receptacle of monstrosities' (V.891) where the deviant has become the norm. Like a Hieronymus Bosch of the novel, Balzac takes his rich verbal palette and paints a hell peopled by strange, disgusting creatures, 'a vast field, incessantly stirred by a tempest of selfish desires beneath which swirls a harvest of men that death mows down more often than elsewhere . . . whose deformed, twisted faces give off the desires, the poisons which have burdened their minds through every spiritual pore; not faces, masks rather – masks of weakness, masks of strength, masks of misfortune, masks of joy, masks of hypocrisy; all exhausted, all marked with indelible signs of panting avidity' (V.1039). The 'almost infernal complexion of Parisian faces' is explained by the frequently mentioned fact that 'Paris has been termed a hell' (V.1039). The horrors would do Bosch proud.

Across all the classes, in all the professions, there are only two ages: youth and decrepitude. This is a society where the young rapidly burn themselves out. The remaining empty shells use cosmetics liberally in the vain attempt to bring back the springtime years they so briefly enjoyed. Paris is a volcano, pouring fire from its crater and consuming its inhabitants so rapidly that one might think they were nothing but moths condemned to self-destruction in the flame. Balzac returns repeatedly to the central vision of a gray, worn-out people, the husks of ardent youth, sickly in color, with rings around dead eyes above sensual mouths. For the narrator, there is no mistaking the signs of debased thought churning in deteriorating minds. These people are unable to rise to the more elevated forms of mental exercise, whether generalizing, making deductions, seeing the bigger picture, or generating new ideas. Corruption, depravity, pestilence bathe an empty people of ephemera who pass away leaving a world the worse for their passage.

By the second paragraph of the introduction, the narrator promises to 'explain the causes' (V.1039) of the horrifying phenomena he has signaled. Later, almost in passing, he will mention several, for example: 'These [middle-class] people [of the third social circle] live, almost all of them, in foul studies, in stinking courtrooms, in small barred offices' (V.1046–7). Farther on he becomes even more precise, and graphic: '[I]n addition to this stench the forty thousand houses of this large city bathe their foundations in filth. . . . Half of Paris goes to bed in the putrid exhalations of courtyards, streets, and sewage' (V.1050). As usual, of course, Balzac is most interested in moral explanations, and he pauses repeatedly to insist on the 'general cause': the deep, pervasive, dominating lust for 'gold and pleasure' (e.g., V.1040). '[T]his universal master, pleasure or gold,' (V.1045) constitutes the root cause for the horrifying destruction at work from bottom to top in each circle of Parisian society.

Balzac's description, which justifies this introductory conclusion, may be far too lively to pass as good scholarship, though the narrator tries to be thorough, pursuing the matter up the social ladder: from the bottom, where workers are turned by love of gold and pleasure into dull beasts of burden for six days a week so that they may remain blind drunk the other, to the top, where the very rich pass their every moment, not in amassing wealth, but in satisfying their self-centered desires. They succeed only in abusing their senses, until they settle into a besotted bestiality. Where the bourgeois, '[h]aving started early in the attempt to become remarkable men . . . become mediocre and crawl on the world's heights' (V.1048), the rich merely intensify the process of becoming vacuous... lacking ideas, lacking love, lacking the very pleasure for which they have abandoned every virtue.

With several lapidary formulae, the narrator pauses to reiterate the lesson: passion destroys. We already know from the preceding page that '[I]n Paris, vanity sums up all the passions' (V.1048). Now we see once again that these destructive passions, this vanity, in fact '[a]ll passion can be broken down into two terms: gold and pleasure' (V.1049).

Of course, the narrator hastens to assure us, there are rare exceptions. These unusual phenomena of virtue, characterized by a magnificent ability to combine thought and action, occur only among the young, the newly arrived, and those who for one reason or another remain temporarily innocent – fools, loafers (*flâneurs*), and women who live in an oriental fashion, rarely going out, thus preserving their beauty.

The narrator then brings this introduction to a close, and he does so in a most amazing way: 'If this rapid glance at Paris's population causes one to grasp the rarity of a Raphaelesque countenance, and the passionate admiration it must at first sight inspire, the principal significance of our story will have been born out. *Quod erat demonstrandum*, that which was to be demonstrated, if one may apply scholastic formulas to the science of customs' (V.1054). An introduction of some 6,000 words to make the reader sense the rarity of Raphaelesque beauty! The temptation is perhaps to wax ironic over mountains moving mightily to produce a mouse and, certainly, judging from the criticism, to conclude that the introduction fits poorly, if at all, with the story of Henri and Paquita.

Experienced Balzacians will pause, however, because they know that when Balzac becomes ponderous, waving a professorial index finger, there is usually more going on than the surface would indicate. If one resists the temptation to dismiss the introduction and treats it rather with the seriousness that Balzac's overtures demand, one could summarize and say that his central point was somewhat different than a first glance at the above passage might indicate, though it indeed leads to a recognition of the unusual nature of beauty in such surroundings. The narrator has covered the various levels of Paris to show that at every level, in every category, people 'ask for glory, which is pleasure, or love, which requires gold' (V.1052). Whether it is because of the moral decay in these people who have committed themselves totally to 'gold and pleasure' or whether it is the physiological deformations that result from the Parisian pollution, one expects to find nothing but moral and physical monsters. As the narrator says, 'This vision of the moral fiber of Paris proves that the physical nature of Paris could not be different from what it is' (V.1051). Exceptions are indeed amazing.

Only after completing the story, and reconsidering it in detail, does one realize that the rarity of Raphaelesque beauty is by no means a trivial point. And while one may view Henri de Marsay with admiration, the narrator injects a note of caution when he calls him an Adonis. Few nineteenth-century readers would fail to remember that despite Adonis' effeminate beauty, he was the result of an unspeakable act and caused no end of trouble before being gored by a stag. Balzac has introduced the themes of androgyny and incest with one comparison. Rapidly the reader learns that Henri is a moral monster, born out of wedlock, provided with a purchased name and an inattentive, substitute father. Furthermore, he was taken in hand and formed by a conscienceless priest who attempted to 'replace his mother in a virile way' (V.1056). 'Henri was as courageous as a lion, as dexterous as a monkey' (V.1057). Adept with weapons, he 'rode horses so well that he brought the fable of centaurs back to life' (ibid.). Centaurs were, of course, the flesh-eating, rapist monsters who symbolize brutal violence, the image of a ruling unconscious.[17] Not surprisingly, '[H]e believed in neither man nor woman, in neither God nor the devil. Capricious nature had begun to bless him, a priest had finished him' (V.1057).

Later, Henri introduces the central image of the story. He compares Paquita to 'the delirious painting called *a woman caressing her chimera*' (V.1065). The chimera was a hybrid monster with a lion's head, a goat's body, and a dragon's tail. Paul Diel, for whom the monster is a complex symbol of imaginary creations or desires which come from the depths of the unconscious to seduce and destroy those who submit to them, relates the serpent's tail of the chimera to the spiritual perversion of vanity, her goat's body to perverse and capricious sexuality, her lion's head to a tendency to domination which corrupts all social relations.[18] Henri's pride is unequaled. His beauty, wit, moral force, and wealth have made him irresistible to others and have left him sated. 'For him to feel the emotions of true love, he would have had to have, like Lovelace, a Clarissa Harlowe. Without the magical shimmer of this unknowable pearl, he could have nothing but passions stimulated by some Parisian vanity, or private decisions to see how much he could corrupt a woman, or adventures that stimulated his curiosity' (V.1070). We remember that he later pays for the right to rape the abducted Lydie Peyrade (VI.661). Physically vain, he spends two and a half hours preparing to go out (V.1071–2). His dominant feature is perhaps his vanity; it is certainly the reason he decides to 'execute' (V.1097) the *girl with the golden eyes*. The narrator emphasizes and affirms Henri's identification with the chimera when he shows us Paquita mistakenly confusing him with 'one of these angels I had been taught to hate and in which I saw nothing but monsters, while you are the most beautiful creature on earth' (V.1099). He symbolically summarizes those penchants, catalogued in the opening pages, that are destroying Paris and Parisians: 'For a woman to see [Henri] was to be crazy about him – you know, it created one of those desires which sink their teeth deep into a woman's heart' (V.1057).

At this point one has perhaps a fuller sense of the purpose of the story's opening pages. In them Balzac has given us the causes for products like Henri de Marsay. While such monsters are normally as ugly as they are morally repugnant, exceptions are the more dangerous. The monstrous Henri, and his sister (whom Paquita terms a

monster – V.1099), were engendered by the self-centered English Lord
Dudley in search of pleasure. The latter's title is quintessentially
appropriate, as Shoshana Felman has pointed out, since French
pronunciation makes it a homonym of gold, l'or.[19]

While few would question Michel Nathan's evaluation of Henri de
Marsay's monstrosity, there might be more hesitation when he likewise
calls Paquita a monster ('Zoologies,' 193). Nathan's insight is justified
if we recall that physical beauty may, as in M. de Marsay, mask a
loathsome reality. We remember that Paquita's mother was once
'bought for her rare beauty in Georgia' (V.1081). It is perhaps not an
accident that her name, Concha, is Spanish slang for the female
genitals.[20] A compulsive gambler, she has sold her daughter and, the
final events imply, her soul to gratify her thirst for pleasure. Now,
'[t]his decrepit woman was like a possible conclusion and configured
the horrible fish tail with which the Greek geniuses of symbols ended
the Chimeras, the Sirens, who were so seductive, so deceptive in the
bodice, as are all passions at the beginning' (V.1080). The monster
Echidne had a woman's body ending in a snake's tail.[21] She gave birth
to numerous monsters, among whom was Chimera. If we accept Diana
Festa-McCormick's suggestion that 'the old woman . . . symbolizes
Paris' manipulative force,'[22] one might wonder whether she does not
also serve as a figurative mother to Henri, while actually fulfilling that
function for her 'monstrous' daughter, Paquita.

Certainly, just as gold is a medium for acquiring one's desires, so is
the girl with the golden eyes. She has but one function: to bring pleasure.
Paquita invites Henri to help himself to the gold in the house, a
suggestion he rejects out of hand. 'It is not mine' (V.1102). Understanding perfectly that in taking her, he might just as well have taken gold,
Paquita insists on the parallel: 'Didn't you take me?' she asks (ibid.).
Like her mother, she comes from a land where women are merchandise, not human beings. They are bought, sold, or killed, as the owner
wishes. '[A]fter all . . . you use them for your caprices, just as you use
your furniture' (V.1108). Paquita's golden eyes reflect her value. In
search of pleasure she dispenses herself – property she does not own
– for Henri, the alluring and monstrous offspring of a sick civilization.
Likewise, the whole of society spends its gold to pander to its vices.
Henri believed in neither man, God, nor devil and, consequently, has
unlimited destructive power. The narrator puts it succinctly: 'Morality
has no force against a dozen vices which destroy society and which
nothing can punish' (V.1097). It is only when the two panels of Balzac's

diptych are seen as one composition that readers understand the degree to which Henri de Marsay incarnates vice and, further, the degree to which Paris' frenetic need for pleasure and gold encourages, indeed causes, the most unnatural depravity. We know that Henri's sister is a lesbian; we sense that his natural father is bisexual. As Le Yaouanc demonstrates, while Lord Dudley's passion for women leaves numerous siblings for his unknowing children, it is doubtless his homosexuality that makes him a fugitive from English justice.[23] When he is forced in 1816 to take refuge in Paris and sees Henri, he asks the identity of 'this handsome young man.' 'Ah! it's my son. How unfortunate!' (V.1058). Few would not understand that he is attracted by the boy, though he draws the line at incest. Henri is not so scrupulous. When his sister, Mme de San-Réal, announces her imminent departure, he protests. ' You're still too young, too beautiful, said Henri taking her in his arms and kissing her' (V.1109).

While the more or less veiled suggestions of homosexuality, lesbianism, bisexuality, and incest have been recognized by numerous critics,[24] the importance and thrust of an element uncovered by Gaubert has not. Paquita has dressed her lover to resemble a woman (his femininity has been well established[25]). Henri suspects that he has been used. An earlier version may indicate what he had in mind: '[W]hy are you worshipping me in a shawl, why are you doing everything in your power to establish your illusion. You have deceived me; you have prostituted me. You don't know what a man is. Well, you are about to get to know one in all his majesty' (V.1566). When he is in Paquita's arms and actually understands the depth of her love, he wonders, 'Am I the one she prefers?' (V.1100) The possibility makes him consider forgiving her offense, at least until she cries out, 'Oh! Mariquita!' (V.1102) in a moment of passion. Then the possibility of pardon dissipates forever, since Henri's vanity suffers immeasurably. He concludes that, after dressing him to resemble her lesbian lover, Paquita has called out to her, and knowing no Spanish, he is then outraged on making the obvious assumption that he has been nothing but a substitute, a mere stand-in. Readers, as the criticism shows, have echoed Henri's mistake.[26] They understood 'Mariquita' to be a pet name for Margarita de San-Réal, Paquita's lesbian mistress and Henri's sister, and they interpret Paquita's cry, 'Mariquita!' as proof that he has failed to supplant the unknown mistress. All of which emphasizes the brilliance of Balzac's find.

As Gaubert pointed out, *Mariquita* is a name given in Spain to effeminate men and homosexuals.[27] Paquita's 'Mariquita!' is a passionate recognition that Henri is not one of these men she has been trained to hate (V.1099). Henri has succeeded in bridging the gap. Neither man nor woman, Henri is an androgynous being, an Adonis.[28] What he understands to mark his failure, in truth proclaims his total victory. Indeed, if Paris constitutes a maker of monsters, and the overture indicates as much, then Henri represents its most perfect work.

Perhaps at this point the genius of Balzac's conjunction becomes apparent. By themselves, the two panels of this work are interesting, though I suspect neither would ever rise much above the general run of, on the one hand, journalistic commentaries and, on the other, pulp fiction. The brief glimpses of various worlds in the first section are too brief to allow a reader to become deeply involved. It is indeed but an overview, and a brief one at that. The second panel might at first seem to be a close-up of one of the realities that passed so rapidly under the narrator's eye in the introduction. Were that the case, one would expect a series of similarly microscopic treatments. That, of course, does not happen. And the more one considers the actual story of the *girl with the golden eyes*, the better one understands why only one example is provided, why only one was necessary.[29]

Just as the first part concerned Paris, at every level and in all its parts, so we see, by the juxtaposition, the second. Paquita is the fresh-faced, beauteous, youthful newcomer, avid for new experiences, ready to break the rules of her upbringing. Her status as merchandise is signaled by her golden eyes. Though a human being, she has lost all value except as exchange in this world ruled by a vain desire for gold and pleasure. Unlike the inconsequential Paul de Manerville who is unable to commit himself fully, Paquita hazards everything she has and is, everything she ever will be. Her mother, on the other hand, already has gone as far as one may go. Now reduced to preying on the helpless, she is ready to glean by whatever means the wherewithal for her remaining pleasures.

In *La Peau de Chagrin*, the skin graphically symbolizes expending one's energy. Here, Paquita illustrates a society self-destructing as its members frantically run after their own and others' self-indulgent pleasures. The further result of this activity is perhaps more frightening: Henri de Marsay. We see him as a monstrous *mariquita* willing to destroy another human being for a frivolous revenge or a moment's pleasure. That he was later responsible[30] for Lydie Peyrade's madness and death is to be expected, and in a society that would choose a Vautrin for chief of police, it is no surprise to see Henri de Marsay as prime minister.

The first panel of 'La Fille aux yeux d'or' is related to the second as cause is related to effect. The narrative has two elements that make a complete narrative 'clause,' in Balzac's grammar of fiction. Not past and present, not beginning and end, but cause and effect. The narrator first sets the stage by describing a society where at every level people have sold themselves for gold and pleasure. Because it lacked the narrational exemplar which gives life, this vision by itself would have been incomplete, at least in the Balzacian world (though it can and did stand alone for a time). As it is now arranged, the overture of 'La Fille aux yeux d'or' is similar to most of Balzac's famous descriptive openings. It differs not in length, since many of his introductions are long, but rather in that the setting it provides for the subsequent narration is the whole of Paris, instead of a considerably more limited place like Saint-Symphorien or the Pension Vauquer. This expanded setting indicates one of the laws of conjunction in *La Comédie humaine*: description is always illustrated by one or more narrations. In this story it is only with the second panel that we see where such a society leads. It eventually generates monsters, which turn on the very society that gave them birth.

While one must acknowledge the importance of recurring themes, motifs, and vocabulary,[31] Balzac seems to have had the vision of a more important fictional morphology underlying and joining the superficially unrelated sequences. 'La Fille aux yeux d'or' is, however, unified within a symbolic Paris considered a 'receptacle of monstrosities,' just as *Le Père Goriot*, *Splendeurs et misères*, and *La Femme de trente ans* were unified within their emblematic titles. This view requires some reordering of expectations, however, since Balzac was not primarily concerned with telling tales. As he insisted over and over again, he was engaged in creating 'the picture of Society' (I.12). Either the narratives are repeated until the armature is established and the normal movement of narration is stilled, or they dramatically illustrate the descriptions. In general, the descriptive passages are subsumed to the dominant idea, 'the reason or reasons for these social effects, . . . the hidden meaning in this immense assembly of figures, passions, and events' (I.11). In Balzac's creations the descriptions are accompanied by dramatic illustrations (little Hélène causes her baby brother, Charles, to drown, for example), by symbols (whether monsters, courtesans, or gold), or by major images (such as the prophetic voices of

La Femme de trente ans, which often, as in Henri's murderous rage in 'La Fille aux yeux d'or,' portray the effects deriving from causes revealed in loving detail across some expository passage). All three works considered in this chapter have noticeable seams, if not gaps, in their plots. Still, despite many opportunities to rectify the 'problem,' Balzac's revisions did not generally affect the narration, but rather were directed toward strengthening the major ideas and images through the repetition of important elements. This repetition constitutes an important indication of what he thought important. One needs to bring more modern techniques of reading to his creations. Had Balzac written in the twentieth century, we should no more complain about his transitions than we do of those in Proust's *A la recherche du temps perdu* (1913–27) or Pinget's *Clope au dossier* (1961). We should simply fit the various parts into the image of the whole. Other principles of conjunction govern collective works like *Histoire des Treize*, *Jésus-Christ en Flandre*, or *Autre étude de femme*, but within individual novels or novellas Balzac always rounded out his expository descriptions with narration, explanation with demonstration, cause with effect. With the completion of the narrational example, and within an illuminating symbol, Balzac's practice was to complete what, under the name of Félix Davin, he elsewhere called 'pictures' (I.1146) or 'paintings' (I.1147). Such paintings were destined to be included within the 'frame' of Paris (ibid.) or society as a whole and, eventually, of his cycle. Before setting a particular novel or short story into *La Comédie humaine*, he worked to make it a coherent unit in and for itself. The rough rock had to lose its sharp edges before taking its appointed place as a stone in the edifice of the whole.

CHAPTER FOUR

Conjoining the Disjoined

Collections of fiction seldom have more than the most rudimentary unity. If there are any characters reappearing in the volume's stories, they are few in number and their reappearance has little significance. Usually, there is no plotline running through the collection, stringing the incorporated units into some sort of a continuum. Stylistic resemblance no deeper than that caused by a common author may provide a certain homogeneity, perhaps even a limited unity. Frequently, there is a frame – in the next chapter, I shall deal extensively with frames and how Balzac used them – but collective frames are suspect. All too often they are nothing but an excuse, an afterthought, a poorly integrated box into which authors and editors toss stories of little similarity for the unique purpose of putting together a volume and thus earning a little extra money from previously published work.

As an example, one might think of Maupassant's collection of stories, the *Contes de la bécasse* [*Stories about Woodcocks*] (1883). The lead story, 'La Bécasse [The Woodcock],' introduces the baron des Ravots whose life once turned actively around hunting, but who is now too old and infirm to go into the fields. Every autumn he nonetheless joins the hunt vicariously from his windows or from an easy chair on his front steps. He continues to invite his friends, since even though he himself is confined to the house, he likes to hear the gunfire in the distance. And he loves the long ritualistic dinners in the evening after the hunt. The baron prepares a kind of roulette, where a woodcock's beak is spun and stops to designate someone to eat a plateful of the birds' brains and, in return, to tell a story. 'Here are a few of these stories.' But the frame fiction is quickly forgotten, and the reader moves from one masterly story to another, content with the value of each one, unconcerned with the collection as a whole. The first few stories include a phrase or two which might recall the frame: 'Say,' for example, M. Mathieu d'Endolin exclaims, 'the woodcocks remind me of a sinister war story.' By the fifth tale, however, the host's physical incapacity is apparently forgotten, as is the traditional storytelling around the dinner table, and 'They walked up onto the bridge after dinner.' The frame's fiction is no longer operative.

Cycles are considerably more of a piece. Forrest L. Ingram is primarily concerned with distinguishing short-story cycles from novels in his consideration of the former. He builds his definitions by looking carefully at such pairs as Faulkner's *Sartoris* (1929), which he terms a novel, and the same author's *The Unvanquished* (1938), which he views as a short-story cycle. Ingram distinguishes between the two in the following fashion:

> The unity of a short story cycle, then, is the unity of discrete pieces juxtaposed in such an order that the significances of each story deepen and expand as the reader moves from story to story, in a particular order. The full significance of the cycle is realized only after the final story has been read. In *Sartoris*, on the other hand, multiple actions intertwine to form a multiweave continuity, exhibiting the development of a number of concomitant 'actions' in the course of the book, each of which actions moves forward piecemeal. Each story of a cycle is, to some degree, self-sufficient, self-contained, because its action is a complete unity. No part of the traditional novel, however, is a truly discrete, self-contained unit, but an integral part of some larger action.'

Unfortunately, things are not always as clear as Ingram believes. I think of *Un Amour de Swann*, part two of Marcel Proust's *A la recherche du temps perdu* (1913–27). It has a complete action and is easily isolated from the whole. Teachers regularly separate it from the rest of Proust's 3,000-page masterpiece and use it alone in courses on twentieth-century literature. Of course, the practice is not necessarily justifiable. The remainder of Proust's novel regularly refers to *Un Amour de Swann*, making it an integral part of the whole, a part whose meaning changes significantly in the course of *A la recherche*. One could even argue that it constitutes one of two sources (the other being *Combray*) from which the whole fiction flows. Ingram also seems more committed to 'complete actions' than a more recent view of fiction would allow. Contemporary fiction, for example, abounds with examples of incomplete, fragmentary, and trifling actions, which, moreover, lack important characters. All one may state with any assurance is that the stories of a short-story cycle seem relatively more discrete than the chapters of a novel. Just as the chapters of a novel are comparatively more dependent on the whole than are stories in a cycle, so the collective whole of a novel is less capable of standing without all of its constituent parts. Ingram is right, however, in pointing to the many devices that are available to short-story writers to bring unity to their collections and cycles.

Since we have considered the techniques Balzac used to bring unity to individual novels and short stories, it is appropriate now to study creations made by assembling other works that have stood and could still stand alone. *Autre étude de femme* (1832–45), *Jésus-Christ en Flandre* (1831–46), and *Histoire des Treize* (1830–9) are considered in order of the thoroughness of their integration, from least to most successful, though at first glance it might seem that *Histoire des Treize* could most easily and at lowest cost be broken into the three constituent stories. As we observe how Balzac brought these stories and essays together, how he welded integrated stories together and with other elements that were in fact little more than bits and pieces, thus making a new unit, it seems possible to gain a more complete grasp of the devices and principles functioning to bring the components of *La Comédie humaine* into one unified work.

The criticism reveals that competent readers have found little or no unity in *Autre étude de femme*. Nicole Mozet in a typical evaluation discusses the 'disparate character of the pieces gathered together.'[2] Balzac would not agree. It is clear that for him the work was unified; for us, with the insights we are developing here, it seems possible to demonstrate the mechanisms functioning to bring the various developments into a whole.

The intimate gathering where the stories are told includes not high society but the déclassé and racier world of socialites. This fact is important, since as Armine Mortimer and Lucienne Frappier-Mazur have understood in excellent and complementary articles, *Autre étude de femme* deals with a society in transition, to some degree the hybrid offspring of Napoleon's sweeping societal changes, but to a large degree due to the decreasing power of the old line aristocracy.[3] We immediately recognize Henri de Marsay, Mlle des Touches (Camille Maupin), Rastignac, the marquise d'Espard, Blondet, the Dudleys, the princesse de Cadignan, etc. The light, familiar tone of the raconteur is appropriate to the group and the late hour, as indeed is one of the major topics: vengeance exacted on unfaithful women. This theme raises an issue of some importance, however: Henri's revenge on Charlotte seems trivial when compared with the immurement of 'La Grande Bretèche' or the pyre on which wife and lover were burned alive in Montriveau's story. Such a disparity is almost enough to bring one to agree with earlier negative evaluations of the work.

Perhaps only at second remove do we realize the actual horror of Marsay's vengeance. He is attempting to degrade Charlotte, a great lady, a true grande dame, and turn her into a mere *femme comme il faut* (a genteel lady), thus hastening a deplorable societal change: 'The last fifty or so years have brought the continuing collapse of all social distinctions. We should have saved women from this shipwreck, but the articles of the Civil Code have leveled their heads las well]' (III.689). A little farther on, Henri de Marsay continues his explanation, establishing the opposition that explains *la femme comme il faut* better than my translation of 'genteel lady': 'We will no longer see grandes dames in France, but for a long time there will be *des femmes comme il faut*' (III.692). Blondet explains that they are living in 'a time when nothing successful resembles what is disappearing, when transitions lead to nothing, when there are nothing but nuances, when great figures are fading away, when distinctions are just of a personal variety' (III.700).

On considering the little that M. de Marsay actually does, one may find the explanation rather overblown. When Henri learns that his mistress has become interested in someone else, he takes up with another woman. He lets Charlotte know that while she has been arranging her marriage with the duke, claiming deathless love for Henri all the while, he has known, been unconcerned, and is nonchalantly capable of simultaneously seducing another young woman. He thus equates the duchess and their love with a flour merchant's daughter, now banker's wife, and an affair. In thus demonstrating his lack of jealousy, he diminishes his love of Charlotte and, indeed, Charlotte herself.[4] As Henri understands, 'When jealousy is true . . . it is the obvious sign of a unique love' (III.680). 'Avenging yourself on a woman,' he asks later, 'isn't that recognizing that there is no other for us, that we cannot get by without her? . . . If she is not indispensable, if there are others, why not give her the right to change which we give ourselves?' (III.683). Henri feels that the jealousy of Othello is 'stupid' and 'in bad taste' (III.681), 'the act of a child' (III.682). In short, if there is no such thing as a single, unique, all-encompassing love, there is no need for vengeance. If love is unimportant, if women can be interchanged without loss, if love calls for no significant distinctions, then jealousy is silly. But the larger subject concerns the whole of society. Henri de Marsay tells his story to explain how he developed the character traits that make him a statesman. In fact, we soon understand that he has revealed the degree to which he has helped the new ideas to succeed. He has become a man of his time, the male counterpart of the *femme comme il faut*, and, as we shall see, a man incapable of making significant distinctions.

Lady Dudley advances a curious defense of Charlotte: 'Men never want to distinguish between constancy and fidelity. I know the woman whose story M. de Marsay has told us, and she is one of the last of the grandes dames' (III.688–9). Henri agrees. He has already called Charlotte a '[g]rande dame' (III.679). He goes on to suggest that 'the grande dame . . . died with the grandiose milieus of last century' (III.689). Although one might momentarily wonder whether he and Lady Dudley mean the same thing by 'grande dame,' his two uses of the term show both that his usage is knowing and that he recognizes his failure in the attempted reduction of Charlotte to her vulgar, modern counterpart, *la femme comme il faut*. Despite Henri, Charlotte lived and died a 'grande dame.'

Today, it is difficult to perceive the subtle differences that seemed so clear to Balzac. The characters chatting at his gathering go to great lengths to explain the difference. Because of undisciplined minds, the Napoleonic code, society's inability to preserve the propertied classes, and journalists turned loose to wreak their will on society, such superior women have disappeared. Now, with the dearth of grandes dames, there is a pullulation of *femmes comme il faut*. Balzac distinguishes the latter, a 'genteel' lady, from *des femmes comme il en faut* (women you have to have), who are the nocturnal imitations that take to the streets after five, and from the grandes dames, who facilitated the birth and formation of the *femme comme il faut* by retreating to their provincial estates and refusing to contend with the new ideas. A grande dame had taste, wit, grace, and distinction – a distinction that had nothing to do with either learning or knowledge but was protected by name, position, and fortune. *Les femmes comme il faut* lie between the bourgeoisie and the aristocracy, the product of one or the other:

'Neither completely bourgeois nor completely noble, [they] slide along without brilliance between the middle-class and the nobility' (III.691). They are 'the expression of our day, where good taste, wit, grace, distinction are gathered together into one last, somewhat faded image' (III.692). Unlike the grande dame, the *femme comme il faut* hints at elegance without attaining true distinction; she hesitates in all things, is virtuous, but may change her mind. She is the product of study and learning. Though quite pretty, her modest budget is apparent. The grande dame might have taken a lover, but she was faithful to her family responsibilities. She was capable of making distinctions between matters of importance, could be distinguished from others, and was then worthy of jealousy. The *femme comme il faut* was easily replaced with another woman of no significant difference. Jealousy and vengeance were then useless and idle, a waste of emotions and effort.

The princesse de Cadignan comes to womanhood's defense. We remember that she had been so thoroughly tainted by a profligate life that only a great love was capable of reclaiming her. Despite her lineage, her beauty, her sense of style, her wit, only d'Arthez was able to find the core that distinguished her from the *femme comme il faut*. Her defense of her sisters is then suspect, though interesting, since she claims that despite the pettiness of her epoch human beings have not changed: 'Are we then really as diminished as these gentlemen believe? . . . Just because today people tend to shrink everything – you like small dishes, small apartments, small pictures, small articles, small newspapers, small books – does that mean that women are also reduced?' (III.701-2). Balzac seems rather to have wanted his reader to conclude that in a period of little real distinction, the *femme comme il faut* has been paired with the *homme comme il faut*.

Montriveau leaps in, however, to agree with the charming princess: '[T]he women of our day are truly grand,' he says (III.702), and he offers to tell a story to prove it. Given his claim, one would have expected the main characters of his exemplum to be chosen from the period of the July Monarchy, since the late dinner where the stories are being told seems to have taken place in 1831. Instead, when he takes center stage, he draws from his recollections of the much earlier French army retreat from Moscow in 1812. This was anything but a typical time. Montriveau talks of 'this variety of egotism which made our rout one of the most horrible dramas of personality, of sadness, and of horror which has ever taken place on this earth' (III.708). And he tells, not of Frenchmen, but of Italians. We remember that Othello, who has already been mentioned several times, served the Italian city-state of Venice. If M. de Marsay can correctly describe Shakespeare's noble Moor as a child ('a big kid'), and killing Desdemona 'the act of a child' (III.682), then the same terms are suitable for Rosina's husband and his vengeance. Of course, Henri de Marsay is mistaken. There is something wrong with a society unable to understand great fury and great love. However reprehensible the results of such passion, it seems better than the lusterless world Henri praises.

Where Henri de Marsay begins by making distinctions and only subsequently learns not to make them ('Healed,' he says, 'of my cold and of pure, absolute, divine love' – III.683), Rosina's husband, the captain, begins by not making distinctions and ends by making them. A 'Piedmontese gentleman,' he is characterized by 'good-hearted mockery. . . . Courageous, educated, he seemed unaware of the affair which had been going on between his wife and the colonel for about three years' (III.707). Rosina is careful to respect the conventions. When the colonel brazenly calls her to share his bed in front of her husband and the other people in the farmhouse, she is clearly annoyed: 'And so the young woman made an indescribable gesture which gave away the annoyance she must have felt to see her subservience exhibited without any respect, and the offence against her feminine dignity or against her husband' (ibid.). Unfortunately, the colonel has no patience and calls again, overcoming Rosina's hesitation. Montriveau laughs, thus publicly acknowledging the situation. When he apologizes, the husband responds, 'You are not the one who is wrong; I am!' (III.708). The next morning everyone slips away, subject once again to the terrible disorder which encourages every individual to worry about his own skin, with little thought for his neighbor. The captain barricades his wife and her lover within the house, which he then sets afire. Despite the colonel's roar and Rosina's cries, the husband takes public pride in what he has done. ' "Son'io!" he said!' (III.708).

M. de Marsay's understanding is limited: 'There is nothing more terrible than the revolt of a sheep' (III.709). Lord Dudley's reaction is more productive, however, since it elicits a very interesting comparison. He asks about Charlotte. We learn that she did marry the duke, died nobly, and was indeed a grande dame. Henri's attempt to reduce her to *une femme comme il faut* failed. The adventure does, however, emphasize M. de Marsay's limitations and his status, not as a great lord, but as *un homme comme il faut*, one of the bizarre hybrids that mark this period of transition.

Bianchon goes on to complete the cycle. He tells the story of 'La

Grande Bretèche,' another tale emphasizing distinctions and horrible vengeance. Once again the events considerably predate the July Monarchy. Early in 1814 countesse Joséphine de Merret has taken a lover, a prisoner of France and 'a Spanish lord' (III.720). The countess has the trappings of a grande dame. She is rich, beautiful, and widely respected. When M. de Merret returns unexpectedly one evening, he hears a suspicious noise in his wife's dressing room. He asks if there is someone there, and his wife swears, eventually on an elaborate crucifix, that there is not. The husband (a 'cruel gentleman' – III.729) has the door walled up and stays with his wife for twenty days, until he is certain that the lover is dead. To his wife's protests, he responds, 'You swore on the cross that there was no one there' (ibid.).

The progression across the three primary stories of the triadic husband-wife-lover complex is clear. Henri refuses to make distinctions and be jealous. The captain learns to do both, and his vengeance is fierce. He is a 'gentleman,' as is M. de Merret, of whose jealousy and vengeance there is never any doubt. Numerous minor traits also link the three stories. Henri asked Charlotte whether she had a guest, and she lied, as did Joséphine when asked a similar question. Henri attempts to enclose Charlotte in the mold of the *femme comme il faut*, thus denying her status as a grande dame. The captain immures his wife and lover, as does M. de Merret. Unlike innocent Desdemona, however, if the women are not unfaithful in Lady Dudley's terms, they are certainly inconstant. And three of the men attempt, with varying degrees of success, some sort of revenge.

All three stories deal with a kind of love and a kind of woman that no longer exist. The duchess is moreover actually dead, as of course are Rosina and Joséphine. The thought that *une femme comme il faut* would elicit such a love and such a vengeance is inconceivable, and one is left to mourn the passing of the great families and the magnificent women who peopled them. Despite the fact that the stories of neither Rosina nor Joséphine do anything to counter the suggestion that the French grande dame no longer exists in the society of the July Monarchy – given that Rosina was a passionate Italian and Joséphine's adventure took place in 1814 – one can nonetheless find some encouragement in Diane de Cadignan's defense. 'Why should the human heart change just because you change your clothes' (III.702). She is of course right, though just as *Gobseck* warned about the danger threatening the great French families,[5] so the present warning is very clear. There is also some comfort in remembering that a grande dame will several years later be resurrected in the princesse de Cadignan. Diane is living proof that there remains sufficient time to correct the conditions that have placed one of the most important of French social institutions at risk.

If it is indeed possible to view Diane as an encouraging factor, it is the only reason for any optimism. Overall, the conclusion is negative. We remember that the narrator stressed from the beginning the importance of conversation to the society of bygone days. Only a very few places remain where people delight in wit and the spoken word. Mlle des Touches's salon is one of them. But as Armine Kotin Mortimer has sensed, the drastically shortened ending of the last version of 'La Grande Bretèche,' as it appeared in *Autre étude de femme*, is extremely important, since it emphasizes a further conclusion: conversation is no longer possible. Certainly, the abrupt ending of Bianchon's tale has extraordinary force. Bianchon tells that whenever Mme de Merret was about to plead with her husband, he cut her off with: 'You swore on the cross that there was no one there.' These lines follow immediately and conclude the story: 'After this tale, all the women rose from the table, and the charm with which Bianchon had held them was dissipated by the movement. Nonetheless a few of them had been half chilled on hearing the last word' (III.729). There is no further conversation. Even in this intimate, late-night gathering, which represents the last refuge of former pleasures, an authentic story of the old-style manners leaves the participants with nothing to say. As Mortimer puts it, the new realistic tale overpowers the joys of conversational give and take.

The activity of putting fragments together into a larger whole was an aspect of Balzac's entire career, but it was particularly strong in the mid-1840s, when he took a minimum of trouble with rendering his unifying principles clear. Not until the 1845 republication of 'La Grande Bretèche,' which was composed in 1831, did Balzac put it with Henri de Marsay's and Montriveau's stories. The new arrangement is not announced by a substantial, apologetic essay, which would allow me to state with authority his reasons for making the combinations. Balzac simply added a subtitle in the Furne edition: 'Conclusion to Autre étude de femme.' A manuscript note in his personal copy of this edition completed the development by directing the story's placement with the other two panels of what then became a triptych. Still, the result leaves little doubt that Balzac was clearly aware of his unifying principles.

All of the stories are subsumed to the idea that the former glories of great women are passing and being replaced by lusterless counterparts. Each of the stories makes use of the triadic complex in which husband-wife-lover are related by the themes of love and revenge. Finally, the details, in their repetition, provide further unification. The familiar tone of the raconteurs is important for this unity, as is the limited context of the telling of all three tales and the fact that all are told during the July Monarchy but are set late in the Napoleonic era. The lack of reappearing characters or narrative linking has little if any negative impact. This is then not a novel, but rather is a cycle. The frame brings the stories into a unit. It does more than merely gather them together; it turns the outstanding traits of earlier women, the point of the stories, into the point of the whole. As the audience confronts the dazzling contrast of the past, their own mediocrity is evident to all. Though, as mentioned, there is a certain progression from one story to another, this change should not be exaggerated. The unity of *Autre étude de femme* comes not from diegesis but from the description of what Balzac saw as the reality of his day.

Jésus-Christ en Flandre has a similarly long history and late conclusion. Though part of what was to become the work as we now know it was published in 1831, the final fusion of the two panels did not take place until 1846. Here, as in *Autre étude de femme*, the reader is left to divine the principles of the gathering. Indeed, its very meaning is anything but evident. Albert Béguin terms it 'rather difficult to interpret' and 'enigmatic' (FR XII.103). Although the end result may not be as successful as the *Histoire des Treize*,[6] which I shall consider next, it seems possible to make out some of the master's most sophisticated techniques.

Jésus-Christ en Flandre implies a narrator from the first sentence and introduces him soon afterwards. The character is not sure when the story he will tell took place. He does not even know the names of Brabant's, Belgium's, or Flanders's rulers at the time of the episode. He merely knows that the story belongs to an old tradition and that, despite the changes each subsequent period has wrought, the tale continues in all its versions to suggest the fantasy and vagueness that are so appealing to Flemish storytellers. He will tell it 'with the audacities that history disavows, with its morality that religion approves of, its fantasy, flower of the imagination, and its hidden meaning which the wise can make the most of' (X.312). While the narrator is unquestionably a nineteenth-century man, since he is aware of the erudite if destructive work that scholars of his day were working on the oral tradition – 'this chronicle . . . would be the despair of faultfinding commentators who pick at words, events, and dates' (X.311–12) – by his own admission, he believes the story. His belief has considerable importance. It couples him with what he calls the superstitious Flemish, and it prepares the hallucination – or vision – he has in the concluding panel, since it presents him as a fit subject for such an experience.

The opening story begins by introducing the ferry joining the isle of Cadzant and the burg of Ostende. It describes its passengers and crew, which can be split into four camps: the rich and arrogant, the poor and lowly, the self-confident skipper, and a stranger who arrived 'without a purse or a sword' (X.313) – unlike Christ's disciples who were instructed to carry both (Luke 22.35–6). The stranger is soon identified as Jesus Christ himself, come back to help his people. When the threatening storm strikes, raises the sea, and swamps the boat, Jesus announces salvation for those who believe: 'Have faith . . . and you will be saved' (X.319), and again: 'Those who have faith will be saved; let them follow me!' (X.320). He then leaves the vessel, walking on the water. The fortune hunter, the young maiden who abandons her mother, the mother who trusts not in Jesus but in the bishop, the bishop whose prayers are mixed with thoughts of his mistress and other worldly pleasures, the wealthy bourgeois who might have been saved had he not tried to bring his gold, and the worldly-wise 'man of science, a doctor at the University of Louvain' (X.313) – in short, the high and mighty situated at the rear of the boat – all drown. The professor from Louvain behaves as the biblical book of Proverbs and the first chapter of Paul's Epistle to the Romans would lead us to expect of educated fools: '[W]hen he saw the stranger proposing that the passengers walk on the sea, the learned man began to laugh and was swallowed up by the ocean' (X.320). The narrator's comment about the bishop and the rich woman seems appropriate for the lot: 'heavy with crimes, perhaps, but even heavier with incredulity, with confidence in false images, heavy with devotion, light in giving and in true religion' (ibid.).

The crew of rowers amidships is represented by Thomas, who like his biblical namesake 'doubting Thomas' manifests something less than steadfast faith. It takes him several tries before he succeeds in following Jesus. It was Thomas, who for the love of God allowed the old woman onto the boat. He had been acquainted with her long before when she was rich and beautiful, if immoral (X.319). She is, in short, a Mary Magdalene figure. Now impoverished and filled with repentance, '[t]he sinful old woman, believing in an all-powerful God, followed the man and walked on the sea' (X.320). So too the peasants, the old soldier, and the humble mother and child. In what is perhaps a nineteenth-century gesture to the entrepreneurial spirit, Balzac also had Jesus save the skipper who had discouraged cries to the Holy Virgin in favor of assiduous bailing with the 'holy' scoops. He tied himself to a plank and was at the mercy of the sea. Retrieved from the angry ocean, he is told by 'the MAN,' 'the Savior' (X.321), 'It is okay this time, but don't try it again; it would be just too bad an example' (ibid.). For a long time people claimed that it was possible to see the footprints Jesus left in the sand at the site of the fisherman's hut that welcomed the survivors. There the convent of Merci was built.

In the second panel the narrator finds himself in this church centuries later. He enters depressed and tired to observe his surroundings without enthusiasm. Little by little, 'my perceptions became confused. I found myself at the limit of illusions and reality, caught in optical illusions and almost stunned by the multitude of their effects,' (X.322). Through a golden cloud, the sun ignites fires in the stained glass's scintillating colors, and it seems to him that the columns begin to move, slowly at first, then more vigorously, until he compares the vibrating church to a 'dance,' initially dignified, then a 'strange sabbath,' and finally a 'hot bacchanalia' (X.323). Having recently seen the fall of Charles X, an event he had previously believed impossible, nothing astonishes him. An enormous statue of Christ smiles with mischievous benevolence. Then a divine power raises the narrator, and he is plunged into infinite joy. He would have given his life to prolong this 'phantasmagoria,' but a shrill voice enters his ear, 'Wake up, and follow me!' (X.324). 'You have to suffer, you have to suffer,' she says as she leads him out of the church and across the filthiest streets of the city. They enter a dark house where she draws him to her, crying, 'Defend me, defend me!' (ibid.). Upstairs they go into a room, past a mute man reminiscent of the Inquisition. She points to a tapestry full of holes, old linen, faded muslin, and gilded copper, saying, 'So it is with eternal riches' (X.324). He realizes that she is but recently resurrected from the grave, and he tries to escape, but her skeletal arm grasps him firmly. 'With this movement, a cry from millions of voices, the hourra of the dead, resounded near us! "I want to make you happy for ever," she said. "You are my son!"' (ibid.).

If there was any doubt, the fleshless old woman is explicitly identified at the end of the story as the Church (III.327). Suddenly the narrator too recognizes her, and he realizes that, though she was once 'young and beautiful, dressed in all the grace of simplicity' (III.325), she prostituted herself, thus abdicating '[h]er primitive power, [h]er intellectual supremacy for the powers of the flesh' (ibid.). She became a Messalina, famous for her injustice and debaucheries. Suddenly, before the narrator's eyes, she casts off her rags and like a butterfly shows herself again as a young and beautiful girl. 'See and believe!' she says (III.326). In the distance, he sees thousands of cathedrals like the one he just left but filled with art, places where scientists work to save books and manuscripts, where almost everyone studies, where the poor are served, where delightful concerts are performed. And from the midst of the surging crowds rise three statues labeled: 'SCIENCE, HISTORY, LITERATURE' (III.327). The beautiful young maiden slowly reverts to her previous state. 'People no longer believe!' he hears. He awakens in the convent church. 'Wake up, sir, we are locking up,' the old crone who passes out holy water says. He understands that he has been called: 'Believe! . . . it is to live! I have just seen the funeral procession of a monarchy. I must defend the CHURCH' (III.327).

Once one understands the particular language that Balzac is using, it becomes clear that he has raised the constituent units of the work from minor pieces of little interest to a work of some significance. The first panel was previously a rewriting of a tale by Erasmus.[7] The second started in 1830 as an anti-clerical allegory entitled 'Zéro.' Within the year, whether because of the revolution that installed Philippe d'Orléans, or the pillage of the archbishop's palace, or the influence of Lamennais, Montalembert, and the group around *L'Avenir*, Balzac rethought his position. When 'Zéro' was republished as a part of *L'Eglise* in 1831, his sympathies had shifted considerably, and he had moved far to the right. Though 'Zéro' and *L'Eglise* have a certain interest for those drawn to the author's thought processes, they have little esthetic value. When these two texts were joined to the legend in 1846, thus constituting the *Jésus-Christ en Flandre* we know today, this combination became an unusual item in Balzac's work, since it created a narrative structure progressing significantly from first to last.[8]

The obvious link between the two panels of the legend, on the one hand, and 'Zéro'/*L'Eglise*, on the other, is the boat. Churches had long incorporated within their structure the shape of an ark, an allusion to Jesus' comparison of His second coming to Noah (Matt. 24.36–9). The architectural symbol is also manifested in certain nautical *qua* ecclesiastical vocabulary. I think, for example, of the main body of churches, or 'nave,' a term Balzac used twice within the first few lines of the second part. The agitation of the sea is perhaps reflected in the church's increasingly violent movement, as is the narrator's feeling himself 'raised by a divine power which plunged [him] into infinite joy' (III.323–4).

Turning to the characters, one immediately sees changes from part one to part two. Jesus is miraculously active in the legendary first story, while He is virtually immobilized in the second. There He seems able only to smile. The biblical Thomas known for his doubting is reincarnated in the ferryboat crewman with the same name who similarly lacks faith. The latter's 'faith faltered; he fell into the sea several times, got up. Then after three attempts, he walked on the sea' (III.320). When the old woman is metamorphosed into a youthful beauty and says to the narrator, 'See and believe!' she brings several biblical episodes to mind, but Madeleine Fargeaud is correct to direct attention to St Thomas.[9] After stating flatly, 'Except I shall see in His hands the print of the nails . . . I will not believe' (John 20.25), the biblical Thomas is allowed to see. Jesus said, 'Because thou hast seen Me, thou hast believed' (John 20.29). Consequently, Balzac's visionary figure's command to see and believe in part two forms a link with the Thomas of part one.

The old woman of Balzac's legend is more interesting. She has a scandalous past, which serves admirably to establish a relationship with the similar figure in part two. The character of the vision has also prostituted herself. It is worth remembering that while churches were often related to the ark, the body of believers, also called the Church, is most often compared to a woman, from the Sulamite of the Song of Solomon to the Bride of Revelation 19.6–9. Connecting the old woman with the Church is inevitable, and appropriate. It is important, however, to notice that she calls attention to several significant differences. Christ was active in part one; the old woman in the ferry depends upon him for her salvation. In part two, while Christ is virtually immobilized, the old woman is active. The miracle-working Christ saves His people in the first panel, but the Church of the last needs a new messiah. She calls the narrator to defend her, and where on two occasions the biblical God the Father announced to those in attendance, 'This is my son,'[10] Balzac's representative of the Church tells the narrator, 'You are my son!' (III.324). The narrator, who is a writer and an artist, has been called to the defense of the Church, not necessarily of the faith.[11] He remembers that when Charles X lost his throne, in effect one of the institutions of society crumbled, leaving society without the guiding hand of the monarchy. If the Church grows weaker and less capable, there is little hope for the future. But if artists gather around the Church, the vision suggests that she can rise anew and thus provide a new impetus for science, history, and literature. Left to herself she will die.

In *Autre étude de femme*, Balzac depended primarily on repeated narrative patterns and character types to unify the three stories. All the stories took place more or less in the same chronological period. *Jésus-Christ en Flandre*, however, spans five or six centuries and brings together completely different genres of the short story: legend and allegory. Moreover, it has an almost non-existent frame: the narrator of the legend comes to the church that commemorates the legend. While there, he has a vision. In short, there is neither chronological nor causal linkage. Part one in no sense causes part two. Nonetheless, if part two is read as an allegory, one discovers an interesting variation on what was found in *Autre étude de femme*. The character types seem to develop as they reappear, whether narrator or Mary Magdalene / Old Woman, thus suggesting a history and a future. The narrator is receptive to the miraculous events occurring in the early legend. Later, he experiences his own miracle: he receives a seemingly divine call to serve as a messiah to the Church. In the early days of Christianity, after Christ was taken out of the world, the Church was strong and powerful. She then had glorious days. Unfortunately, she fell on bad times and now needs another savior. She calls the narrator, suggesting that the Church's past glories are once again possible, should he be willing to hear her and rise in her defense. The need for ecclesiastical rebirth is highlighted by a series of contrasts, most significantly the miracle-working, active Jesus of part one and the passive Christ in a moribund church of part two. Balzac frequently used contrasts to join narrative blocks. He does so in *Jésus-Christ en Flandre* and thus creates a cycle.

Histoire des Treize [*History of the Thirteen*] uses such repetitions, and indeed adds to them other far more profoundly integrated elements, though a first and perhaps a fifth reading of *Histoire des Treize* might leave one wondering why Balzac would put the three novellas of this strange collection together. 'Ferragus,' 'La Duchesse de Langeais,' and 'La Fille aux yeux d'or' differ radically from each other. Of course, Balzac is not alone in gathering together ill-assorted works. While the history of joining tales with some sort of a frame is old and honorable, the vast majority of collections show little if any desire to create a cycle of stories. Based on normal practice, Balzac had no need to collect these three stories with anything in mind but a convenient vehicle for their publication. It is then surprising, because unnecessary, that the author would insist on the ties that bind them one to another.

The narrator/author of the work's preface – I shall call him the *auteur* – stresses that there has been selection. 'He was told stories dripping with blood, plays full of terror, novels where secretly severed heads roll' (V.788). Unlike Bouvard and Pécuchet, he has not merely served as a recorder of any and all information which passed his way. While there is no question that the ending of 'La Fille aux yeux d'or' is 'dripping with blood,' there is no decapitation. We have then been deprived of, or spared, some of the material at his disposal. In a passage written in 1833, before he had composed what became 'La Fille aux yeux d'or,' he goes on to say, '[The *auteur*] preferred to choose the milder adventures, those where limpid scenes follow storms of passion, where the woman is radiant with virtue and beauty' (V.788–9). In addition, he claims to have but recently received permission to tell 'a few of the adventures which have happened to these men' (V.788), and he indicates in a 'Postface' to the 1833 *Revue de Paris* version of 'Ferragus' that he has permission to release nothing but the three that eventually made up *Histoire des Treize*: 'These three episodes . . . are the only ones that the author can publish' (V.904). Obviously, if that is so, there has been no selection, and the *auteur* is not uniquely responsible for the moral or esthetic excellence of what follows. Perhaps that is why Balzac subsequently deleted the passage and found other reasons for the choice of texts.

One can be certain only that the *auteur* attributes the particular stories to somewhat different motivations in the preface accompanying the volume in 1834: 'Now, he is allowed to begin the tale of the three episodes which captivated him particularly in this history because of the Parisian fragrance of the details and the bizarreness of the contrasts' (V.792). Several points should be made about this passage. Most important is the indication of a 'history' behind the 'episodes' included in the volume. He makes no claim for exhaustiveness. Indeed, a significant portion of the preface turns on background information which gives the reader a fuller understanding of the *Treize*. Without the prefatory remarks one might not have realized that the group's power was pervasive, that indeed 'the whole of society was secretly subjugated [by these thirteen men]' (V.788). In addition, while taking some trouble to justify bringing the tales together as three 'episodes' of a larger 'history' (V.789), Balzac has also indulged in a blatant use of the post-partum preface to render the fiction more verisimilar.

In the course of reading the various versions of this preface one becomes increasingly aware of this *auteur* as a distinct person, considerably more than the vague but omniscient narrator one knows from so much of Balzac's (and other nineteenth-century writers') work.[12] He exists in the larger society within which the three episodes occur. The societal frame has much importance to the whole of *La Comédie humaine*, and I shall return to it. Here, the *auteur* is motivated from without and from within. We know very little of the external forces, the anonymous person or persons who told him the various adventures, though he does describe the apparently young man who gave him permission to tell the three tales we have before us. The author of the preface suspects that 'a vague desire for fame' (V.788) might be responsible for the group's uncharacteristic openness, but the reader is left without any other insight into why they would have allowed him to repeat certain stories but not others. The *auteur* provides somewhat more explicit explanations for his own choices: he settled on those stories that attracted him because of the (1) form (bizarrely contrastive – V.792) 'where scenes of purity follow storms of passion' (V.788), (2) characters (beautiful and virtuous women – V.789), and (3) details (mild, Parisian – V.788, 792). Nonetheless, though such traits might justify a collection of stories, they leave the reader indoctrinated with the Balzacian credo of unity dissatisfied.

Perhaps that is why critics, with the notable exception of John R. O'Connor, have viewed with something less than enthusiasm Balzac's various claims that *Histoire de Treize* constitutes 'a modern epic'[13] and that 'Ferragus . . . is connected by invisible threads to the History of the Thirteen.'[14] Still, on reading and rereading the work, one is struck by quite a number of elements that, in their repetition and development across the three novellas, seem to serve as unifying elements. Balzac's repeated insistence that 'details alone will from now on constitute the merit of works which are improperly called *Novels* [*Romans*]' (I.1175), might encourage us to notice some of those details that reappear in the various stories: for example, the color red, which, while relatively limited in 'Ferragus,' explodes in the burst of poppy-red and blood of 'La Fille aux yeux d'or.' Comparisons to demons and the devil, references to the Orient and 'Asiatic pleasures' (V.791), images of fire, branding, masks and veils, themes of youth, monsters, suicide, revenge, and condemnation are notable in all three. The Hispanic peninsula reappears, though in various guises. The escaped convict, Ferragus, takes the Portuguese name and identity of M. de Funcal in his attempt to become a respectable member of society, and the Spanish convent of los Dolores to which Mme de San-Réal plans to retire is perhaps the same one to which the duchesse de Langeais withdrew.[15] After explicitly referring to Caligula and Nero in the first two novellas (V.840, 979), the author introduces us to a world of comparable depravity in the third. With each rereading the common elements multiply. The volume includes a veritable plethora of orphans, either real (M. Jules, Auguste de Maulincour, Armand de Montriveau) or functional (Mme Jules, Henri de Marsay, and his sister, Margarita de San-Réal). If Paquita's mother's unnatural willingness to sell her daughter into slavery and, subsequently, her death qualify the girl to be a functional orphan, one can say that most major characters of the *Histoire des Treize* fall in the same category. While the dissolution of the family was dealt with at length in *Le Père Goriot*, here, several thousand pages later, we are treated to the results. Some of these repetitions remain motifs and do little but recall preceding contexts. Others, like youth, blood, orphans, masks, serve as symbols.

On the most accessible level, the three stories are joined by reappearing characters the most important of which are members of this terrifying and secret league of 'thirteen men who start the Society of Jesus over again for the benefit of the devil' (V.791–2). In each of the stories we make the acquaintance of one or more of these exceptional beings. As a group they are very gifted, completely amoral, and intensely loyal to each other (Balzac does not fail to cite Otway's tragedy, *Venice Preserved*, which for him symbolized perfect friendship in Pierre and Jaffier's relationship). By cooperating, their powers are multiplied, as their progenitor foresaw: 'Immense with their actions and intensity, their secret power – against which the social order is doubtless defenseless – casts down obstacles, overwhelms others' wills, and gives to each one of them the diabolical power of the group' (V.791). The self-serving lack of vision and the frivolity that characterize the adventures in which the Thirteen manifest their powers become an important theme, highlighting society's failure to exploit these and other exceptional beings who could preserve it from the debilitating social decay that condemns it to lackluster mediocrity. While Auguste de Maulincour, the vidame de Pamiers, Madame de Sérisy, the Nucingens, and Ferragus are mentioned in two of the three novellas, Ronquerolles and Henri de Marsay appear in all. The duchesse de Langeais is quoted in 'Ferragus' and, of course, is central to the middle panel of the triptych, which bears her name. Ronquerolles and de Marsay are particularly important, since they signal the continuing influence of the Thirteen and intensify the linkage provided by the group's actions. Ferragus is also one of the Thirteen, so even though he only appears in two of the stories, his impact continues in the occult league he represents.

Because Balzac knew his audience and was perfectly willing to give them what they wanted, whether tales of violence or sentimentality, it would be wrong to neglect the popular side to the author's plots and characters. But it would be equally wrong to limit his fictions to such a role. Balzac suggests considering the characters at a more abstract level when he points out that each of the tales contains a radiantly beautiful and virtuous woman (V.789). He consistently emphasized his calling to create not just memorable characters but rather a vast canvas of man in society. Pierre Barbéris put it this way, 'The stories of men and woman are not Balzac's expedient for taking up the history of his century, but it is in the history of his century that he discovers or rediscovers the stories of men and women.'[16] His characters are important only insofar as they represent an idea. Félix Davin quotes Balzac as saying, 'It does not suffice to be a man. You have to be a system' (I.1151). If we follow well-established narratological practice and view the characters as empty of individual significance in their roles of master, victim, or violator, and the plots as armatures, other comments seem appropriate.

Following O'Connor's remarkable insight, one notes that each of the three stories constitutes a penetration.[17] In 'Ferragus,' though Auguste de Maulincour never enters the home of M. and Mme Jules, his surrogates do. When he sees Mme Jules in a notorious neighborhood, he immediately assumes she is having an affair. Since she has repulsed him, he decides to punish her by revealing her infidelity to all. He infects M. Jules with his jealousy. No longer able to trust his wife, M. Jules takes over the role Maulincour had initiated and continues the destructive work. Mme Jules, for example, has barred her husband from her inner sanctum, '[the] dressing room where she took off what she wore to the ball and from which she came dressed for the night, mysteriously adorned for the mysterious celebrations of her heart' (V.840). Wild with jealousy, M. Jules 'went into the dressing room' to seize the proof of his wife's mendacity (V.849). His wife's decline and eventual death is thus assured: her husband's failure to trust has broken their life-sustaining union. By thrusting himself into Mme Jules's most private place, he has effectively violated her. Convinced by Auguste de Maulincour that Mme Jules has stolen her lover, Ida Gruget soon comes storming into the couple's salon. M. Jules pursues his penetration until he has uncovered not just his wife's but Ferragus's secrets. It is a constant of Balzac's world that destruction awaits those foolish enough to allow their lives to be penetrated. The most famous example is doubtless Pons's self-betrayal in inviting strangers to visit his collection. Likewise in 'Ferragus,' as with Mme Jules, so Ferragus himself proves the rule. M. Jules subsequently recognizes Ferragus in the pathetic old man who has become 'something horrible to see' (V.903). Though Maulincour is the only violator who pays the ultimate price of death, all suffer.

The sexual nature of the penetration plot, which remains muted in 'Ferragus,' resonates in 'La Duchesse de Langeais.' Montriveau wishes to rush her off to bed, while Antoinette devotes all her skills to retaining her lover without submitting to his will. Montriveau is invited into her boudoir, forces his way into her bedroom, lies his way into the convent's visiting room, and breaks into her cell. He fails to ravish her only because she has died. One suspects that God, 'a jealous and vengeful God' (V.913), might have killed her as Margarita did Paquita. An early chapter title, later deleted, reads, 'GOD ARRANGES THE CONCLUSIONS.'[18] Finally, in 'La Fille aux yeux d'or,' Henri de Marsay's penetration also occurs in several stages, though unlike the others it culminates in the physical act of love (one might say it results in complete penetration). It echoes the preceding stories in that the object of desire dies.

When viewed abstractly, the progression in the stories cannot be mistaken. The penetrator of the first story is repulsed; that of the second almost preferred to God; and that of the third deified: '[M]ay your holy will be accomplished!' Paquita tells Henri. In each of the stories the violation is progressive, and from first tale to last the seduction is more successful. The victims are increasingly guilty, though not of the 'crimes' of which they are accused. Mme Jules failed to trust her husband; Antoinette was tempted to commit adultery before taking the veil, and subsequently she both deceived her mother superior and put God in competition with her carnal lover. Paquita was unfaithful to Margarita. In short, within the plot armature of penetration, one sees on an even higher level of abstraction a more complete narration of penetration.

Nonetheless, while giving due credit to these developments, one is more struck by the similarities between the 'episodes' of this 'history.' In each of the stories a seducer becomes an intruder/violator before turning into what the story repeatedly calls a villain (*bourreau*.)[19] Each of the stories recounts a tale of seduction, which includes a seducer/violator, a master, and the object of desire, a beautiful woman who becomes the victim. The seducer, in all cases an intruder, is unwelcome in the first story. While increasingly welcome in succeeding accounts, he is always illegitimate. Mme Jules is happily married, and, while Antoinette de Langeais can by no means be said to be happy, she is married. During the second phase of Montriveau's assault, she belongs to God. Paquita, of course, is the property of Mme de San-Réal. In each case the intruder's activity arouses the master, who is then responsible for the victim's death. The victims are in fact innocent of the accusations that hang over them. Mme Jules has no lover, only a father. The duchesse remains chaste. And Paquita gives herself only to her mistress's alter-ego, as Margarita realizes when it is too late: 'She was as innocent as possible' (V.1108). If the victims are guilty, it is but of the appearance of evil.

One should not minimize appearance, for the narrator emphasizes its importance, especially in the society of his day. The princesse de Blamont-Chauvry leaves no doubt. One may do as one wishes, but one must 'skilfully get around the laws of propriety rather than violate them' (V.1019). Still, the real guilt clearly lies elsewhere than in the victims, rather in the violator/villain.

If one follows this well-established narratological practice and views the characters in their roles of master, victim, or violator, empty of individual significance, further observations are possible. The masters are divine and human, both male and female. The victims come from each of the classes: proletariat (slave), bourgeoisie, and aristocracy. And the violators are in every case young and aristocratic. They have no legitimate right to intrude, but, when frustrated, each feels justified in seeking revenge, becoming not just judge but executioner as well. At this level of abstraction, I have both stressed the similarities in the roles of each story and pointed to several important themes: appearance and social classes. It is then time to rise to the next level of abstraction, that of idea. We are reminded that when *Même histoire* was still a series of apparently unconnected episodes, before they were brought together as *La Femme de trente ans*, Balzac insisted that they were unified. True, the same character was not to be found in each of the episodes: 'The character who so to speak crosses the six pictures with which *Même Histoire* is composed is not a figure; it is a thought' (II.1037). From detail, I have gone to the empty *forms* of characters and narrative armatures, and now to the *content* or ideas that inform them.

'Ferragus' begins with a description of Paris, a setting of enormous importance to each of the three episodes. Paris is a monster, 'the most delicious of monsters' (V.794), and we are pointedly given to understand the monstrousness of her foster children. The vidame de Pamiers, Auguste de Maulincour, Mme de Langeais, Henri de Marsay, Paquita, all are either compared to monsters or explicitly termed unnatural or monstrous.[20] Nor have M. and Mme Jules escaped the contagion. After introducing the image of the androgyne – 'Is not the treatise of *yes* and *no* one of the most beautiful works of diplomacy, philosophy, logography, ethics which remains to be done? But would not an androgynous genius be required to accomplish this diabolical work? Consequently, it will never be accomplished' (VI.835) – the narrator phrases his descriptions of the couple in ways that highlight their unnaturalness. 'How,' he asks, 'could two heads which are so closely tied remain on the same pillow when one of them suffers and the other is tranquil' (V.842). Furthermore, Mme Jules is happy that they are childless, an attitude that would certainly have shocked the general public of Balzac's day. This marriage has not and will not bear fruit.

Paris makes an appropriate setting. As Félix Davin says of *Les Scènes de la vie parisienne*, 'A capitol city was the only possible framework for paintings of a critical period, when infirmities afflict the hearts of men no less than their bodies. Here, true sentiments are the exception and are crushed by the play of self-interest.'[21] One would almost think he is paraphrasing the introduction to 'La Fille aux yeux d'or,' a work that, with 'Ferragus' and 'La Duchesse de Langeais' serves most importantly to introduce the *Scènes de la vie parisienne*.

Given that the first character to come on stage is an aristocrat, one might consider what it means to be a noble. For Balzac, the members of this class were called to rule. That they no longer have power has less to do with the Revolution than with their failure to see that the forms of power have changed while the substance of power remains the same. '[I]deas wear different garb, and . . . the conditions of political life completely change their form, without essentially changing their reality' (V.927). The weapons of leadership have changed. The lance no longer dominates; now 'art, science, and money form the social triangle within which the shield of power is inscribed, and from which the modern aristocracy must proceed' (V.928). When the aristocracy lacks the character necessary for leadership, it should open its ranks to those who have the required qualities (V.928–31). The faubourg makes fun of plebeian officials but fails to provide sufficiently superior nobles. Unfortunately, 'far from possessing this redemptive political insight which goes looking for strength where God has put it, these great little people hate all strength which does not issue from them. In short, far from rejuvenating themselves, the aristocratic circles of Saint-Germain have grown old (V.931). Mistaking money for power – in fact, the narrator says, 'Money . . . is only a sign of power' (V.930) – they sold their lands to play the market. 'Instead of demonstrating the protectiveness of a great lord, the Saint-Germain quarter showed the avidity of a parvenu' (V.930). In sum, the narrator asks, 'What would a marshall's baton be without the intrinsic force of the captain who holds it in his hand? Saint-Germain played with batons, believing that all the power was in them' (V.928). The aristocracy confused form with substance, and '*Form carried off the real content*' (V.1013, italics in original). Mme de Chauvry, who encourages her niece to keep up appearances regardless of reality, recognizes that the dishonor occuring under the reign of Louis XV, came because witnesses revealed the truth. 'The people, who are badly placed for judging anything at all, saw the reality of things, without seeing the form' (V.1020). With an aristocracy incapable of leading, the bourgeoisie seized power. This class is of course unsuited for leadership, since it is by definition oriented toward personal gain rather than public good.

Youth might hold some hope. Napoleon, Louis XIV, all the great kings looked to the young to make changes in society (V.1049). But the France of Balzac's day chose rule by gerontocracy. 'The youth, which in everything was uncertain, blind, and clairvoyant, was completely disregarded by the old men who were jealous of keeping the reins of state in their feeble hands, whereas the monarchy could have been saved if they had retired and allowed this young France to come to power' (V.801). But youth will not be denied. Lacking constructive outlets for its energy, it expends itself in self-indulgence. This is the lesson highlighted by the *Histoire des Treize*: a society devoted uniquely to personal gain has no force to hold itself together. Exceptional people will continue to appear. Lacking direction, however, they become plagues on society, victimizing it at every level. The Thirteen are in fact motivated by the same faith as the society that gave them birth: 'this religion of pleasure and selfishness' (V.791). Because they are exceptional and because they have been willing to band together, 'the social order is without defense' (ibid.). Balzac held out some hope in the virtuous work of Mme de La Chanterie's band, the counterpart to that of Ferragus, with which he planned to end the *Scènes de la vie parisienne* (VI.426), but it seems rather weak after the extensive description of a society in the process of self-destruction.

Having moved from detail, to armature, to idea, it is now possible to return to the form of *Histoire des Treize*. In truth, Balzac has given us all that is necessary in these three loosely related episodes; in their very lack of obvious links to each other, they reflect the fragmented reality of the society that permits the Thirteen to operate. Félix Davin discusses '[t]he mysterious union of the Thirteen and the gigantic power that it assures them in the midst of a society without any ties, without principles, without homogeneity' (I.1169). If, as Balzac's spokesman also says, 'the distinctive task of art is to choose the scattered parts of nature, the details of truth, in order to create a homogeneous and complete whole' (I.1164), Balzac has indeed taken scattered 'episodes' which come together to make up one 'history.'

In the three works that have concerned me in this chapter, it is possible to see some of Balzac's most important devices for bringing his 'fragments' into relationships of coherence and unity. Should we take Todorov's definition of plot – as a movement between two states of equilibrium[22] – one might even suggest that a sort of plot links several of these creations. Though *Autre étude de femme* is more interesting for the variation on the eternal triad of husband/wife/lover than for any development from start to finish, just the same there is a certain progression in horror, if nothing else. The development of *Jésus-Christ en Flandre* and *Histoire des Treize* is, however, considerably more significant. These abstract 'narrations' lack developing characters; one sees rather a developing figure or plot system. And, as usual, the plots are subordinated to the vision of society as a whole. Symbols like the metal, gold, the Magdalene figure, the ship repeated in the church's nave, motifs like fire, demons, or veils, types like victims and villains, details like the color white and small intimate rooms, all are undoubtedly important in weaving the parts of these collections into wholes which have far more significance than the separate stories, but the overriding ideas remain the most important vehicles for the collections' unification. We are encouraged to conceive of an orphan society, cut off from its traditional, institutional roots, helpless before the monstrous violations of exceptional youth that is both unexploited and uncontrolled. It is a society of no great distinction, but in desperate need of a savior. Balzac's *auteur* has heard the call, and he details his terrifying vision for all to see.

CHAPTER FIVE

Unframing Frames

Narrative frames are analogically, if not directly, related to the frames and borders around many paintings. Consequently, a study of the frames of the visual arts provides useful perspectives on those of narratives. Frescoes are a good place to begin. Most often, of course, they were carefully planned, integral parts of walls and ceilings making use of architectural features like arches and columns to separate scenes or subjects. Plenty of examples exist, however, where the required architectural feature was not located exactly where the artist needed it. Judging from what we find in still extant frescoes, artists did not hesitate to invent whatever the particular setting might lack and to paint the needed columns, walls, arches, floors, ceilings, thus providing his fresco with the necessary enclosure. Perhaps the very idea of a frame came originally from the enclosures provided in walls and openings of various kinds. Whatever the origin, numerous paintings, frescoes, and mosaics, still extant from the time of Byzantium, Greece, Rome, have applied borders using the same medium as the enclosed works. Even the pebble mosaics from the fourth and fifth centuries BC incorporate such borders, as did the earliest remaining example of a Greek illustrated book, the Ambrosian Library's copy of the *Iliad*, dating from sometime between the third and fifth centuries AD. The book's plate XXIX includes a battle scene surrounded by an excellent example of a neat, painted border of two colored bands.

Such borders bring the enclosed material into focus and separate it from what surrounds it. In respect to this tradition, E.H. Gombrich says pertinently, 'Any hierarchical arrangement presupposes two distinct steps, that of *framing* and that of *filling*. The one delimits the field or fields, the other organizes the resultant space.'[1] Frames can become extraordinarily complex. The early twelfth–century *Last Judgment* of Autun surrounds the Christ in judgment with figures which form a border while completing the frieze. The curvature of the tympanum represents the firmaments, and the tetramorph immediately framing Him forms an open border, with angels, prophets, and apostles on the one side and demons on the other. Beneath are human beings awaiting the dread moment of His decision. While in this case the figures of the frame seemingly bring the events into the lives of the people, the border thus serving to open the work, other similarly constructed pieces have quite the opposite effect. The twelfth-century Torcello *Madonna*, for example, isolates the Madonna high in a dark cupola above a line of prophets and saints. The congregation in prayer is found even further below. As Mary Ann Caws puts it, 'To frame in is also to frame out, so that the notions of grid and selection, of inclusion and exclusion, are constantly in play.'[2]

Numerous works of the thirteenth century multiply scenes around a central figure. I think of the Master of S. Martin's *Madonna*, now in the S. Matteo Museum of Pisa. Here the various scenes recount the most important events of the Virgin's life, seemingly completing the central picture with narrative content. Cimabue's *S. Trinità Madonna* in the Uffizi has several prophets portrayed below the Virgin, which encourage the spectator's eye to rise to the Mother and Child sided, right and left, with angels. Likewise, Giotto's *Ognissanti Madonna* and many other works of the period deploy figures to make similar frames.

Fourteenth- and fifteenth-century miniatures that adorned various kinds of books most often had borders painted around them, sometimes of a highly complex, intricate nature. And even later, Renaissance painters perhaps derived the important architectural motifs of their works from those features that had surrounded earlier friezes and frescoes. Such borders set off, isolate, and often contrast with the enclosed material.

Michelangelo, of course, was a master of frames, as he was of so much else. The Sistine Chapel shows him isolating scenes with borders, which are then violated by figures spilling over into other scenes and thus visually connecting material that the Bible connects narratively. Frames isolate, integrate, and explode, apparently sending the figures and subjects cascading into the lives of those spectators staring upwards in awe. In this masterpiece the frames open into the context; the individual scenes then refuse to be confined to the ceiling of the Sistine Chapel. Similar effects are achieved in other, modern works, where, because of minimal or absent frames, the artist implies that the surrounding environment – whether gallery or room or the whole of reality – provides the frame. Although when we talk about frames, we usually mean something explicit, Michelangelo and recent painters and sculptors make us aware that the context may become the frame.

So it is with narrative frames. When explicit, they serve most obviously to isolate, to illustrate, to highlight, to exemplify, but they may also open an enclosed story to ramifications that extend far beyond the work. What we call a narrative frame is in fact a clearly stated context for the telling or finding of the principal story. The frame need not be explicit. As sophisticated readers begin to wonder about the narrator, narrative tone, and point of view, the implicit context or frame may be considerably more interesting than the explicit. In a way, all fictional works have a frame, some more than one. Mme de La Fayette's *La Princesse de Clèves* (1678) is framed by exact references to the historical French court of 1558–9. Names and events leave no doubt about the dating. But the social customs and practices provide a second, implicit frame of Louis XIV's court which held sway at least 100 years later. Indeed the latter gradually overcomes the former. Mme de Clève's eventual decision to refuse Nemours and retire to a convent makes sense only in relation to seventeenth-century distrust of passion. Although taking place in a sixteenth-century setting, Mme de Clève's withdrawal is justified in terms of the prejudices of those seventeenth-century readers for whom it was written.

In Marguerite de Navarre's *Heptameron* (1558), the frame introduces the ten people who each agree to tell a story each day, and the reader immediately understands that here we have a French *Decameron*, though the intended goal of 100 tales was never reached, thus requiring a modified title. Not only does the fiction that encloses the tales establish the collection in a tradition going back at least as far as the Westcar Papyrus (1991–1786 BC?), where each of the sons of King Khufu or Cheops tells a tale of magic, in addition, by introducing the tale-tellers, we have their personal guarantees of the veracity of the stories told. The frame of the *Heptameron* then serves as a means of rendering the stories more verisimilar and, as well, of intensifying the moral lessons to be drawn, since one quickly perceives from the discussions following each tale that the characters and the relationships between them establish parallels with the narratives and offer additional insights into human beings and their affections.

Indeed, it seems that when a work does not suggest a frame, the reader imagines one nonetheless. The inventions must have a context, whether fantastic or historical, and readers are seldom hesitant to provide the necessary. Recent authors have attempted to establish frames that have nothing to do with either history or humanity. Jean Ricardou's *La Prise / Prose de Constantinople* (1965), for example, takes as its frame the incorporating book rather than society, print and paper rather than characters. But for the most part, narrative frames fix the enclosed story into a society of greater or lesser extent and more or less explicitly.

Eighteenth- and nineteenth-century frames most commonly served as tools of verisimilitude. At the beginning of Marivaux's *La Vie de Marianne* (1731), we are told, for instance, that with the exception of changing the names, the text we are about to read is the same as that found in the wardrobe of the country house the narrator recently bought. Especially in the case of supernatural tales, some sort of a frame was apparently considered indispensable, since it is so commonly a part of such fiction. The narrator who is introduced in the opening lines may be a man of such probity that one cannot doubt his conclusions. I think of the narrator of Theophile Gautier's 'Omphale: Histoire rococo' (1834), who skeptically reviews some events of his youth. When he is incapable of finding a reasonable explanation for the miraculous events he remembers, the reader is encouraged to submit (or suspend) his disbelief. The narrator then is a model for the reader. Similarly, in Maupassant's 'La Main' (1883), one is impressed with the narrator's impeccable credentials – he is an examining magistrate and tells the story with such objectivity that one would show ill will to doubt the account. When, however, his rationalistic explanation is patently unconvincing, readers are encouraged to join his fictional audience and reject it, thus taking a cautious step toward believing in the supernatural.

Balzac's narrative frames do all this and more, for I have by no means exhausted the potential of such frames. There is no doubt, for instance, that one is more willing to accept the stories told by Derville and Bianchon in *Gobseck* and *Autre étude de femme* because they are such solid citizens and so very credible. Still, although the Master never passed up an opportunity to increase the realism and thus the believability of his work, his frames usually serve more important ends. Most significantly, they provide a powerful device for unifying *La Comédie humaine*. But they do much in addition.

Ross Chambers has argued in a fine article that 'Sarrasine' (1830) represents a double rupture of contractual agreements. In the frame the narrator promises to tell Mme de Rochefide the story of Sarrasine. In return she agrees to become his mistress. She has been attracted by the lovely painting of an Adonis stretched out on a lion's skin, which is in fact a portrait of a statue Sarrasine did long ago of the now aged Zambinella. Clever readers like Chambers understand that the story of Zambinella parallels the broken contract with which Mme de Rochefide rewards the narrator who has tried to sell his artistic narrative for a night of sexual pleasure. Zambinella, whose lovely voice and physical beauty were the source of the family fortune, is a castrato. He is thus a work of art fashioned by the hands of men. Once, long ago, his friends encouraged him to entice the young French sculptor, Sarrasine, into believing they could love one another. On discovering that he has been misled, Sarrasine disdains killing the castrato. 'You are nothing,' he pronounces. Then he considers the beautiful figure he has sculpted of Zambinella. '[A]nd that is an illusion!' he concludes (VI.1074). Mme de Rochefide has likewise been enamored of a painting that represents this same illusion and by the story of the aborted love between Sarrasine and Zambinella, which, of course, is nothing but the narrator's creation of a similarly artistic fabrication. She, like the singer, breaks her contract, leaving the artist with nothing. The contract of the frame between the narrator and Mme de Rochefide then parallels the implicit contract that Zambinella offers Sarrasine.[3] And the permutations continue. The aged castrato gives his ring to the young, charming Marianina, for example, establishing an implicit betrothal, which he cannot fulfill.

In 'Sarrasine' the frame is important in that it sets up a *mise en abyme* and thus a vibrant relationship with the incorporated story. While by no means a constant, the more interesting uses of frames establish and play on such patterns. This particular example does little to open up onto the rest of *La Comédie humaine* or onto the reality of Paris and Parisians. Most commonly, however, Balzac's narrative frames provoke an outward movement, establishing a link to a broader world, and suggesting a generalized truth or particular reality that will subsequently be deepened.

La Maison Nucingen provides a pertinent example. The external frame introduces the narrator, who is eavesdropping on the gathering in the cubicle adjoining his. The partition separating him from his neighbors both screens him and, for the reader, establishes the central image of the following story. In the first few lines, the reader learns that the narrative 'I' is dining with a companion at an unnamed but elegant restaurant. Though the partition between him and his neighbors is thin, 'thanks to our remaining very quiet' (VI.331) the four guests in the adjoining room act as though they think themselves alone.[4] Emile Blondet, Finot, Couture, and the malicious, verbal pyrotechnician, Bixiou, allow the wine and their supposed privacy to lull them into a free-flowing discussion of the fortunes of Nucingen and that of those, like Rastignac, whom the banker used and either rewarded or discarded. The conversation starts with a question about Rastignac's 40,000-franc income which, we learn, came to him as a consequence of Nucingen's third liquidation. In order to understand that transaction, one must understand a whole series of events, which encourages Bixiou to launch into an episodic tale, where each tale incorporates another. Couture has a hard time following him: 'In all of the tops that you set spinning, I don't see anything at all which is concerned with the origin of Rastignac's fortune.' But Bixiou reassures him: 'We are getting there. . . . You followed the course of all these little streams which created the forty thousand pounds of income which so many people envy! Rastignac then held the thread of all these existences in his hands' (VI.369).

As Armine Kotin [Mortimer] makes clear in an excellent study, the structure of *La Maison Nucingen* is a good deal more complicated than a simple 'aventure à tiroirs' (an episodic tale where each story incorporates another, rather like Chinese boxes).[5] After the introduction, where we meet the mute, eavesdropping narrator, Bixiou begins with the story of Rastignac and his fortune, which is interrupted with the account of Nucingen's fortune, which is hardly begun when we are given some background on M. de Baudenord, which is broken off to tell about the d'Aldrigger family, which is left incomplete with Bixiou's word play in a set piece describing the people at M. d'Aldrigger's funeral, which leads into a digression on Desroches, which is also left undone to begin the story of the Matifats.

By this point, of course, the unbroken string of incompletions has established a pattern, and we expect the story we are reading to be broken off. Readers are trained, however, to search for order. They expect it. And they are constantly positing future order rooted in past history, a need that, though based on structural patterns, builds a kind of suspense. Here, our expectations are intensified, since with the beginning of each new story, we wonder how and when it will be interrupted, and with each new interruption, our curiosity about the various outcomes grows. For both structural and narrative reasons, then, the interruptions raise suspense rather like that elicited by detective stories. Roland Barthes could have included it in what he called the *hermeneutic code* ('the set of unities which have as their function to articulate, in different ways, a question, its answer, and the varied accidents which can either prepare the question or retard the response; or – another possibility – to formulate an enigma and to bring about its deciphering'[6]). Barthes was thinking only of narrative questions, but, as artists have sensed from the beginning of time, structures of repeated sounds or phrases can elicit similar responses. In this case, not only does the reader come to expect *narratio interrupta*, his curiosity is increasingly aroused, and he awaits the resolution of the various mysteries that Bixiou has strung out, one after the other.

Suddenly, the series of new stories is arrested, and instead of having the resolutions presented in series, either repeating or reversing that of the original pattern, 'the course of all these little streams' (VI.369) arrive in a sort of basin where all work together. As Mortimer puts it, 'The confusion in the structure of the conclusion results from the fact that the scenes influence each other and that all the stories are telescoped and combined.'[7] To summarize, Nucingen's third liquidation defrauds his stockholders in order to establish his bank on a solid financial footing. Rastignac, though he apparently does not understand his role in the complicated hoax very clearly, serves as the promoter who makes the fraud work. He receives a comfortable reward for his pains. The by no means obvious pattern accompanied by seemingly impenetrable camouflage is pierced only by the already mentioned Bixiou, and by Palma, Werbrust, and du Tillet. These were 'the only ones who understood' (VI.388), and that only after the fact. Nucingen had carefully arranged everything well in advance. No one had seen through what he had done until it was over, and then only the cleverest were able to penetrate his machinations. He had no confidants, only tools: 'Nucingen's salient trait is to use the cleverest people around for his projects without telling them what he is doing' (VI.371).

However obscure this revelation may remain, it is lucidity itself compared with the story prepared by the restaurant partition separating the narrator from Bixiou and his friends. The partition repeats and reintroduces the motif of the veil, which has been so important throughout the *Scènes de la vie parisienne*. As the first few lines of the novella certify, the narrator can see nothing taking place in the room next door. He recognizes the voices, however, and, knowing the names and their circles, he is able to make sense of Bixiou's seemingly nonsensical (but, as we know, carefully constructed) narration. Indeed, the mute scribe has such a firm grasp that he does not hesitate to posit certain actions which accompany the words. Occasionally, he gives the impression that he can actually see through the partition.[8] At one point, for example, we read, ' "Couture, a crown!" said Blondet, putting a twisted napkin on his head' (VI.378). We do not know whether the narrator shares the extrasensory powers of the narrator in 'Facino Cane,' whether Balzac wanted to suggest that the eavesdropper was so keenly attuned to Bixiou and his friends that, despite his inability to see them, he could confidently posit accompanying gestures, or whether, finally, Balzac merely made a mistake. The last hypothesis is the least plausible, given that the narrator's acuity parallels, thus supports, the main thrust of the story having to do with Nucingen: though after the fact Nucingen has been penetrated.

Nucingen has a considerable reputation. The four friends consider '[t]his elephant of Finance' (VI.339) the ideal banker, since he views a bank as a business center involved in everything from large-scale commerce to politics. 'The Bank contemplated in this fashion became a whole set of policies. It required a strong mind, and encouraged a sturdy man to put himself above the laws of integrity, in which he feels too cramped' (ibid.). Elsewhere, for example, in *Les Employés*, he is termed the Napoleon of finances (VII.1058), which perhaps explains the military imagery that frequently accompanies descriptions of his activities: 'The banker is a conqueror who sacrifices masses for hidden results; his soldiers are the desires of individuals. He has his strategies to work out, his ambushes to set in place, his partisans to launch, his cities to take' (VI.339–40).

Blondet goes on to give a little history of other bankers. Through the ages, there have been many colossal men of finance, men whose names remain but whose fortunes no longer exist. Necker, Samuel Bernard, the Paris brothers, Law, Bouret, Baujon, each held sway for a time, but now all are gone: 'As Time does, the Bank devours its children' (VI.340). The narrator explains that all these men became involved in politics, which swallows up their fortunes. But for the reader who has experienced and pondered the lessons of *La Comédie humaine* there is another story, a harbinger of Nucingen's future: Nucingen has allowed himself to be penetrated. In the past, because he has been able to focus his will and dominate his passions, he was master of all situations.[9] Now, however, others have been able to see through the veil that once disguised him and his activities. Like Cousin Pons, who opened his collection and was thus destroyed, it is only a matter of time until Nucingen will meet his fate. It comes through his senses rather than through his financial empire, and, as we read in *Splendeurs et misères*, he falls victim to Vautrin and the latter's carefully prepared tool, Esther. It does not seem an exaggeration to suggest that, though Nucingen was to a minor degree affected by Vautrin's machinations, he was preserved from bankruptcy or worse by Esther's suicide.

In *La Maison Nucingen* the reader finds a frame that highlights a central image by suggesting that Nucingen's protective veil has been torn, violated by the piercing looks of fellow speculators, by Bixiou, by the latter's friends. In Balzac's world the banker has then become defenseless against predators. Balzac uses Bixiou's well-known maliciousness to emphasize the danger to Nucingen, though in fact any penetration provides a potentially dangerous wound which tends to worsen. As the last words of the story indicate, Bixiou may well know that he is revealing all to an audience wider than his three friends. ' "Say, there were people next door," Finot said on hearing us leave. "There are always people next door," responded Bixiou who must have been drunk' (VI.392). Bixiou may have foreseen that his story would be spread abroad, which, of course, is the eavesdropping narrator's function. In short, the frame mirrors the penetration motif and the danger such piercing implies in *La Comédie humaine*; it explains how the narrator has learned what he tells in the pages before us; and it suggests an opening onto the web of Balzac's fictional world. As has been frequently pointed out, this novella constitutes an intersection where numerous characters pass fleetingly and where one learns much of Rastignac's and Nucingen's background.[10] By directing the reader outward, the frame emphasizes the interconnected nature of *La Maison Nucingen* and the rest of *La Comédie humaine*.

Throughout the length and breadth of Balzac's enormous cycle, there are vestiges of other neighboring or distant creations. Most obviously, the characters themselves encourage us to recall where we know they have been or are going. Our knowledge of characters' lives has nothing to do with the placement of the particular work we are actually reading, since the ordering Balzac imposed on *La Comédie humaine* had nothing to do with chronology. Nor will all readers remember the Eugène de Rastignac of 'Etude de femme' when they come across a younger version of him in *Le Père Goriot*, but for those who read the *Scènes de la vie privée* from start to finish (or who, for whatever reason, have the background), his youth is enriched in the latter work by knowledge of his subsequent life as a socialite. Elsewhere, for example on making the acquaintance of Mme Tiphaine in *Pierrette*, we remember other members of the Roguin family, whether her mother and the longstanding affair with du Tillet or her father and the disasters his philandering caused in *La Rabouilleuse* and *César Birotteau*. But important systems of image and narrative motifs do as much. When Antoinette de Langeais begs to be branded, who does not recall the horrifying *TF* (for *Travaux forcés* or 'hard labor') burned into Vautrin's back? Even thematic developments are capable of recalling other comments or other illustrations. The references to the July Monarchy's gerontocracy in 'Un Prince de la Bohème' recall, for example, its results as painted in *Histoire des Treize* or in 'Z. Marcas.'

Occasionally the reverberations are so subtle and complicated that few if any readers notice them on a first or even on a second reading. I wonder, for example, whether the just mentioned 'Prince de la Bohème' has not suffered from the overly esoteric nature of Balzac's echoes. Judging from the dearth of secondary literature, almost no one has given the work a second glance. Patrick Berthier is one of the exceptions. In no uncertain terms, he announces, 'This product of haste is to be taken seriously . . . taken seriously because [the work] in all of its parts is a true critical summation.' With 'Z. Marcas,' Berthier sees it denouncing 'the way that the gerontocratic July regime has abandoned intelligent people and the stagnation to which the "Romantic malady" ["*le mal du siècle*"] has condemned ambitious youth' (VII.797). Denis Slatka adds to this comment the suggestion that Balzac's jabs at Sainte-Beuve can be justified esthetically in that 'Sainte-Beuve is the perfect expression of the middle-class mediocrity' under attack here.[11] Pierre Citron merely calls it the first of the new series of comic short stories which Balzac was to write for his *Revue Parisienne* (CI V.278).

'Un Prince de la Bohème' (1840–6) included a frame in its earliest version as 'Les Fantaisies de Claudine,' a frame that changed significantly in 1846, when the story was incorporated into *La Comédie humaine*. The differences between these two versions provide insights into what Balzac asked of frames. The tale introduces us to Charles-Edouard Rusticoli, comte de La Palférine, an impoverished dandy who spends his time in ever more outrageous episodes highlighting his insolent, cynical uselessness. He considers his posture justified in a mediocre world where aristocrats are no longer able to take their rightful place at the head. *Burlesque, satirical, journalistic, exaggerated* are terms that come to mind when one attempts to summarize the story's character. Though Pierre Citron is probably right to conclude, 'Balzac does not attach too much importance to it' (CI V.278), the work *was* included in the *Comédie humaine*, which gives it a certain significance, and, for the present purposes, its frame has considerable interest.

The body of the tale concerns Claudine's infatuation with the arrogant La Palférine, who rewards her submissiveness with increasingly difficult demands and capricious treatment. Poor himself, his perverse pride leads him to insist that she be surrounded by all the accoutrements of wealth. ' "Well," La Palférine said to her one day, "if you want to remain the mistress of a La Palférine who is poor, penniless, without a future, at least you must represent him in a worthy way. You must have a carriage, footmen, livery, a title. Give my vanity all these enjoyments that I cannot have for myself" ' (VII.824). While this may seem impossible for someone like Claudine, who after all is little more than a former dancer now married to a reasonably successful writer of vaudevilles, she manages to accomplish his every demand. To make her success more realistic, Balzac gives her a substantial inheritance which arrives toward the end of her efforts. She drives her husband, du Bruel, to become an increasingly renowned playwright. Consequently, especially because of Claudine's cruel taskmaster, La Palférine, her husband succeeds beyond his dreams, leaves the theater, and, financed by the inheritance, enters politics. Finally, he gains a title, all of which Claudine lays at La Palférine's feet. As the narrator points out, '[I]f it had not been for his wife's fantasies, du Bruel would still be de Cursy, a mere vaudevillian among five hundred others' (VII.837).

Anthony R. Pugh takes us back to the 1840 version. There, Raoul Nathan is telling the story to Delphine de Nucingen's daughter, who has become Rastignac's wife. When Nathan finishes, she says, 'My dear Nathan . . . I know of another household where it is the husband who is loved and the wife who is du Bruel.'[12] Nathan explains, 'I had forgotten . . . that after a fifteen year long affair, and after having tried out . . . her son in law, Baroness Delphine de Nucingen had married her daughter to Rastignac. The female financier ruled the latter absolutely, though without his being aware of it, and the young baroness finally learned everything' (ibid.). Pugh rightly terms the *mise en abyme*, which has the young Mme de Rastignac identifying with du Bruel, a 'delicate idea' (ibid.).

Balzac changed the title to 'Un Prince de la Bohème' in 1844, an obvious allusion to Charles Nodier's pessimistic, though farcical, *Histoire du roi de Bohême et de ses sept châteaux* of 1830, but it was in 1846 that the author of *La Comédie humaine* made a startling revision. He jettisoned the young Mme de Rastignac and replaced her with Dinah de La Baudraye. Dinah, the former 'departmental muse' is now living a life of poverty in Paris with her lover, Lousteau. The latter squanders the household's money on various women and other debaucheries, leaving Dinah no choice but to succeed as a writer. If there is to be any financial security, it depends on her. Having heard Nathan's story of La Palférine when he told it to Mme de Rochefide, she has used it as the basis for a short story. She reads it to Nathan, thus creating a new frame that distances Nathan. Now he becomes not precisely *the* narrator, but the narrator in a story written by Mme de La Baudraye, who, moreover, takes Mme de Rastignac's role and whispers in the poet's ear, 'I know of another household where it is the woman who is du Bruel' (VII.838).

The 1846 frame is considerably more complicated than that of 1840. Though Dinah's lover, Lousteau, is a philandering mediocrity, and, as she points out, the sexes of the two triads are reversed, the narrative pattern of driven/driver/taskmaster, du Bruel/Claudine/La Palférine is repeated far more exactly in Mme de La Baudraye/Lousteau/Fanny Beaupré and others than in the earlier Mme de Rastignac/Rastignac/ Delphine de Nucingen. In the 1846 version, both of the 'driven' are writers. Because of Lousteau's incapacity and intemperance – Lousteau 'shamelessly committed one infidelity after another' (IV.773) – Dinah is forced to take up her pen. Her whispered comment to Nathan then becomes a statement of faith. Like du Bruel, she intends to write her way to success.

Readers who have been reading from the beginning of *La Comédie humaine* or who have already met Mme de La Baudraye in *La Muse du département* have surely sensed a growing number of resonances as they listened to her read the story of Claudine and La Palférine. It becomes increasingly obvious why Dinah would have been attracted to Nathan's story in the first place. Had 'Un Prince de la Bohème' ended there, it would have provided an admirable, if sketchy, *mise en abyme* which mirrored the main story, thus supporting and strengthening it with a strong resemblance. It does not, however, end there. Dinah's budding parallel with du Bruel's life will not bear fruit. Instead, Dinah will return to her husband and accept the obligations of her name. Nathan suggests as much when Dinah bemoans her inability to repay him for his many kindnesses:

> 'Who knows? Perhaps you will have the same good fortune as Mme de Rochefide.'
> 'Do you think it is good fortune to go back to your husband?'
> 'No. But it is a fortune!' (VII.807)

Lousteau, who had arrived near the end of his mistress's reading, wants to know how the story ends. Dinah disclaims any interest in conclusions, only to have Nathan tell her, 'But there is a conclusion' (VII.838). It seems that, when Mme de Rochefide first heard him tell the story, she became curious about the arrogant La Palférine, then fell in love with him. As the 1846 prologue, now the definitive version, makes clear, Béatrix de Rochefide had returned to her husband. Unfortunately, her husband, Arthur, is still involved with Madame Schontz, and Béatrix's attention is wandering. In the conclusion of the definitive 'Un Prince de la Bohème,' however, Nathan announces that La Palférine and Maxime de Trailles plan to break up Arthur's extra-marital affair and reunite him with his wife. The narrator explicitly encourages us to read *Béatrix* – '(See *Béatrix*, Scènes de la vie privée),' (VII.838) – where not just the Rochefides are reunited, but the du Guénics as well, and, wonder of wonders, Maxime de Trailles promises to be faithful to his new wife. Those who have read *La Muse du département* will also remember that Dinah will shortly be reintegrated into her family – '[T]he Sancerre Muse returned openly to the Family and to Marriage' (IV.790).

This fairy-tale ending is perhaps enough to remind us of the way Balzac concluded the introductory panel of the 1846 frame. Mme de La Baudraye has set her story in the luxurious salon of 'a very famous marquise' on the Rue de Chartres-du-Roule, almost certainly Mme de Rochefide's residence before she moved back in with her husband. The marquise de Rochefide encourages Nathan to tell his story: 'I am listening to you the way a child listens to her mother tell the story of *Le Grand Serpentin vert* [*The Big Green Serpent*]' (VII.808). The tale, in reality titled *Serpentin vert*, is by the seventeenth-century fabulist Mme d'Aulnoy and had recently been reedited (1835). Balzac uses the allusion to recall other 'conclusions.'

The heroine of *Serpentin vert*, Laidronnette, was cursed by the evil fairy Magotine to be 'perfect in ugliness.'[13] After numerous adventures Laidronnette agreed to marry the king of the Pagodes, not only sight unseen but also promising that she will not look at him for another two years. Naturally, as these things go, she is eventually unable to resist. She faints on seeing her husband: 'she saw the awful Serpentin Vert [Green Snake] with his long hair standing on end' (12). As a result of her broken promise, Laidronnette's husband disappears, and she falls into the hands of the wicked Magotine. The malevolent fairy delights in imposing one painfully impossible obligation after another on the contrite young woman. The result is unexpectedly beneficial. Laidronnette is changed by her misfortunes and by her recognition of the mistakes she has made. '[S]he was washed in the water of discretion' (20–1), gains the new name, Queen Discrète, and successfully retrieves her husband from Proserpina's dark kingdom. The enchantments are broken, enabling the king and queen to regain their throne. Their newly handsome countenances reflect their virtues as they live happily ever after.

Whether or not Balzac was justified in expecting his readers to remember *Serpentin vert* well enough to recognize the new patterns he establishes is of course moot. Those who can remember the requisite background are led to understand that the author changed the entire thrust of 'Un Prince de la Bohème' with his introductory allusion to Mme d'Aulnoy's tale, which, in addition, highlights incidents in *Béatrix* and *La Muse du département*. V. Propp would identify several functions (a function resembles a mathematical function or quantity whose value varies according to the value of one or more related quantities). He would surely have pointed to the cruel master and his demands, the attractive slave accomplishing the impossible tasks, and the blessings that pour out on the slave and loved one(s). As Propp understood, the sex of the characters in the respective functions is immaterial, for they are often reversed without changing their function. When du Bruel is later inundated with wealth, is named a deputy, academician, commander of the Legion (of Honor?), peer of France, and count, all because La Palférine sets impossible conditions in the attempt to brush off the importunate Claudine, the absence of a fairy godmother making everything possible does not render Balzac's story any less fantastic.

The frame uses the allusion to *Serpentin vert* to open onto *La Comédie humaine*, both to remind us of all the broken marriages, which will shortly be reconciled, and to insist on the benefits gained from the difficulties afflicting the wives while they were separated from their husbands. We trust, though we cannot be sure, that their experience will brighten the renewed marriages. Remembering that Family constitutes one of the foundational institutions for *La Comédie humaine*'s ethical system – in 'Catéchisme sociale' Balzac wrote that 'the basic social unit is not the individual but the family' (HH XXIII.118) – it seems worth mentioning that Béatrix and Dinah, like Claudine, gain their advantages only within the family. Dinah's benefits come not from her pen, as she had dreamed, but rather from her husband's success in accumulating fortunes and titles. Balzac, I suspect, wanted the frame to emphasize that true success only comes through the institution of Family.

I doubt that Balzac's comic tale can bear the weight the author imposed on it in 1846. It is quite enough to use the new frame to establish a parallel between Dinah and Claudine. It is excessive to go further and not only break the frame by reminding readers that Dinah's dream of success as an author came to naught, but moreover suggest new parallels: like Claudine, like Béatrix, like Maxime de Trailles, Dinah will find success and apparent happiness while accepting the traditional role *en famille*. Still, whether or not one believes Balzac has gone too far in establishing such conflicting patterns in so few lines, the story's frame correctly indicates what the author expected of such devices. It was not enough to parallel the enclosed narration with a simple *mise en abyme*. Balzac wanted more: the reminder of a lesson, the highlighting of a theme, an opening outward either onto his fiction or onto reality itself.

'Le Chef-d'œuvre inconnu' exemplifies such an opening that is narrowly focused beyond *La Comédie humaine* onto reality.[14] Granted, the story's themes also have importance to Balzac's cycle, but the characters and plot are projected most directly onto history itself, since it is set in seventeenth-century France. The story, thus, provides the opportunity to move beyond those frames that encourage the reader to consider Balzac's fictional creation to those that suggest a reality outside of illusion in the actual world.

As the first few words of the work reveal, the reader is taken out of the normal, nineteenth-century setting of *La Comédie humaine* and transported back several centuries, '[t]oward the end of 1612, on a cold

December morning' (X.413). The initial dating and detailed description make it clear that we have not left the conventions of Balzacian creation behind. Detail remains important at levels far removed from that of concrete reality. December, for example, is anything but propitious for a love story, and the physical setting of the Rue des Grands-Augustines suggests the past: it lies across from the Ile de la Cité at the heart of 'Old' Paris, just off the Quai des Grands-Augus-tines. The street and quay were named for the monastery that was once situated there. On rereading 'Le Chef-d'œuvre inconnu,' with the recognition that the story sets up a series of oppositions between life and art, German draughtsmen and Italian painters, Dürer and Titian, two and three dimensions, line and color, Balzacians might remember that Saint Augustine, whose rule was followed by the Grand-Augustine monks, is remembered for his masterful treatises which for centuries explained the relationships between the great oppositions of his day: faith and works, good and evil, belief and reason. Balzac's story is situated precisely between life and art, love and science, heart and mind. Though he would in most cases valorize the former over the latter, as he does here, he understands, sympathizes with, and occasionally recommends pursuing art to the detriment of everything else.

The central opposition of love and art is raised in the first sentences. A young man paces before the door of a building 'with the irresolution of a lover who does not dare present himself at the home of his first mistress' (ibid.). It is of course not a question of his mistress, and, as already pointed out, it is not the season of love, but is, rather, December. The character, who turns out to be Nicolas Poussin, paces before the home of François Porbus, a well-known painter. Although Poussin does not yet know it, he is in the process of choosing between love, in the person of his mistress, and art.

The Faustian aspect of the bargain that will be presented to Poussin is highlighted by 'something diabolical' (X.414) that he sees in Master Frenhofer,[15] the bizarre character he follows into Porbus's lodging. Magnificently dressed in dazzlingly white lace, a black doublet, and a heavy gold chain, Frenhofer wears a gray goatee beneath green eyes, which were doubtless 'capable of casting magnetic looks' (X.415). Not surprisingly, he is soon revealed as the fount of esthetic knowledge and skill. With a few deft brush strokes he raises Porbus's latest work, '*Mary the Egyptian* getting ready to pay for her boat passage' (X.416), from the ordinary to the glorious. While making the few changes, he lectures, explaining that Porbus has failed to integrate the German and Italian schools, and he brags about his own masterpiece, a portrait of Catherine Lescault, which no one has seen. Finally, 'the demon stopped' (X.422).

Frenhofer gained his knowledge from Mabuse in what was chronologically the first exchange to which the reader is privy.[16] 'Having become his friend, his savior, his father, Frenhofer sacrificed most of his treasures to satisfy Mabuse's passions. In exchange, Mabuse bequeathed him the secret of relief, the power of giving to figures this extraordinary life, this flower of nature which causes our unending despair, but which he did so skilfully' (X.426–7). Within the time span of the story, Frenhofer initiates another exchange when he purchases Poussin's sketch for two gold coins. This give and take is only preparation for the central exchange. Frenhofer needs a perfect model against which to judge the perfection of his painting of Catherine Lescault. 'Oh, I would give my entire fortune to see just once, for a moment an example of nature in her perfection, of the ideal! I would go to limbo itself to find you, celestial beauty!' (X.426) Poussin, on the other hand, feels he will learn essential lessons if he can study Frenhofer's work. '[F]or the enthusiastic Poussin, by a sudden transfiguration, this old man had become art itself, art with its secrets, its ardor, and its dreams' (ibid.). Given that Poussin's mistress is available and has the needed perfections, the possibility of an exchange arises.

The theme of the sacrifice of modesty was introduced in Porbus's painting, mentioned early in the story. We are told that the work shows St Mary the Egyptian getting ready to disrobe to pay for her passage across a river. Gillette's modesty is well established, and, whatever the sins of earlier editions in which Catherine was repeatedly called 'la Belle-Noiseuse [*the beautiful party-girl*].' Balzac later deleted these sobriquets to insist on her virginal nature – 'Born in my studio,' Frenhofer insists, 'she must remain virgin, and cannot come out until she is dressed.'[17] Gillette is purified by her joyous, selfless passion, and Mary the Egyptian is a saint.

Despite the sacred example, neither Frenhofer nor Gillette is happy with the proposed arrangement. Although Frenhofer has always been willing to pay anything necessary to gain knowledge, materials, or paintings, this bargain requires a personal sacrifice of him. 'What!' he says, 'reveal my creature, my wife? tear the veil with which I chastely covered my happiness? That would be a horrible prostitution!' (X.431). Gillette is already upset because of what happened when she first modeled for Poussin. She recognizes that he looked at her in quite a different way, his eyes no longer guided by love but by esthetic demands, and she flatly refuses to pose for anyone else. She has promised, she points out, to give her life for Poussin, but she has never agreed to renounce her love. 'If I showed myself this way to someone else, you would no longer love me. And I myself would feel unworthy of you' (X.429). Poussin raises the issue of his future glory, which he sees as bound up in the chance to see Frenhofer's work, and he proclaims, 'Excuse me, my Gillette. . . . I would rather be loved than glorious. For me, you are more beautiful than a fortune and honors' (ibid.). Gillette gives in, sure that Poussin no longer loves her. In addition, 'She felt as though she already loved him less, since she suspected he was less worthy' (X.430). In short, despite both Fren-hofer's and Gillette's hesitations, an exchange is arranged. Gillette explains, '[I]f our love perishes, and if I open myself to deep regret, won't your fame be the price of my obedience to your desires?' (X.433) Porbus pronounces a sort of justification, 'The fruit of love passes rapidly, those of art are immortal' (X.434). Of course, while this may be true in the greater scheme of things, it does not mean that Balzac believed art more worthwhile than love. We have seen the contrary message in *Les Secrets de la princesse de Cadignan*. Nonetheless, Poussin chooses to risk his love for what he hopes to learn from Frenhofer's painting.

Sadly, it is all wasted, since little but the dangers of excess can be learned from the painting, once it is put on display. As the master himself said, but earlier, 'Say, too much knowledge, like ignorance, brings one to a negation' (X.425). Frenhofer's masterpiece is a 'chaos of colors, of tones, of vague nuances' from which, however, emerges a 'fragment' – an admirable foot (X.436). The word *fragment* is of course weighty with significance in *La Comédie humaine*. Poets like the naturalist Cuvier were able to reconstruct worlds from such bits and pieces. '[O]ur immortal naturalist reconstructed worlds from whitened bones; like Cadmus he rebuilt cities from some teeth, gave a thousand forests all the mysteries of zoology from a few pieces of coal, redis-covered populations of giants in a mammoth's foot.'[18] As Frenhofer looks at his painting, he sees the process of creation, every touch of his brush, every flesh tone as it quickens and dies in the changing light of the seasons and days. Having compared Gillette to what he sees on looking at his Catherine, he is able to say, 'Come in, come in. . . . My work is perfect, and now I can show it off with pride' (X.434–5).

Especially after having heard his continuing discourse, sensitive readers can perhaps imagine what is denied to those whose imaginations are limited by the paint-caked canvas that remains. Fortunately for us, during his discussions the great artist has already transposed the creation of his mind into words. But unfortunately for him, he was unable to render his vision with paint, since paint is limited and paintings are static. He has forgotten his own lesson, 'The mission of art is not to copy nature but to express it' (X.418). He rivaled nature; he attempted to breathe new life into his work. The result was a process evident only to readers who have followed his descriptions and to the artist himself.

The conclusion of the story leaves many questions unanswered. Frenhofer suddenly sees what is obvious to others, though he finds the strength to deny the new vision and show the visitors to the door. Gillette tells Poussin to kill her, and goes on to deny their love: 'You are my life, and I find you horrible. I think that I already hate you' (X.438). Then, after Frenhofer's chilling 'adieu,' '[t]he next day, Porbus, who was uneasy, came back to see Frenhofer and learned that he had died during the night, after having burned up his canvasses' (ibid.). We do not know whether Frenhofer committed suicide. We cannot spend time before the master's paintings and study them in detail, for his destruction has deprived us of such thorough attention. We cannot know why the artist deprived mankind of his works. We are ignorant of his state of mind while he destroyed his masterpieces and at his death. These things we do not know, for neither the story nor history tells us.

We need not, however, remain completely ignorant about the future of the main character, as does one reader – 'we do not know what became of Poussin'[19] – and we need not wonder how another critic can be so sure that 'Poussin loses Gillette.'[20] Other lovers in *La Comédie humaine* put up with much more and continue to love. But we know that indeed Poussin must have lost his mistress, since history does not mention her, while he goes on to achieve artistic greatness. Given these two facts, it seems fair to assume that Poussin failed to learn his lesson, that even if he did mend their relationship after this episode and placate Gillette, he continued to sacrifice his love for art. Gillette had already noticed what happened when she modeled for Poussin: she took second place. Clearly, Poussin continued his errant ways, depriving himself of a magnificent love, but giving mankind art of genius.

I suggest that Balzac expected his reader to ask questions about Poussin and his love affair. It is only natural to do so. By setting up a situation where the reader's natural curiosity can only be satisfied by leaving the work of art, Balzac effectively connects the illusion to reality. Simultaneously, of course, he increases verisimilitude (the point after all of his frequent mentions of real persons and events across *La Comédie humaine*). The frame then not only opens onto reality, it encourages the reader to accept reality as the ultimate conclusion of the story, and the artful story as real. The unknown masterpiece is then multiplied. Of course, there is the marvelous work Frenhofer destroyed but that readers can imagine from the master's descriptions. There are also those paintings still unknown in 1612, because Poussin had not yet created them, but that we can now study in museums across the world.

Elsewhere, the frame opens onto a much broader social phenomenon. Take, for example, 'Facino Cane.' As is so often the case in *La Comédie humaine*, the original confrontation with the title of the story produces suggestive resonances that can orient the reader appropriately. It has an Italian flavor; thus one is not surprised to find an Italian main character or to discover that he shares supernatural powers of many other fictional foreigners. Nineteenth-century French supernatural tales often either take place in foreign climes or they tell of a foreign power imported into France. The foreign then serves as a supporting image of the strange, the bizarre, the supernatural. Still, one also suspects that while the middle-class audience's well-practiced powers of observation would have greeted such preternatural phenomena skeptically in their own everyday world, authors probably hoped they would accept more easily the possibility of supernatural events outside France, the likelihood of alien events in an alien place or in an alien person.

Facino Cane believes he has the power to sense the presence of gold, even through walls. If names suggest the deeper characteristics of personages, as Balzac repeatedly claimed, Facino's given name may make one think of the French *'fasciner* (to fascinate), which has two related meanings: to master by the hypnotic power of a person's gaze or to charm by the dazzling beauty or power of some object. Certainly, Facino is obsessed by the vision of gold that he carries with him wherever he goes. His family name, Cane, while pronounced [cane] in Italian, would be [can] in French. Given that 'cane' [can] is French for a female duck, it is perhaps not surprising that he is called either *le père Canard* ('old' duck – VI.1024) or *le père Canet* (ibid. – a *canet[te]* is a duckling). That '*un canard*' is as well a musical false note makes the nickname appropriate on several levels, but, given the immediate context, when Facino is being encouraged to talk about Venice and is called '*le père Canard*,' it seems clear that Facino Cane's acquaintances have judged the fabulous story of hidden gold and jewels he likes to tell. 'Don't talk to him about Venice,' the violinist warns the narrator, 'or our doge will start going again, especially since the "prince" has already downed two bottles!' (ibid.) It is for them a '*canard*,' a false story or hoax, and he bears the stigma of their judgment in his sobriquet, whether *le père Canard, le père Canet[te]*, or Cane, pronounced in the French manner.

The story proper begins with 'I [*Je*],' a pronominal designation that shortly introduces himself as a narrator telling a story which happened some years before. 'Facino Cane' is then enclosed in a frame. The narrator has a past. Once, because of his love of 'science,' he lived a monastic life of study, housed in a garret near the Place de la Bastille. His one distraction was to follow other inhabitants of the neighborhood. Impecunious himself, he fit into his impoverished surroundings and was not noticed. He was able to eavesdrop on their conversations and to a surprising degree empathize with them: 'While listening to these people, I could become a part of their lives, I felt their rags on my back, my feet were walking in their holey shoes. Their desires, their needs, everything passed into my soul, or my soul passed into theirs' (VI.1020). He even claims to substitute himself for them, comparing his power to that of the dervish of the Arabian Nights who 'took the body and soul of the people over whom they spoke certain words' (V.1019). This ability is a gift, he says; he wonders whether it is 'a kind of second sight' (VI.1020). While he does not know its causes, it has allowed him to understand the common people in depth (ibid.).

The narrator is invited to a marriage celebration, where he looks forward to losing himself in the 'joy of these poor people' (VI.1021). The celebration takes place on the second floor of a wine merchant's establishment on Charenton Street. The recollection that Charenton was also the name of one of the most famous psychiatric hospitals of the day may explain why Balzac chose that particular street. Certainly, the bright lights, the inflamed faces, and the fact that the area is a 'seminary for revolutions' (VI.1020) lend the scene an air of excess, perhaps even of madness. The narrator watches as the eighty guests dance in their Sunday finery 'as though the world were coming to an end' (VI.1021).

At this point we are treated to one of Balzac's meta-literary comments: 'But neither the physiognomies of this gathering, nor the wedding party, nor anything in this world is concerned with my story. Retain only the bizarre character of the frame. Imagine a vile place painted red, smell the odor of wine, listen to their joyous roars, stay right in this quarter, in the middle of these workers, of these old people, of these poor women, all of whom are given over to a night of pleasure!' (VI.1021–2). The function of disclaimers such as 'neither . . . nor . . . have anything to do with' is not always what the literal meaning would lead one to expect. Whether positively or negatively noted, one should pay specific attention to the object designated. Here, the carousing poor of Paris are specifically highlighted in the frame. One remembers what the narrator says about the lower classes in the introduction to 'La Fille aux yeux d'or': '[T]hey have all exhausted themselves in order to earn this gold that fascinates them. Then, heedless of the future, avid for pleasures . . . great lords for a day, they throw their money away on Monday in the cabarets, which stand in a muddy circle around the city. . . . [T]heir pleasure, their rest is exhausting debauchery . . . which only lasts a couple of days but which steals the future's bread, the week's soup, the wife's dresses, the baby's swaddling clothes, all of whom are in rags' (V.1041). This descriptive frame is, in short, so much a part of Les Scènes de la vie parisienne that one might well believe the story was created explicitly for it.[21]

Practiced readers of Balzac may find what follows anti-climactic, so much is it foreshadowed by the title and introduction. The narrator's eye is drawn to three blind musicians. He quickly dispels any grandiose musical analogies: 'Their music brutally attacked . . . the eardrum. . . . [The] clarinet player. . . . blew at random, not paying the least attention to either the beat or the melody' (VI.1022). It is perhaps pertinent to note that three is the number of spiritual synthesis, though here whatever unity there may be emphasizes dissonance and blindness. The narrator is drawn to one in particular: '[M]y soul passed into the clarinet player's body' (ibid.). He compares him to the plaster cast of Dante, a reference to the latter's death mask, and to the blind poet Homer, but he says that the old man resembled a lion restrained in his 'cage of flesh' (VI.1023).

The clarinetist and the narrator leave the revelry and, seated before the 'black water in the Bastille's ditch' (VI.1031), which as Albert Béguin has pointed out alludes to Venice's canals,[22] Facino's story is soon told. His prevailing passion was determined before his birth –

'[I]t is sure that my mother had a passion for gold during her pregnancy' (VI.1026) – but his initial difficulties were of a more carnal nature. He had fallen in love with Bianca, an eighteen-year-old married woman. When the young woman's husband discovered them, if not exactly *in flagrante delicto* at least talking of love, he tried unsuccessfully to kill Facino, who then leapt on the husband and killed him. Forced to flee, he soon lost his estates in the Venetian condemnation proceedings and his more portable fortune in gambling. And so he returned to Bianca, where on being discovered once again he was captured and imprisoned. He uncovered a partially completed tunnel in his cell and determined to finish it. While working, however, he was afflicted by strange visions: 'I heard the sound of gold; I saw gold in front of me; I was dazzled by diamonds!' (VI.1028). The tunnel completed, he found himself in the secret treasure trove of the doges. He used the treasure to bribe his guard, and he escaped, carrying fabulous wealth with him. Later, after he went blind (perhaps as a direct result of his strange ability to sense gold), his mistress robbed and abandoned him in London. Somehow – the narrator does not explain the precise methods – he made his way to Paris, where he has remained.

We understand that his continuing vision of the gold that he stumbled across makes him feel at home in Paris, since his obsession is shared at all levels of this society. Even the narrator, whose love of 'science' has condemned him to poverty, feels overwhelmed by the vision of mountains of gold, a vision shared by the rest of his world. Although Facino does not know the exact location of the treasure, his extrasensory gift will surely lead him to the place, and the seduced narrator cries, 'We will go to Venice' (VI.1031). Unfortunately, whether because the narrator regains his senses or because it is necessary to amass funds to pay the expenses of the trip, old Facino Cane dies before they leave.

Like the best of Balzac's frames, it shimmers with suggestive reflections from the incorporated story of the past. While the monastic narrator is charmed (*fasciné*) by the Venetian's temptation, the story seemingly melts into the frame, which is the society as presented by *La Comédie humaine*. Thoroughly prepared readers no longer need a long discourse on society's obsessive focus on gold. The mere fact of the man of science's seduction by the vision of gold – however momentary – is quite enough to bring the thematic backdrop from elsewhere in *La Comédie humaine* and, moreover, to reflect this further emphasis back out onto the fictional and real worlds.

'Z. Marcas' begins without any preparation. The first word, 'I [*Je*],' identifies the character who begins to tell the story. One understands that he is a law student and that he rooms with a medical student named Juste. The two are impoverished, though not disagreeably so, since they enjoy their studies and each other, pleasantly passing the hours discussing the society that surrounds them, sharing their thoughts, walks, and tobacco. Next door in even more complete poverty lives a mysterious man of lionesque features: Z. Marcas. He earns the 30 sous needed to keep him alive by doing copywork by the page. Eventually the two young men make their neighbor's acquaintance. Brilliant, well trained, filled with ambition, he had looked for a rich deputy whose career he could establish, thus establishing his own. Twice he succeeded, with the same person, but, when on each occasion the deputy betrayed him, he managed to bring about his fall. Now, reputed to be dangerous, he is unable to find suitable work or a new protector, and he is left to the marginal life of a copyist. One night the narrator and his roommate, Juste, overhear the traitorous deputy acknowledging his sins and proposing a third attempt to gain power. The boys talk Z. Marcas into accepting the proposal, which succeeds only temporarily before he falls back into poverty, takes sick, and dies. Throughout, the story has been sprinkled with comments on the July Monarchy's disdain of youth as it embraces mediocrity.

The frame is keyed by the narrator's 'I' and his present. (The story of Marcas took place in the recent past.) We learn early on in the story that not only has Juste left the country to make his fortune in Asia, but the narrator is about to leave France. As Marcas's tale is recounted, we understand that it is an exemplum of what is happening to French young people. They have seen their talented elders rejected, disdained, and destroyed. They have judged France and found it wanting. In 1790 such young people fomented a revolution; this time they merely turn away.

The last few lines of the story cast further light on the frame, however, since the narrator is identified. He is Charles Rabourdin, the son of the brilliant administrator, Xavier Rabourdin, who had dedicated his life to the state, and who was destroyed, on the one hand, by mediocrities and, on the other, by Bixiou's almost random viciousness. In defeat, Xavier planned to turn to commerce and make a fortune. So he promised his wife in 1824. The fact that his son lives in poverty in 1836 gives a reasonably reliable indication of the father's lack of success. Charles has had the lesson of futility from two tutors: his father and Marcas. Outstanding men have no future in politics, in the administration, or in business – at least not in France. In the words of des Lupeaulx: calumny is the daily bread of remarkable men. '[T]here are two ways to take [calumny]: if overwhelmed, you need to pack your bags and retire to the country; or to stay in control, proceeding fearlessly, without paying any attention at all' (VII.1096–7). If not just slander but failure as well await the outstanding and the talented, there remains nothing but to try one's fortunes outside France. The motherland, of course, is the loser.

The original frame is deepened as the narrator recounts the story of Marcas. We learn about the narrator as we learn about his now-dead neighbor. Little by little the frame becomes an integral part of the story of Z. Marcas. Near the beginning we are told that 'Z' stands for Zéphirin, after St Zepherin (or Zephyrin), who was martyred in the second century. No wonder the narrator comments, 'This "Z" which preceded Marcas, which appeared on letters addressed to him, and which he never forgot in his signature, this last letter of the alphabet suggested something strangely fatal' (VIII.829). We remember the old German word, 'marca' or boundary, a meaning that is also found in the modern Spanish 'marca' (boundary or frontier region). Especially in the light of the narrator's commentary on the fatality of Marcas's name, which he expands a few lines after the above cited passage, it may be appropriate to suggest that Z. Marcas is the last of his kind, the last of the remarkable and brilliant who will stay in France, continue to struggle, and be destroyed. He marks the outer edge. As Marcas says when approached about joining the opposition, 'It is too late' (VIII.854), thus echoing Puyraveau's frustrated cry at the tardy attempt to amend the edicts which served as the most immediate cause for the riots leading to Charles X's downfall in 1830.[43]

The conditions detailed in Les Employés have not changed. Xavier was forced to resign from his position in the ministry, though if his superiors had possessed foresight, he might have revitalized all the governmental bureaucracies. Z. Marcas has had no more success in the political realm. Rather, he is destroyed. And we can gather from what we know about Charles's financial condition that, on attempting to storm the world of commerce, his father has found a situation similar to the one he confronted while in government. Balzac seems to be telling his readers that the youth that could have saved the country either has been destroyed or has fled what he elsewhere condemns as a 'gerontocracy' (VII.808). France is then left defenseless against the revolution that finally arrived in 1848.

Readers understand that while 'Z. Marcas' is framed by the story of the students, the implicit but much more significant frame is in fact *Les Employés*, which, though a part of the *Etudes de mœurs* is included in the *Scènes de la vie parisienne* rather than the *Scènes de la vie politique*, where we find 'Z. Marcas.' But more important, as we perceive the thrust of this rapidly expanding frame, it seems that France herself, and not *La Comédie humaine*, encloses the story. 'Z. Marcas' has then become, not the story of one particular, political failure, not the story of a young man of potential who abandons France for Malasia, but the story of France herself, wasting away and thus losing her greatest resource – her youth. In the account of Z. Marcas, we see the boundary with which France is constrained. We learn once again the lessons the boy, Charles Rabourdin, has had from both his father and Z. Marcas, and the inescapable conclusions he himself makes are emphasized. It is too late for France. Outstanding young men must expatriate themselves.

As with the frames that surround mosaics, frescoes, illuminations and paintings, Balzac's frames serve to limit, to define, to intensify, but they also orient the reader's attention to things going on outside the frame. In many cases we are clearly expected to think of events, characters, activities, phenomena in *La Comédie humaine*. The cycle then serves as the frame which borders, like pillars around a fresco, and concomitantly organizes the enclosed material. The work, whether *La Maison Nucingen* or *Le Père Goriot* or 'Sarrasine,' is organized rather like a painting in a exhibition. It has its place, and while Balzac tried many different arrangements, in the end he generally settled on what we currently find in most editions. Seldom are museum goers given the opportunity to see a show of all of a major artist's works which is, moreover, hung by the artist. *La Comédie humaine,* however, provides readers with that experience. The cycle as a whole serves the function of a museum with a number of galleries. Each gallery, carefully chosen for its suitability, constitutes a second frame with individualized lighting and context for each of the works included. The museum itself, of course, exists in society, subject to its moods and passions. In a sense, museums are always without walls, for they both are defined by and define the larger world in which they are found. So it is with *La Comédie humaine*. Though explicitly framed by the various *scènes*, it also opens onto the author's and our world, gaining and giving definition and intensity.

CHAPTER SI X

Configuring the Whole

In the first chapter, I introduced six principles which are operative in the organization of *La Comédie humaine*. They are by no means discrete, though I have attempted to separate them sufficiently to show how they function within Balzac's masterpiece. It is time to look at them as a group, and this chapter will be concerned with the way they all work together to provide his *Comédie* with coherence and unity.

1. *Narration is subordinated to description, though description is usually illustrated by one or more narrations.*
2. *Description is keyed by one or more central images, which are subordinated to what Balzac called* l'idée mère *(generative idea). Whether as concept or image, Balzac consistently sought some sort of a principle that would unify all aspects of his works.*
3. *Images are linked to each other and to the whole by repetition, which is played out through parallels, opposition, development, and systematic variation.*
4. *The unchronological arrangement of* La Comédie humaine *can be explained by the consistent esthetic vision of the entire work.*
5. *Balzac's works, often placed within an explicit frame, are always set within an implicit context, which is essential to the creation.*
6. *Balzac was the master, not of collage – the construction of a whole from isolated pieces – but of montage: he regularly constructed wholes from other wholes.*

Readers cannot, of course, limit consideration of *La Comédie humaine* to technique, any more than with other nineteenth-century writers. The novel genre was long a stranger to any conception of 'art for art,' and Balzac in particular insisted on the importance of meaning.

Those who have finished *La Comédie humaine* have a curious privilege. They can look back across the thousands of characters, the hundreds of stories and settings, and they can see a world that is surprisingly comprehensive, so much so that they may confidently dismiss any charge that Balzac was presumptuous when he invited comparison to Dante's *Divine Comedy*. Lukács put it simply: 'Balzac gives a larger foundation to his work than any writer before or after him.'[1] There are things we do not know: characters whose future or past is beyond our ken. Still, there is no doubt that Balzac really did create a self-consistent world of impressive proportions, which for all its mysteries seems unified and complete. From the perspective of the entire *Comédie humaine*, we look back at a society ruled by egotism and greed, where the conservative institutions of Church, King, and Family are rapidly losing what little influence they have left. As Barbéris writes, Balzac has created 'an epic of selfishness and separation. No character obeys anything but himself, defined not as belonging to a group but uniquely in respect to selfish interests, consequently interests which are opposed to those of other men.'[2] Indeed, this is a world in the process of disintegration, since individualism out of control destroys virtually everything in its path. Balzac insists on his point of view in the 'Avant-propos,' though it is evident throughout his oeuvre: 'Man is neither good nor evil. He is born with instincts and aptitudes. Society, far from corrupting him, as Rousseau claimed, perfects him, makes him better, but self-interest develops his bad tendencies a great deal' (I.12). Ordinarily, built-in systems with a long tradition suffice to orient people toward serving the greater good, but in wrenching times of change, old constraints cannot be relied on. Balzac recognized what history has subsequently verified: the old order was passing away, and while the new one was not yet born, its shape was becoming all too apparent.

The Church had lost its power and was well on the road to what many call the post-Christian world. Furthermore, having lost its king, the French state was decapitated, though some semblance of life continued because of corrupt politicians, pandering to a greedy, self-centered populace. 'In every creation, the head has its indicated place. If by chance a nation drops its chief at her feet, sooner or later she will note that she has committed suicide' (V.926). And, finally, the family was disintegrating. With every passing day there was less to restrain and mold those forceful individuals able to focus their energy and bend the world to their desires. Though Balzac regularly defended himself from the charge of painting only the depraved, the criminal, the reprehensible (he claimed that *La Comédie humaine* included as many virtuous creations – for example, I.15–16), there can be no doubt that demonic figures like Ferragus and Vautrin overshadow by a considerable margin angels such as Mme de La Chanterie and Benassis.

La Peau de chagrin is frequently chosen to demonstrate how focused human thought in its guise as will, passion, and idea can become a powerful force to serve good or ill. The capacity to concentrate to such a degree raises one above the norm, but it also destroys the individual who commits himself so intensely. The title presents the central image, the magical skin, which satisfies the owner's every desire, though at the cost of a shortened life, graphically illustrated by the shrinking skin. When Raphaël de Valentin fully understands the payment exacted for the power the skin gives him, he attempts to imitate the antique dealer and restrain his will. Such a man as Raphaël is of course incapable of living without desire, and with every desire he sees the skin shrink and his life slip away.

Critics have long felt that the book turned around a choice that the antique dealer – a type of guide or wise man – presented him: between a life of 'WANTING and BEING ABLE [*VOULOIR et POUVOIR*],' on the one hand, and '*knowing* [*SAVOIR*]' on the other (X.85). The old man has observed the high cost of the first choice: '*Wanting* burns us and *Being able* destroys us; but KNOWING leaves our feeble organization in a perpetual state of calm. So it is that desire or wanting is dead in me, killed by thought' (X.85). He has placed his trust in 'the brain which does not wear out and survives everything' (ibid.). The antique dealer is remarkably similar to Gobseck, as is his glorification of the advantages of the withdrawn, detached life of the observer. When Raphaël tries to adopt the recommended passivity, he applies to himself an image that was previously associated with Balzac's usurer: he says he wants to '[b]ecome one of the oysters of this rock.'[3] It is, of course, impossible. As I suggested in *Novel Configurations*, Balzac illuminated his feelings about those who attempt to deny the qualities that are central to life itself by the conclusion he appended to *Gobseck* in 1835: the miser dies surrounded by his hoarded food which creates an intolerable stench as it rots.

Life cannot be denied. Just as water that does not flow is not a stream, so life without aspiration and action is not life, and a life lived has its price in its physical and mental suffering. There is no doubt that the *chagrin* of the title (and central image) means a 'wild ass' (X.83, 239–40); nor is there any doubt that the novel exploits the homonym of *chagrin*, with the sense of *distress, affliction, suffering, shame*. The text uses the word with this sense a number of times.[4] Remembering the association that the narrator attributes to M. Martellens – '*Châagri* is a stream' (X.241) – readers should also recall that Raphaël earlier compares 'the human will [to] a material force that resembles steam' (X.149). When Raphaël 'abdicated life in order to live' (X.217), he denies his humanity: 'In the midst of luxury, he led the life of a steam engine' (ibid.). We remember from Balzac's 'Catéchisme social' that the novelist distinguished machines from what they do – '[T]he steam engine,' he says, 'is distinct from the movement it produces' (HH XXIII.119) – and, as is clear from *La Peau de chagrin*, Raphaël has become a machine, running empty. The will remains, but it is useless, since it is not translated into action. For the accomplishment of anything worthwhile, there must be activity. 'Could you,' he asks in 'Théorie de la démarche,' 'find a great human accomplishment for me that did not also have some excessive movement, whether material or moral?' (HH XXIII.621).

Curiously, despite Balzac's repeated emphasis on the importance of egotism to *La Peau de chagrin*,[5] critics have concentrated on other issues, generally agreeing that the novel centers on the opposition between energy and passivity, between Aquilina/Euphrasie and the antique dealer, between intense, short-lived pleasure and dispassionate but long life, between pleasure/consumption and renunciation/contemplation, or between Raphaël and the antique dealer. Emile J. Talbot, however, offers a persuasive new reading. For Talbot, the opposition I have just detailed is in fact 'merged into a single egotism.' He argues that 'the symbols of the novel's real options are . . . found at the antique dealer's: the portrait of Christ and the magic skin, symbols of altruism and egoism.'[6] It seems to me that the skin is rather symbolic of life,[7] thus leaving the antique dealer or Fœdora to symbolize egotism and oppose Christ. In the painting Christ's 'suave, magnificent smile . . . seemed to express this precept: . . . *Love one another!*' (X.80). The dealer tells him, 'I covered this canvas with gold pieces' (ibid.). What he means is of course that he paid a great deal for the painting, but the words he uses imply that he has tried to veil Jesus' message. He has chosen gold and selfish withdrawal from life.[8] When he offers Raphaël the talisman, the *Peau de chagrin*, the young man makes a similar choice, symbolized by his rejection of Pauline for Fœdora.

The names are important. 'Pauline' is the feminine form of 'Paul.' Given the novel's emphasis on the painting of Christ, this young woman's name points to the 'apostle to the gentiles' and author of the Pauline Epistles, which were primarily responsible for formalizing the practices of the Christian Church. Pauline, who exemplifies altruistic love in action, will sacrifice anything to help Raphaël; she prefers his life to her own. But Raphaël turns away. '[Y]es, I want to live in excess' (X.87), he declares. He choses Fœdora. The text tells us she is one of those 'profoundly egotistic women' (X.164), 'lacking a soul' (X.169). '[S]he is everywhere. If you wish, she is Society' (X.294). Talbot suggests that her name might make us think of the Latin *foeda* (shameful), if not '*faite d'or* [made of gold]' or '*fée d'or* [golden fairy]' (78). The self-centered hero not only rejects Pauline, the personification of love, he also spurns other traditional values. He no longer wants to devote his life to mankind. When given the power to accomplish anything at all, his 'first desire is vulgar' (X.88), and subsequent ones are no better. He could have finished his treatise and arranged for it to have the impact to change the course of human history. He could have solved problems of hunger and sickness. In one drunken moment, he promises great things: 'I will wrestle with yellow, blue, green fever, with armies, with scaffolds' (X.203). Before being given the skin and thus being granted this awesome power, he was so devoted to his father that for years he sacrificed his pleasures to help him, and he eventually signed away his property to pay the family debt. His refusal to part with one small island where his mother's tomb is located symbolizes his commitment to traditional values. Believing that he was destined for great things (X.128), he wants to cover himself with glory (X.132), to 'scramble to heaven without a ladder' (X.133). The vehicle was to be his philosophical treatise, *Théorie de la volonté* [*Theory of Will Power*]. He dreamed of using it to lay out 'a new path for human science' (X.138), of a life of significant service to humankind. Instead, he settles for a life of luxury where his egotism is emphasized by selling the island containing his mother's tomb (X.201) and by killing a young man in a duel (X.275–6).

In the first flush of excitement about the skin's power, now under his control, he asks, 'Who would not be good if he could do anything?' (X.202), but when he almost immediately compares himself to Nero

(X.203), he foreshadows his own ignoble future. Blondet prophesies: 'I wager that within two months you will become disgustingly egotistical' (X.211). Little more than a month later, he thoughtlessly wishes his teacher, M. Porriquet, well, and, realizing what he has given of himself in the process, he screams, '[I]f all the Porriquets in the world were to starve to death, what difference would that make to me?' (X.219–20). He vows, 'No more beneficent thoughts! No more love! No more anything!' (X.220). M. Porriquet is right to be 'prey to acute uneasiness about Valentin's moral health' (ibid.). Elsewhere Balzac says, 'You are judged on your ways and means' (HH XXIII.104), and, as the narrator comments, 'Raphaël had been able to do everything; he did nothing' (X.276). Confronted by a choice, he could have expended his life, and a part of the skin, in either egotistic or altruistic ways. The antique dealer's passive egotism is opposed to the painting of Christ, Fœdora to Pauline. Raphaël turns from Christ and Pauline first to follow Fœdora, then to imitate the dealer.

An extensive allusion to the biblical accounts of Nebuchadnezzar and Belshazzar emphasizes the themes of egotism and self-sufficiency, what Balzac termed individualism. Raphaël is twice compared to Nebuchadnezzar (X.203, 205). In the Bible, Daniel tells the Babylonian king, '[T]hy greatness is grown, and reacheth unto heaven and thy dominion to the end of the earth' (Dan. 4.22); Balzac's Blondet announces that Raphaël 'is king. He can do anything; he is above everything as are all rich people' (X.210). When the biblical Belshazzar and his courtesans drink from the gold and silver vases that belonged in the temple in Jerusalem, toasting false gods, the king sees the *Mene, Mene, Tekel*, and *Upharsin* written on the wall. He pales, quivers, and his imminent death and the division of his kingdom are prophesied (Dan. 5). A similar orgy given in response to Raphaël's desire is explicitly contrasted with virtue and Family (X.206–7). At the instant the young man's wish for wealth is also fulfilled through an unexpected inheritance, he suddenly remembers the golden writing on the *Peau de chagrin*, assuring him that his life has been shortened as a direct result. 'The heir grew horribly pale, the muscles of his face stood out, his features contracted, . . . and his eyes grew fixed. He saw death' (X.209). Later, Raphaël explicitly refers to '*Mene, Tekel, Upharsin*' (X.237).

Similarly to Nebuchadnezzar, who dreamed a dream that Daniel interprets as the history of mankind to come (Dan. 2), Raphaël 'left real life' (X.70) on entering into the antique dealer's shop. He sees not the future, however, but the past: 'the bones of twenty centuries. . . .

a confused picture, in which all human and divine works clashed. . . . The beginning of the world and the events of yesterday married each other. . . . All the countries of the world seemed to have brought some debris from their sciences, some samples of their arts' (X.69). Rising from floor to floor, he eventually arrives at the apex, where 'under the sway of these inexplicable hallucinations' (X.77), he meets the mysterious old antique dealer and is exposed to the choice between egotistic passivity and hedonistic excess, on the one hand, and Christ on the other. The positive side of the novel's opposition is encapsulated by the beggar, crying 'Ah! good sir, *carita! carita! catarina!*' (X.66). *Carita* is of course Latin for 'affection' or 'love of neighbor,' while *catarina* doubtless derives from the Greek *katharos* meaning 'pure.'

Absolute power corrupts, however, whether in the hands of Nebuchadnezzar or Raphaël. Any opposition or resistance to those whose every whim is granted raises frustration or worse. Nebuchadnezzar's fury grows when the wise men are unable to tell him what he wishes to know, and he wants to kill them all (Dan. 2.12). Later, frustrated by Shadrach, Meshach, and Abednego, who proclaim allegiance to their God, refusing to do as the king commands and bow to the statue he raised to his own glory, the enraged monarch has them thrown into the fiery furnace (Dan. 3). Raphaël has a little more control. On leaving the three scientists who are unable to help him, he is simply 'prey to cold rage' (X.252).

Daniel explains what happened to Nebuchadnezzar: '[W]hen his heart was lifted up, and his mind hardened in pride, he was deposed from his kingly throne, and they took his glory from him: And he was driven from the sons of men; and his heart was made like the beasts, and his dwelling *was* with the wild asses [*onagres*]: they fed him with grass like oxen' (Dan. 5.20–1). Made unwelcome at a resort near Aix, Raphaël goes to live with peasants near Mont-Dore. Because of the name, 'Golden Mountain,' we may reasonably suspect that the choices Raphaël makes here are as egotistical as those he exhibited when rejecting Pauline for wealth and social pleasures, even though his orientation has changed. Now he is attempting to achieve the antique dealer's passivity. '[H]e remained . . . in the sun like a plant, like a rabbit in its hole' (X.282). 'He had strangely mixed his life with the life of this rock. He had implanted himself in it' (ibid.). Finally, back in Paris, 'this man . . . descended to the level of sluggish animals who rot in the midst of forests[; he was] like the dead remains of some dead plant' (X.289). Nebuchadnezzar's senses return when he is ready to acknowledge that God has all power over the kingdom of man (Dan. 4.22). Likewise, in full knowledge of what he is doing, Raphaël finally realizes the error of his ways and desires Pauline. We assume that he thereby embraces all his former values as well. He dies in her arms.

It is not surprising that until near the end Raphaël choses against service, charity, and love. His adventure occurs during the July Monarchy and the weakening of the major institutions which, as Balzac says in his 'Lettre sur la littérature [*Letter on Literature*]' of 10 August 1840, are necessary to negate the destructive impulsion of 'individualism. Christianity is a complete system which opposes the depraved tendencies of man, and absolutism constitutes a complete system for the repression of society's divergent interests' (HH XXIV.119). Balzac did not equivocate about the period in which Raphaël lives. Neither a republic, deriving its power from the people, nor a monarchy ordained by God, it is one of these 'vile, bastard governments: unmoving, immoral, lacking foundations, lacking principles, which unleashes all the passions without gaining advantage from any of them' (ibid.). In addition, Raphaël is an orphan, thus without the restraints imposed by Balzac's third important institution, that of Family. It is this society of the July Monarchy that the novelist wanted to paint, a society in process of disintegration. It encourages people to indulge themselves, and until the virtual end, Raphaël goes with the current.

When critics agree that Balzac's *Comédie humaine* is unified, they are usually referring either to his realistic vision or to his philosophy. Although I have not met a historian who claims that one must read Balzac to understand France of the July Monarchy, neither have I met one who denies the nuance and illumination a reading offers. Balzac represented the essence, and often the particulars, of his world with astonishing accuracy.[9] Likewise, his overview is remarkably consistent. Bardèche, Bertault, Curtius, Guyon, Nykrog, Picon, Prendergast, and many others have studied Balzac's philosophical orientation at length and in detail. Despite their real differences, they agree both about the novelist's unified vision, and, in general, about the issues constituting it. I have little to add to their comprehension of the whole,[10] but am drawn rather to what might be called the artistic unification, though I know that one cannot separate form from content.[11]

In the preceding chapters, I have concentrated on those elements, whether details, devices, or characteristics, that have supported the novelist's consistent philosophy and strengthened the cycle's coherence and unity. I do not forget that as far as Balzac was concerned form must be undergirded by some sort of meaningful vision. As he put it, 'In literature, it is not enough to amuse, or to please. You must attach some meaning to the pleasantry. Telling stories for the sake of telling stories is empty' (HH XXIV.157). Too much emphasis on artistry sins in another direction, as well: 'Where Form dominates, sentiment disappears' (III.770). In short, it is for me a matter of emphasis, and, while emphasizing technique, I have tried not to neglect the meaning. There is no doubt that, whether we call Balzac's vision a set of attitudes, a perception, an orientation, or a philosophy, the way he looked at the world ties individual works to each other and to the whole. This part, the 'meaning' or the 'generative idea [idée mère],' can be easily summarized. It appears explicitly in many of his newspaper pieces. The really distinctive things that make Balzac worth reading, however, only become apparent during a sophisticated reading of the text itself. I think, for example, of the awesome horror that builds around the primary motivation in his society... GOLD.

As we move across the scènes and études, Balzac's world gains consistency, depth – one might even say presence. Readers are encouraged to assume it is realistic, if not real. As in life, though subsequent contact may force some revision in our projections, we expect that the people and institutions we meet in one context will continue to act normally, that is, according to the patterns observed during our acquaintance, whether or not we are actively observing. More than a backdrop, Balzac's society is entirely integrated into every part of the cycle. It is nonetheless essential not to minimize society's importance as a backdrop, for it helps to fill in those gaps between the various works. It provides a consistent context or frame for the entire Comédie humaine. Reality is brought in by constant references to real places and real people. I suspect that most of us no longer know in every case which character is historical and which is not, which event actually took place and which did not. The boundaries between the real and the illusory become blurred, and La Comédie humaine gains substance. Within the frame of the whole 'hang' some 120 works, which form a montage of extraordinary complexity. In short, the world created by Balzac incorporates society, which then becomes its context and provides a frame for the works within La Comédie humaine. It does likewise for the whole. In this regard, as in most others, the principles governing the structure of individual works function for the entire Comédie.

When Balzac talked of the whole, he frequently used an architectural analogy. The individual work was for him, and for Davin, a 'stone' (for example, X.1202). Davin felt Balzac was no more concerned about where his works appear in the span of *La Comédie humaine* than an architect 'inquires about the place on the building site where the stones with which he is to make a monument have been brought' (ibid.). For a time it might even have been the way Balzac viewed the matter, but the number of lists in his scrapbook, which repeatedly consider different arrangements, and the many times he actually changed the placement of individual 'stones' indicate that a work's context was indeed important. Balzac did not build his edifice haphazardly. He gives every indication of seeking the perfect fit for every carefully hewn block. In fact, on reading his masterpiece from start to finish, one gains an appreciation for the order he finally chose. Those who read at random, or in the chronological order of the fictional events, lose important pleasures. Balzac was very concerned with the way contiguous creations related to each other, but the major linking devices, on the most obvious level at any rate, have nothing to do with chronology. And while I do not wish to neglect the unity of the whole – the way, for example, *L'Envers de l'histoire contemporaine* constitutes a mirror image of *Histoire des Treize,* thus ending the *Scènes de la vie parisienne* in a way that recalls its beginning – coherence, or the relationship of adjoining elements, was also an extremely important consideration. By following *La Peau de chagrin* with *Jésus-Christ en Flandre,* to pick one of many possible illustrations, the author effectively emphasized the important Christ symbol in both.

I also think of the way the parts of *Les Célibataires* – a trilogy composed of *Pierrette, Le Curé de Tours,* and *La Rabouilleuse* – fit together. In each of the three stories the crux occurs in a different region of France, but the settings resemble each other in that they are outside Paris, thus 'in the provinces.' All three stories, of course, deal with celibates, especially with their selfishness and love of sensual delights. For these characters, other people lose their humanity. Not surprisingly the victims of the first and last panels of the trilogy bear names of stones: Pierrette and Agate. The casualty of the middle story is named Birotteau, which may suggest *virvolter* (to twirl around), something at the mercy of every passing gust of wind. The disinherited are killed by activities of the illegitimate inheritors in the first and last novels and psychologically destroyed in the middle creation. The villains of the three works are, respectively, Rogron, Troubert, and Rouget, names whose phonic similarity marks the characters' profound

relationship. While only the last two novels are to any degree concerned with secret leagues, the first turns around struggles between
groups of monarchists and liberals.

Like all of the *Scènes de la vie de Province*, each story deals with
flocking and the conflicts between provincial insiders and outsiders.
The groups' relationships to those excluded, however, change within
each work and vary in respect to the factions of the other two novels.
In *Pierrette*, the Rogrons, having made their money in Paris, return to
Provins. Though not accepted by the town's elite, they slowly build
their own group. In the process, they invite the disinherited Pierrette
to come and live with them, promising to allow her to inherit. Once she
is within their power, they forget the agreement, and they abuse and
eventually destroy her. By this time their party of liberals has become
so strong that, though charged with responsibility in her death and
brought to court, they get off scot free. In *Le Curé de Tours*, Troubert
comes in from the outside and is rejected by the senior priest and the
little society that has gathered around him. Though never able to gain
entrance to this local group, Troubert brings the *Congrégation* (that
horror of Balzacian horrors!) to bear from Paris and imposes his will.
Birotteau, who has been so entranced with his selfish little pleasures
that he has not kept up his allies, finds himself isolated from his
protectors and loses everything but his life. In *La Rabouilleuse* Agate has
left for Paris and is thus easily disinherited by her half-brother. When
she returns she is unable to stay long enough to gather a support
group and, as the outsider, goes back to Paris with empty hands and
pockets. Her son, Philippe, however, comes to Issoudun and remains
sufficiently long not only to gain acceptance by the local, reigning
group but, as well, to isolate the usurper, Max, an outsider who has
managed to take control of the family wealth. Philippe then inherits.
This turn of events does not benefit Agate, the rightful heir. Philippe
is an unnatural brute, so cruel to his mother that her heart is broken
and she dies. Still, justice will out. Because he remains a celibate
(though of the marrying kind), he neglects his allies and is eventually
rejected and killed.

Today's physicists tell us that, although in one way or another the
smallest particles of reality constantly make order, they move in a random fashion. For Balzac, however chaotic nature might seem, everything adds up. '[N]othing is isolated; everything is connected. . . . [A]ll
facts having to do with ethics are connected as are all material facts'
(HH XXIII .121). At least as early as 1834, he jotted down the idea of

a book 'composed of detached fragments, seemingly without beginning or end, but having a secret, logical meaning' (HH XXIV.675). If we remember that a 'fragment' was for Balzac the indication of a whole, we may find this note particularly suggestive, since it seems to describe with accuracy the organization of *La Comédie humaine*: apparent disorder masks an arcane configuration. In fact, the disorder one sees on first confronting the novelist's cycle may well have been meant as a device of realism, presenting reality as it seems to most people. This is Peter Brooks's point when he writes, 'The *Comédie humaine* is a paradoxical monument to a corpus in dissolution' (*Melodramatic*, 117). Balzac firmly believed that the society surrounding him was in the process of destruction – self-destruction. The problem that faced him can be easily understood on considering his belief in the absolute esthetic necessity of unity: if unity is an artistic imperative, but the subject of the work is in the process of disintegration, how then does one make order of a vision of disunity? The answer did not come to him immediately, and he never explained his solution in detail. As he continued to work, however, his dependence on the most obvious and well-worn devices for giving his readers the sense of a neatly ordered reality decreased.

Balzac, of course, had no doubts about the overriding logic of either reality or his own work. He simply broke the former down into its component parts as he made the latter. As Félix Davin says, 'Before getting to a society composed of men, the author had to apply himself to decomposing man' (X.1213). Balzac started with the detail, the fact, the part. It might be a character, a setting, though just as often it was a statue, a particular kind of wallpaper, a piece of furniture, a word, or a turn of phrase. When the details are repeated they take on additional importance. We would probably then call them motifs, though the term is foreign to Balzac. Increasing repetition adds significance to them, and they become symbols or narrative armatures or 'images,' a word which for the novelist was generic. As he stated over and over again, his task was to generalize. 'Consequently, the writer's task is primarily to come to synthesis through analysis, to depict and to assemble the elements of our life, to posit the themes and to prove them all together' (II.267–8). No detail could be justified for itself alone: 'Literary truth consists in choosing facts and characters, in raising them to a point where everyone believes them true on perceiving them, because each has his particular truth, and everyone has to recognize the complexion of the one he sees within the general coloration of the type presented by the novelist' (HH XXIV.91). When he chose a character, it was because the individual represented a class. '[E]xceptions must never play anything but an accessory role in a novel's action. Heroes must be of a general nature' (ibid.). In fact, 'the mission of a poet is to paint types' (HH XXIV.86). Poor writers 'generalize particular traits, instead of particularizing the general' (HH XXIV.108–9). Balzac expressed the relationship of 'idea' and 'image' on a number of occasions.

From details to motifs, to images, to ideas, such at least was Balzac's hierarchy of the materials of literature. Thinkers who start with the 'idea' to create what might be termed a philosophical reconstruction may not find an appropriate image, since, while '[e]very image corresponds to an idea or, more exactly, to a *sentiment* which is a collection of ideas, . . . ideas do not always result in an image. An idea requires work in development which is not suitable for all minds.'[12] And of course all this must be brought into some sort of unity: 'Whatever the number of accessories and the multiplicity of figures, a modern novelist must . . . group them according to their importance, subordinate them to the sun of his system, an interest or a hero, and conduct them in a certain order like a brilliant constellation' (HH XXI V.89). As Balzac quotes the chemist Vauquelin, '[W]ithout unity, no power' (VI.127).

Balzac did not rely on plot to provide coherence. At the end of *Illusions perdues* and of the *Scènes de la vie de Province*, Vautrin and Lucien are on their way to Paris. Readers close the volume or turn the page, depending on the edition, ready to begin the *Scènes de la vie parisienne,* but the interruption is so radical that one may begin to seek something other than character or plot to tie these two major scènes to each other and to *La Comédie humaine*. Setting provides the most obvious relationship. Some characters are going to Paris. The next tale occurs in Paris, though without the benefit of either Vautrin or Lucien, at least not for many hundreds of pages.

Mme Jules is being spied upon by a potential usurper, Auguste. The purposive character of the names is rapidly highlighted. After Ronquerolles thinks he has killed the young Auguste in a duel, he leans over and whispers, 'Julius Caesar's sister, sir, must not be suspected' (V.829). When she is later compared to Caesonia, because of the latter's proverbial ability to please Caligula by catering to his caprices (V.840), readers may suspect they have been introduced to a world comparable to that chronicled by Suetonius. Certainly, the amorality of the society reflected in 'La Fille aux yeux d'or' is well prepared. Not surprisingly, the duchesse de Langeais's toying with Montriveau is compared to Poppaea's playing with Nero (V.979). By the time we arrive at the title of the next work, *Histoire de la grandeur et de la décadence de César Birotteau* [*History of the Grandeur and Decadence of César Birotteau*], which begins by recounting Mme César's premonitory dream – she sees herself a widow in rags and begging – the allusion to another dream is too obvious to be ignored: 'And on his last night Caesar dreamed that he was soaring above the clouds, and then shaking hands with Jupiter; while his wife Calpurnia dreamed that the gable ornament, resembling that of a temple, which had been one of the honours voted him by the Senate, collapsed, and there he lay stabbed in her arms!'[13] While there is no doubt that the dream in *César Birotteau* has a number of functions within the novel – highlighting the perfumer's pride, foreshadowing his destruction, for example – one should also note that it joins with various allusions to encourage readers of *La Comédie humaine*, who are able to call on memories of other novels, to compare Paris to decadent Rome and to link the novel to those that precede and follow. The meaning of the allusion is significant, but its function as a linking device is equally so.

I already discussed the weight accorded monsters in *Histoire des Treize*. The image is introduced within the first few paragraphs of 'Ferragus' – which is also, of course, within the first few paragraphs of *Les Scènes de la vie parisienne* – rapidly establishing Paris as a 'receptacle of monstrosities' (V.891) and the metaphor as an important symbol. By the time we come across the following phrase in *La Maison Nucingen*: 'Like Time, the Bank devours its children' (VI.340), monsters have become one of the signs of Paris and of the *Scènes de la vie parisienne*, since it is in this section of the book that Balzac concentrated on the results of the rampant individualism found in the capital city. I do not wish to suggest that there are no monsters in other sections of *La Comédie humaine*, for that is not the case; I only say that monsters are particularly numerous in this portion of the cycle. In addition to its characterization of Paris, the monster image modifies particular individuals (V.802), physical conditions like virginity (VII.152), physical qualities like asexuality (VII.494), or moral qualities like self-interest (VII.427). The repeated use of the symbol has importance, of course, in regard to meaning. When we finally arrive at the silver seal Steinbock gave cousine Bette and imagine the represented Faith, Hope, and Charity with their feet resting on 'monsters which were tearing each other apart' (VII.90), there is little doubt that the multiple contexts that have accumulated around the image make it almost unbearable. Simultaneously, it links *La Cousine Bette* to other novels within this group of creations. By itself, 'monster' as a link is as weak as gossamer. When, however, it is combined with others – the 'dance [*bal*]' where Auguste imposes himself on Mme Jules, the 'dance' from which Antoinette de Langeais is kidnapped, César Birotteau's 'dance,' with 'devils' and 'demons,' masks, disguises, incognitos, and pseudonyms, with 'villain[s]' (for example, VIII.39, 406), with the brands on Ferragus, Vautrin, Chaussard, and Vauthier (only the first two characters were invented by Balzac), with orphans, with gold, with hundreds of other motifs and images, the mutually supportive filaments converge and work together to create a fabric of astonishing strength.

Themes repeat and weave similar fabrics. I think of the way Auguste de Maulincourt judges and condemns Clémence Desmarets (Mme Jules) without trial. In doing so, he prepares his own condemnation at the hands of Ferragus. More importantly, the theme of judgment, which reappears throughout the *Scènes de la vie parisienne*, is set in motion. I think of the kangaroo court Montriveau held for the duchesse de Langeais, the bankruptcy judgment and subsequent rehabilitation of Birotteau by the Royal Court, the less formal but perhaps more powerful way society gossip is used as judge, jury, and executioner in *Les Secrets de la Princesse de Cadignan*, 'Sarrasine,' *Les Parents pauvres*, and *Les Employés*. I think of the way justice is used and abused in *La Maison Nucingen*, *Splendeurs et misères des courtisanes*, 'Facino Cane,' and *L'Envers de l'histoire contemporaine*. It is in this portion of *La Comédie humaine* that readers gain their fullest understanding of speculation, of the driving desire for self-gratification through gold, power, and pleasure, of idle youth, of the gerontocracy, of attractive masks covering horrendous decay and vice, of passion having nothing to do with love. Novels and short stories included in other *scènes* and *études* may touch on one or more of these themes, though never in quite the concentration or quite the same mix, rather like a single fleece which can be spun, dyed, and woven into different wool tartans and then sewn either into kilts or vests. It is easy to understand why Balzac considered putting *Le Père Goriot* with other *Scènes de la vie parisienne*, for example, though the work's emphasis on family was doubtless important if not decisive in his final decision to include it with the *Scènes de la vie privée*.

As it is with details and themes, so with plot systems. A few pages back, I mentioned that all the works in the *Scènes de la vie de Province* turn around factions organized by the apparently primary function of exclusion. To distinguish it from the penetration armature of the *Scènes de la vie parisienne,* I call it a defense plot system. *Ursule Mirouët* sets the pattern. The wealthy Dr Minoret retires to Nemours with his wife's niece. Though born in the town, where he has many relatives, he has been gone for so long that he has become an outsider. By education, experience, and inclination, moreover, he feels distant from his relatives and from most of the locals. He is determined to leave his fortune to his wife's niece, Ursule, which poses a problem. Unlike most Parisians, he understands provincial life, and he knows that without a supportive group strong enough both to protect Ursule and to impose his will, his despised relatives will disinherit the girl after his death. Ursule, unfortunately, is related to the good doctor only through his wife and by means of an illegitimate birth. Before the law, the relatives cannot be completely disinherited. The wily doctor prepares to leave them the minimum and hide a fortune for the girl between the leaves of one of his books. Without the group, which he carefully prepared, however, the girl would have been left with nothing, for Minoret-Levrault steals the cache. The doctor's friends gather around her. Bougival, her nurse and the doctor's housekeeper, accompanies her to an inn, then to a small house that Bongrand helps her purchase with the inheritance from M. de Jordy. Bongrand also has the legal knowledge necessary to trace the assets Minoret-Levrault stole. Father Chaperon advises her in adversity and when she confronts the supernatural. But the most important friend is God, whom Dr Minoret met at his conversion and who apparently permitted Dr. Minoret to return from death both to tell his ward about the theft and to threaten the thief. The fact that everything ends happily is directly due to the strength of the league Dr Minoret was able to establish before his death. Otherwise, the opposing faction of relatives and locals would have been victorious. As Madeleine Ambrière-Fargeaud says, 'The struggle between the temporal and the spiritual ends in victory for the spiritual, and heaven manifests its presence by conversions and phenomena which profane people qualify as supernatural, but which, according to the novelist, are explained naturally' (III.735).[14]

In the next novel the rigorously limited world of Eugénie Grandet is disrupted when her cousin Charles arrives from Paris. Her provincial neighbors surround her diligently, however, and Charles never seems to understand what a marvelous young woman, and fortune, he missed through his own blindness. *Les Célibataires* [*The Celibates*] next introduces variations on the armature as do the other novels in the *Scènes de la vie de Province*. In some the intruder is killed or repulsed, in one Gaudissart is soundly and delightfully tricked, in one Lousteau succeeds temporarily; but in every case we watch families and local groups gather to protect their own from outsiders. While the provincials are not always in the right, they are seldom at the mercy of intruders, unlike those lone, virtually defenseless individuals peopling the *Scènes de la vie parisienne*. One can observe families that continue to operate, though weakened by the diseases being spread from Paris. Désiré Minoret-Levrault, as just one example, 'had . . . acquired ideas [in Paris] which would never have occurred to him in Nemours' (III. 773). The defense plot functions rather like the penetration armature in that it gives the reader a sense of recognition as he moves from one to another of the novels in these scènes. The repetition of details, themes, and narrative systems works to link neighboring novels and short stories, to give *La Comédie humaine* coherence as the reader moves through in an orderly fashion.

One of the problems that comes with consciousness of these repeated elements is a temptation to begin to imagine that they reveal a particular order of generation or creation. I think, for example, of the high incidence of families in *Les Scènes de la vie de Province* (compared with the number of orphans in the next series of *scènes*) Did families generate the idea of defense against outside predators in this sequence, or is it an outgrowth of Balzac's understanding of the provinces? In fact, for those interested primarily in coming to terms with *La Comédie humaine*, rather than the way it was created, it does not matter. All these images and others contribute to tying the elements of these *scènes* together. When readers are aware of the repeating elements, the repetitions become as pivotal as a plot would be to another author.

Still, however powerful the links between the neighboring parts may seem as one reads in the order of Balzac's arrangement, I do not wish to overemphasize coordination. It seems to me that the paradigmatic unity of the whole cycle, how each part is related to every other, is far more important. Most often, readers do not recognize the way a particular novel echoes another until after both are understood thoroughly. Naturally, we see that *Splendeurs et misères des courtisanes* finally carries on the plot that stopped suddenly at the end of *Illusions perdues*. Only when each unity is grasped in and for itself, however, does it fully contribute to the entire *Comédie humaine*. Balzac's system of montage may then require a higher level of abstraction than if he had constructed his cycle of bits and pieces. With a collage, one is encouraged to find the unifying elements that draw the fragments together once and for all. Montage is different, in that one must first come to terms with a constituent unit, fitting its parts together into what might be called a subwhole, before going on to the next important unit, and only then attempting to grasp how these two separated subwholes are related to each other. The process continues until the spectator is capable of conceiving all the elaborate and distinctive subunits as a new, encompassing whole that is separate from and superior to each of the units that make it up, though the constituents are preserved in their integrity. As Proust understood, the process is metaphorical. Each subunit is an image. The images combine to make new images. *Histoire des Treize* then joins *César Birotteau, La Maison Nucingen, Les Parents pauvres,* and others to make the *Scènes de la vie parisienne.* At some point one notices that several motifs, themes, symbols, or armatures are repeated in several subunits, which then combine additionally to make images that differ from the previously discussed subwholes. We become aware, for instance that the despair of Albert Savarus is repeated in Raphaël de Valentin.

Eugénie Grandet, which shows in detail how a repressed girl might build unrealistic dreams around an oblivious young man, varies the elements of *La Vieille Fille,* which casts a glaring light on one possible result of such castles in Spain. *Albert Savarus* is, Balzac told Mme Hanska, '*Louis Lambert* in another form.'[15] *Les Parents pauvres,* in concentrating on the elderly unmarried, recall and fill in the sketches of *Les Célibataires. La Maison Nucingen* opposes *César Birotteau.* As Balzac said, '*Nucingen* and *Birotteau* are twin works. It is lack of integrity and integrity juxtaposed as they are in the world' (HH XXIV.535). *L'Envers de l'histoire contemporaine* sets up a similar opposition, though in a more profound way. For example, it is by no means accidental that, when Ferragus's daughter dies, he is destroyed, whereas the death of Mme de La Chanterie's daughter merely confirms the mother's saintly devotion to the good of others, choosing not revenge, as did Ferragus, but mercy and forgiveness.

Previously, we looked at length at the devices that bring *Autre étude de femme* into some semblance of unity. I did not mention several particularly important elements linking the cycle internally to the *Scènes de la vie privée,* to the *Etudes de murs* and to *La Comédie humaine* as a whole. In her introduction to *Autre étude de femme* Nicole Mozet recalls the 'Etude de femme,' since the title echoes the earlier 'study,' but she concludes that *Autre étude de femme* 'does not correspond well with the first story' (III.658). There is no doubt that the story of Mme de Listomère's temptation does not include the jealous vengeance that would be required for inclusion in *Autre étude de femme*, but one should remember that Balzac's titles are never accidental. He certainly meant these works to recall each other. 'Etude de femme' is told in the *Scènes de la vie privée* by Bianchon, one of the narrators of *Autre étude de femme*, which is also located in the *Scènes de la vie privée*, though more than a thousand pages farther on. 'Etude de femme' turns around Rastignac, who is not only present at Mlle des Touches's late dinner, as is his mistress, but is a recognizable member, perhaps even the sign of the world of socialites on display. Most important, however, 'Etude de femme' presents the portrait of 'une femme comme il faut,' distinguished as we recall from a grande dame. Mme de Listomère is 'one of these young women raised in the spirit of the Restoration' (II.171). Like 'la femme comme il faut,' 'she offers an image of the present day' (ibid.). Her virtue is clearly shallow, for it takes very little to prepare her for Rastignac's plucking. The only reason she retains her virtue ('she is virtuous out of calculated self-interest, or perhaps from inclination' – ibid.) is that Rastignac is fully occupied elsewhere. In short, while the names of Bianchon, Rastignac, Listomère tie the story to *La Comédie humaine*, the title, the subject, and what Jeannine Guichardet calls 'the too light pen of "the bedroom historian"' (II.165) put the two *études* into a unit that allows us to perceive in detail what it means to be a 'femme comme il faut.'

Some of the motifs become images that rise above the very works themselves. Major settings – the conservative provinces, for example, or infernal Paris – and many characters function in this way. This is surely what Balzac had in mind when he wrote, 'Let us admit it frankly, *Gil Blas* is tiring in its form: piling up events and ideas has something sterile about it. When an Idea becomes a Personage, one has something more beautifully intelligent' (HH XXIV.217). While it is doubtless true that *La Peau de chagrin* exemplifies egotism in the July Monarchy, Eugène de Rastignac does as well, though in a different, no less important way. His portrait is painted in *Le Père Goriot* but is broadly brushed in preceding novels and touched up here and there across the entire *Comédie humaine*.

Rastignac provides an example of how Balzac used his characters. If a personage only appears once as a supernumerary, a passerby, some sort of assistant or filler, he would correspond to any other detail that has importance only to the degree that it contributes to its context. If we imagine a reading starting at the very beginning with 'La Maison du chat-qui-pelote' and moving work by work through *La Comédie humaine*, Rastignac's name first appears in *Le Bal de Sceaux* set for the most part in 1825.[16] His name is merely one among others. Some four years before the ball that provides a title for the work, Emilie de Fontaine rejects M. de Beaudenord because he is not noble and is both ugly and fat. She feels no more excited at the thought of Rastignac. 'Mme de Nucingen is making a banker of him, she said maliciously' (1.128). Emilie's 'maliciousness' indicates that M. de Rastignac's particle is more meaningful than Beaudenord's. If it were self-appropriated or purchased, there would be no malice in implying that the young man has allowed his standing within the aristocracy to fall, for in that case he, like Baudenord, would have no standing, and Emilie's maliciousness would be senseless. Here, however, the name serves primarily to emphasize Emilie's unreasonable impertinence in the matter of choosing a husband.

We next meet Rastignac in 'Etude de femme,' set several years later. He is apparently a financially independent, attractive young man about town. In his mid-twenties, he can still be embarrassed and left at a loss for words by an allusion to his long-lived 'faithfulness' to Mme de Nucingen. Repeated appearances of characters indicate somewhat more significance, since like a motif, a character accumulates the previous context and brings it to bear on the present. When Rastignac is quoted farther on in *La Fausse Maîtresse*, he is some ten years older than he was in 'Etude de femme,' and while retentive readers might wonder about him, they need to wait until the next work, *Une Fille d'Eve*, in order to gain a better acquaintance. There, in a fictional setting of 1833, we learn that he remains very close to Mme de Nucingen. In fact, though he has a number of seamy acquaintances, he and his family appear well connected. His younger brother has just been appointed a bishop at the young age of twenty-seven, clearly through influence, and his sister is married to a member of the cabinet. Rastignac himself has become an under-secretary of state. It is rumored that he will shortly marry the Nucingens' only daughter (11.312), which might give one pause, but only if one were sufficiently perceptive to distinguish the daughter from her mother, his mistress, Mme de Nucingen, who is mentioned in 'Etude de femme' and who continues as his confidante.

The next story where Rastignac appears, *L'Interdiction,* takes us back to 1828 where, in a conversation with Bianchon, he considers discarding Mme de Nucingen for Mme d'Espard. The narrator calls him a baron and mentions that he is one of the most elegant men of Paris. Though enjoying a 20,000-franc income, he remains ambitious. Unfortunately, Delphine is aging (she is thirty-six), and he is certain she can carry him no further. Still committed to the belief that he will succeed through his women, he thinks a 'society woman' would do him more good than Mme de Nucingen (III.422). Contradicting Bianchon, who believes that love is irrational – you love because you love [that is, inexplicably]' (ibid.) – Rastignac lists the qualities in Mme d'Espard that cause his 'love.' Prominent in the enumeration are her income and the fact that she can help arrange to have his debts paid.

The words the French language has for a man who uses women as tools to gain wealth or success are as ugly as they are in English, and the reader has a fairly good idea of what Rastignac stands for. Though elegant, witty, an aristocrat, and a socialite, he is also not above making certain compromises. We meet him again in 1831 enjoying a late-night gathering at the home of Mlle des Touches. He helps mark the group as a fast crowd (III.691). The following *Père Goriot* does no more than show us how he became what he is. When does the reader absorb the fact that Eugène is more than merely indelicate, that he is in fact amoral, if not a moral monster? The preface to *Pierrette* tells readers that 'he finally married Mlle de Nucingen' and moreover that '[t]he scandal sheets, the court and the townspeople discussed this marriage at length' (IV.23-24). Here we confront the practices of the novelist's editors. Of the prefaces, Balzac retained only the 'Avant propos' in the Furne edition, and he gives no indication in the notes he made in his own copy of the Furne edition that he would have changed that decision. To the contrary, he specifically indicates his desire to suppress them (I.14). Most modern editors, however, publish them in appendix if not as an actual preface. Should we continue to imagine a reader experiencing *La Comédie humaine* from the beginning and reading in order, the chances are very good that Rastignac's marriage to Delphine's daughter does not make an impression until the first few pages of *La Maison Nucingen*. In this context, it serves to stamp the world of finance as morally ambiguous or worse.

Today, because we tend to be tolerant of anything but egregious blood-letting, we must consider what is said carefully and put ourselves back in the tradition of Balzac's day in order to understand how to take what we read. M. de Rastignac comes off looking very bad indeed.

The reader hears the aging roués, Finot, Blondet, Couture, and Bixiou, laugh about him, since he has for years been kept by the Nucingens. With tongue firmly in cheek, Bixiou asks them to be sophisticated and worldly: '[D]o you dare reproach poor Rastignac for having lived off of the Nucingens, of having been furnished in the same way the Torpille was by Lupeaulx? If you do, you are falling into the vulgarity of Saint-Denis Street' (VI.334). The banker keeps Eugène around because he occupies his wife, thus leaving him free, and because unlike Henri de Marsay he is 'easy to handle' (VI.333). Furthermore, as the reader will soon learn, Rastignac was instrumental in Nucingen's third liquidation, which put the banker on a solid financial footing. But there are worse things than being a gigolo or an unknowing swindler. One might think, for example, of incest.

If there is any doubt about how people viewed Rastignac's marriage to his mistress's daughter, one need only recall that for Chateaubriand and his readers it was not merely the incest between brother and sister, as with René's love for Amélie, which was reprehensible. Other, somewhat more distant relationships were also considered in this category. Neither Racine nor the Greeks doubted that Phèdre's love for Hippolite was also incestuous, even though she was only the boy's stepmother. Or, to mention a more appropriate example, since the roles are similar, John the Baptist's disapproval of Herodias was based largely on the fact that she had left her first husband for his brother. But, when she could no longer seduce Herod Antipas into acquiescence to her wishes, her decision to send her daughter, Salome, to entice Antipas to murder John is proverbial for its immorality (and ready for Flaubert to exploit). To make the reader understand the nature of Rastignac's marriage to his mistress's daughter, Balzac used a more recent example: 'The question is very old. It is central to what caused the famous duel between La Châtaigneraie and Jarnac. Jarnac was accused of being on good terms with his mother-in-law, who provided for the excessive luxury of this too much loved son-in-law' (VI.335). Bixiou takes up the matter a few pages farther on: 'Rastignac wanted to enrich Delphine, though he was poor and she rich. Will you believe it? He succeeded in doing it. Rastignac, who would have fought the way Jarnac did, passed over to the side of Henri II when he said, "There is no absolute virtue; there are only circumstances." That in a nutshell is the story of his fortune' (VI.337). Nothing further can surprise us. He may be rich, he may gain political power, but he is 'a profoundly depraved gentleman' (ibid.). Readers need not wait until they read the unfinished *Le Député d'Arcis* to learn what he is. Every time his name appears it brings the image of the man: a corrupter (VI.965).

Rastignac, like Bianchon, like Diane de Maufrigneuse, like Popinot, like Grandet or Benassis, like hundreds of other characters, is an idea, a complex of meaning, an image, a symbol. It is for this reason that it would be impossible to overemphasize the importance of reappearing characters, for they bring with them known backgrounds and attitudes, a history, a significance. Readers are encouraged to see the 'fragment' before them as a part of a character's life-story and of the unfolding vision of society. It really does not matter whether the reappearing character is real or fictive. Henri de Marsay and Talleyrand, Bianchon and Mesmer – they all bring meaning, and, as they are repeated, they join other similar characters in encouraging the reader to see the way characters like Finot, Blondet, Lousteau create the 'type' of journalist. Other characters combine into type-characters of judge, notary, criminal, neglected wife, master, victim, violator, emptying the generalization of individual significance and creating something new. There is no doubt of Balzac's debt to the *physiologie*, a genre he cultivated expertly.

Félix Davin, generally considered to be a faithful spokesman for Balzac himself, provided the best analogy for *La Comédie humaine*. He compares the *Etudes de mœurs* (I would say rather the entire *Comédie*) to 'a gallery of paintings appropriately divided into rooms each one of which has a particular function' (X.1204). Balzac, as well, used the image, though he did not develop it in quite the same way (I.18). Beginning with "La Maison du chat-qui-pelote" and moving on through the exposition arranged not by curators but by the still living artist, the first series of 'big rooms [which] extend to infinity' (X.1207) are titled *Etudes de mœurs*, and the first 'room' *Scènes de la vie privée*. Each 'picture' is but a 'fragment' of the entire work, which Balzac firmly believed to be an accurate reflection of the entire society, but it is complete in itself. It stands as what I have called an image, though it may include one or more plots. As we move from room to room, pausing before each masterpiece, we begin to recognize elements that reappear – colors, details, motifs, themes, characters, narrative armatures, images – letting us know that we are in a common world and leading us to the next creation. Sometimes the particular work presents so complete a vision of an environment that it needs no further development. I think of *Le Médecin de campagne*. Still, even here, this corner of the world depends on other elements. As Balzac put it, 'Nothing is of a piece in this world. Everything is a mosaic' (II.265). Elsewhere our understanding of a particular concept or type is completed only after we have come, in the case of celibacy, for example, to *Le Curé de village*, and a special category of work stands out from the others. Personages like Père Goriot are, except for passing references to their lives, limited to one work, but there are other characters who gather episodes, portraits, and remarks from many novels and short stories before they, like types, make a separate image of their own. We begin to notice the resemblances between Lucien Chardon and Philippe Bridau or between Lucien and Rastignac. Likewise, both the provinces and Paris move out from the walls, bringing details from across the gallery, to make other images of extraordinary complexity. Balzac is not finished with such paintings until the very end of *La Comédie humaine*. One work leads syntagmatically to the next, so that at the end, the reader has a paradigmatic experience, which readily illuminates the relationships between works that are widely separated across the entire gallery and creates a magnificent image of the whole.

Doubtless, there are gaps. Not only did Balzac announce creations that he never wrote, but he started others that he never completed. For him, however, the gaps are not empty. Just as '[i]ntelligent people' are invited to complete the portrait of David Séchard (V.119), so we are encouraged to imagine what happened to Victorine Taillefer or Augusta de Nucingen. Every work is firmly fixed in society as a whole, and we understand that the entire *Comédie humaine* is framed by that society from which it springs and which gives it its meaning. Balzac's enormous masterpiece is whole and complete in the same way as is society. It presents the tableau of man playing out his perhaps frightening drama in an industrial world where old values are dying and new ones have yet to be adopted ... a human comedy.

Notes

CHAPTER ONE: *Disjecta membra poetæ*

1 Barthes, *S/Z: Essais* (Paris: Seuil 1970), 11–13.
2 The quotations are from Marina May-chun Heung, 'Strategies of Discontinuity: Balzac, Dickens, Sterne, Proust, and the Realistic Novel,' *Dissertation Abstracts International* 40 (1980): 5430A; and Serge Gaubert, '"La Fille aux yeux d'or": Un Texte-Charade,' *La Femme au XIXe siècle: Littérature et idéologie*, ed. R. Bellet (Lyon: Presses Université de Lyon 1978), 167, in that order. See for a more complete catalogue: Gérard-Denis Farcy, 'Les Inégalités de la couture chez Balzac,' *Poétique* 76 (1988): 463–73.
3 Hunt, *Balzac's Comédie humaine* (London: Athlone 1959), 83.
4 Macherey, *Pour une théorie de la production littéraire* (Paris: François Maspero 1966), 287.
5 Barbéris, 'Préface,' *La Duchesse de Langeais; suivi de La Fille aux yeux d'or*, by Honoré de Balzac (Paris: Livre de Poche 1972), 215. Jean-Yves Debreuille mentions the 'inoperative clumsiness' of the story's major transition: 'Horizontalité et verticalité: Inscription dans *La Fille aux yeux d'or*,' in Bellet, *La Femme au XIXe siècle*, 151.
6 C.-A. Sainte-Beuve, 'M. de Balzac (*La Recherche de l'absolu*),' *Portraits contemporains*, Nouvelle édition, vol. II (Paris: Calmann Lévy 1889), 341.
7 Dällenbach, 'Du fragment au cosmos: (*La Comédie humaine* et l'opération de lecture I),' *Poétique* 40 (1979): 421. In the ruminations that

preceded the present book, I was particularly stimulated by Dällenbach's series of articles: the just mentioned 'Du fragment au cosmos' as
well as 'Le Tout en morceaux: *La Comédie humaine* et l'opération de
lecture II,' *Poétique* 42 (1980): 156–69; 'D'une métaphore totalisante:
La Mosaïque balzacienne,' *Lettere Italiane* 33 (Oct.-Dec. 1981):
493–508; 'Le Pas tout de la *Comédie*,' *MLN* 98 (1983): 702–11; and
Lucienne Frappier-Mazur, 'Lecture d'un texte illisible: *Autre étude de
femme* et le modèle de la conversation,' *MLN* 98 (1983): 712–27.

8 As André Allemand says, 'People read Balzac; people have for all
intents and purposes never stopped reading him since the publication
of *Physiologie du mariage*' – *Unité et structure de l'univers balzacien*, Histoire des mentalités (Paris: Plon 1965), 11.

9 See, for example, Barthes, *S/Z* and *Le Plaisir du texte* (Paris: Seuil 1973);
Philippe Hamon, 'Note sur les notions de norme et de lisibilité en
stylistique,' *Littérature* 14 (1974): 114–22, and 'Texte littéraire et
métalangage,' *Poétique* 31 (1977): 261–84; Jacques Derrida, *L'Écriture
et la différence* (Paris: Seuil 1967).

10 Dällenbach returns over and over again in the previously cited series of
articles (n.7) to a passage where Balzac maintains that blanks give depth
and vitality to his work. It is doubtful, however, that the passage will
bear such weight, since when put in the context of the *Physiologie du
mariage*, where it appeared in early editions, the tone is clearly comic.
The author has instructed the reader to reread several macaronic
passages, 'since the author has put all his thought there' (XI.1928). He
goes on to order the reader to equivocate when the material of the book
seems serious or farcical. Then he turns to the aphoristic quality of the
Physiologie and says, 'If, on the assumption that it is an axiom or an
aphorism, you have intensified your attention in reading the passages
between the two rules, you have often accused the author of vanity, not
dreaming that he never claimed these passages were better than the
others. The goal of the large white spaces is to give more depth and
vitality to the book, because it is in a way its sleep, where it is revived.
Moreover, by leaving such blanks, the author more quickly reaches the
delicious words: *End of the first volume*' (XI.1928–9). Nonetheless, despite
my quibble with Dällenbach's use of this particular passage, he is on
firm ground in his assertion that Balzac claimed to have used the blank
spaces in his unfailing attempt to achieve unity. Dällenbach and I differ
on how the novelist succeeded.

11 See the articles cited in n.7, above.

12 John Porter Houston insists on 'how much is left implicit and unstated

in *La Comédie humaine*.' Though Balzac never says that Rastignac has prostituted himself, for example, his speech and actions leave the reader no doubt – *Fictional Technique in France, 1802–1927: An Introduction* (Baton Rouge: Louisiana State University Press 1972), 30–1.

13 Although the articles mentioned in n.7, above, were seminal to my thought leading to this book, I was recently reminded that some twenty-five years ago Anthony R. Pugh called for 'seeing what emerges when the individual novels [of *La Comédie humaine*] are placed in counterpoint to each other' – 'Ten Years of Balzac Studies,' *Modern Languages* 46 (1965): 96. For fine studies which complement my work, see, for example, Max Andréoli, *Le Système balzacien: Essai de description synchronique*, 2 vols (Lille: Atelier National Reproduction des Thèses, Université de Lille III 1984); Roland Le Huenen, 'La Sémiotique du corps dans *La Peau de chagrin*: Le Tout et le fragment,' *Le Roman de Balzac: Recherches critiques, méthodes, lectures*, eds. Roland Le Huenen and Paul Perron (Montreal: Didier 1980), 51–64; Paul Perron, 'Système du portrait et topologie actantielle dans *La Maison du chat-qui-pelote*,' ibid., 29–40; and Roland Le Huenen and Paul Perron, 'Balzac et la représentation,' *Poétique* 61 (1985): 75–90.

14 Letter of 26 octobre 1834, *Lettres à Mme Hanska*, ed. Roger Pierrot, 4 vols (Paris: Bibliophiles de l'Originale 1967–71), I, 270.

15 H.U. Forest, *L'Esthétique du roman balzacien* (Paris: PUF 1950); Allemand, *Unité et structure*.

16 Ethel Preston, *Recherches sur la technique de Balzac. Le Retour systématique des personnages dans la 'Comédie humaine'* (Paris: Presses Françaises 1926); Anthony R. Pugh, *Balzac's Recurring Characters* (Toronto: University of Toronto Press 1974); Martin Kanes, *Balzac's Comedy of Words* (Princeton: Princeton University Press 1975).

17 For a very helpful consideration of the lessons to be learned from Balzac's personally annotated copy of the Furne edition about such matters, see Roger Pierrot, 'Les Enseignements du "Furne corrigé," ' *L'Année Balzacienne* 1965: 291–301. I use Castex's twelve volume Pléiade edition (1976–81) mentioned in the front matter, because it most closely follows Balzac's last desires; problems remain, however, particularly with the placement of *Pierre Grassou*, *Le Lys dans la vallée*, and the arrangement of the *Etudes philosophiques*.

18 See Alexander Fischler, 'Rastignac-Télémaque: The Epic Scale in *Le Père Goriot*,' *Modern Language Review* 63 (1968): 840–8. For other references to consideration of 'fatherhood' and Balzac, see ch. 2, n.7, below.

19 Maurice Bardèche, *Une Lecture de Balzac* (Paris: Les Sept Couleurs 1964), 246.

20 Forest, *L'Esthétique*, 207.

21 Henry Miller, 'Balzac and His Double,' *The Wisdom of the Heart* (New York: New Directions 1941), 244–5.

22 HH XXIV.253. Balzac believed, I think mistakenly, that *La Chartreuse de Parme* was a political novel. I have argued at length that it centers rather on Fabrice as he changes from a selfish boy to a religious devoted to meditation on the divine – *Novel Configurations: A Study of French Fiction (Stendhal, Balzac, Zola, Gide, Huysmans, Proust, Robbe-Grillet, Saporta, Cortázar, Ricardou)* (Birmingham: Summa 1987), 27–50.

23 A point James W. Mileham makes in his fine study, *The Conspiracy Novel: Structure and Metaphor in Balzac's* Comédie humaine. Lexington: French Forum 1982.

24 Priscilla P. Clark, 'The Metamorphoses of Mentor: Fénelon to Balzac,' *Romanic Review* 75.2 (1984): 200–15.

25 The reference to the FR edition under the direction of Béguin and Ducourneau is given in the front matter under 'Abbreviations.' Earlier, Claude Mauriac had said, 'I dream of another complete edition laid out in a new way: the diverse parts of *La Comédie Humaine* being deliberately placed according to the fictional chronology, rather than where Balzac, who was still too involved in his work to see it as a whole, put them. . . . Each reader will little by little learn to make up his own *Comédie Humaine*. There is no better organization than the one which grows from the original disorder of our first readings' – *Aimer Balzac* (Paris: Table Ronde 1945), 45–6. David Bellos maintains that 'there is no more reason to read [*La Comédie humaine*] in the order of the published volumes than by choosing titles at random' – *Old Goriot* (Cambridge: Cambridge University Press 1987), 25 – and in a certain sense he is right. Balzac expected his reader to make a whole that rises above contingency. Still, I shall argue that Balzac worked a special magic by his ordering. For others who question the importance of Balzac's final arrangement see Diana Festa-McCormick, who says, '[Balzac] often switched works from one group to the next, however, inventing new categories, reestablishing old ones, for these were indeed interchangeable in mirroring the complex existence of an epoch' – 'Paris as the Gray Eminence in Balzac's "Ferragus," ' *Laurels* 51.1 (Spring 1980): 33; and Michel Butor: 'It is a question of what one might call a novelistic mobile, a grouping formed of a certain number of parts which we can take up in the order we wish' – 'Balzac et la

réalité,' *Répertoire [I]* (Paris: Minuit 1960), 83–4. Other arrangements can, as well, have a certain interest – see, for example, Pugh's *Recurring Characters*, which studies the sequence of actual composition. Still, for the present purposes, I agree rather with Kanes: 'One of Balzac's chief intentions was that the *Comédie humaine* should constitute a totality and be read as such. Yet the organization of the *Comédie humaine* has nothing to do with the order of its composition, the chronological order of its events, or even the progressive development of its themes' (*Comedy of Words*, 9).

26 See especially Proust, *Contre Sainte-Beuve*, Bibliothèque de la Pléiade (Paris: Gallimard 1971), 263–78.

27 Proust, *A la recherche du temps perdu*, ed. Jean-Yves Tadié, 4 vols, Bibliothèque de la Pléiade (Paris: Gallimard 1987–9), III.666.

28 Koestler, *The Act of Creation* (New York: Macmillan 1964). Derrida's comments referred to here appear in 'La Structure, le signe et le jeu dans le discours des sciences humaines,' *L'Ecriture*, 427–8. Variations on the reader I posit are to be found in the work of Charles Altieri, for example, *Act & Quality: A Theory of Literary Meaning and Humanistic Understanding* (Amherst: University of Massachusetts Press 1981), and that of E.D. Hirsch, Jr, for example, *The Aims of Interpretation* (Chicago: University of Chicago Press 1976). I am not, however, suggesting the necessity, or even the possibility, of an absolute interpretation, since I am quite happy if I approach a view that corresponds, more or less, with that of others who know and love *La Comédie humaine*.

29 (*Satires*, I.4.56–62). Balzac perhaps purposely misquoted Horace's '*disjecti membra poetæ* [limbs of the scattered poet]' and made it read '*disjecta membra poetæ* [scattered limbs of the poet].' I am grateful to my colleagues John T. Kirby and Karl Rosen for their help with these passages.

30 Sergei Eisenstein began his essay 'Montage in 1938' with the statement: 'There was a period in our film art when montage was proclaimed "everything" ' – *Notes of a Film Director* (New York: Dover 1970), 62. In fact, that is so, and, as Andrew Tudor points out in *Theories of Film* (New York: Viking 1973), 38–9, it was Eisenstein who did the proclaiming. Eisenstein's most important dissertations about montage occur in the discussion just mentioned and in the earlier, 1929 essay, 'A Dialectical Approach to Film Form,' *Film Form: Essays in Film Theory* (1929: New York: Harcourt Brace 1977), 45–63.

31 Ilya Prigogine and Isabelle Stengers, *Order out of Chaos: Man's New Dialogue with Nature* (New York: Bantam 1984); Ilya Prigogine, 'Order

out of Chaos,' *Disorder and Order: Proceedings of the Stanford International Symposium (Sept. 14–16, 1981)*, ed. Paisley Livingston, Stanford Literature Studies 1 (Saratoga, Ca: ANMA Libri 1984), 41–60. See also Stephen W. Hawking, *A Brief History of Time: From the Big Bang to Black Holes* (New York: Bantam 1988).

Transition to a non-sequential or non-linear mind set has not been easy for western readers, perhaps because of Aristotle's seminal influence. Hideki Yukawa has noted that in Japan Niels Bohr's complementarity looked evident: 'You see, we . . . have not been corrupted by Aristotle' – Philip Morrison in his review of *Niels Bohr: A Centenary Volume, Scientific American* 254 (March 1986): 27. Post-structuralist criticism's insistence on instability and fragmentation, despite fallacies and inconsistencies, can be seen, however, as a step toward a new world view, where Gestalt rather than sequence reigns, where paradox, parallels, movement, and rest all can be integrated by larger wholes. By bringing readers' attention to the non-mimetic levels of texts, artists attempt to encourage readers to see systems of organization that have nothing to do with our physical world. Plot, character, setting, narrators, point of view, themes, images, various rhetorical devices are renewed, because their significance as device is emphasized, rather than the effect they may cause. Readers and writers are no longer limited to the Aristotelian reality of linear chronology and causality.

32 I am indebted here to John R. O'Connor's excellent analysis – *Balzac's Soluble Fish*, Studia Humanitatis (Madrid: José Porrúa Turanzas 1977), especially part I.

CHAPTER TWO: Image Structure

1 P.-G. Castex, ed., *Le Père Goriot*, by Honoré de Balzac (Paris: Garnier 1963), xi. For other similar conclusions, see, for example: 'Above all . . . it is Rastignac's first function and appointed task, to search out the secrets that surround the life of Goriot. *Le Père Goriot* is first and foremost a tragedy of paternal affection' – Charles Gould, ed., 'Introduction,' *Le Père Goriot*, by Balzac (London: University of London Press 1967), 52; 'the main theme of the book – the obsession with his daughters which brings him to destruction' – Martin Turnell, *The Novel in France* (London: Hamish Hamilton 1950), 231–2; 'The true hero is unquestionably the grievously stricken Goriot' – Jean-A. Ducourneau, ed., 'Introduction,' *Le Père Goriot* (Paris: Club du Meilleur Livre 1957),

iii; Gretchen R. Besser quotes the initial idea of the self-sacrificing Goriot, as Balzac noted it in his notebook, and adds, 'To this pivotal theme he added two secondary plots, one being the "education" of Rastignac, the other the unmasking of Vautrin' – 'Lear and Goriot: A Re-evaluation,' *Orbis Litterarum* 27 (1972): 30; 'In Balzac's eyes, Rastignac is not the principal character of this novel; this quality belongs to no one but that fellow, Goriot' – Albert Prioult, ed., *Le Père Goriot* (Paris: Cluny 1937), xix; 'As the novel progresses, it is Goriot's lamentable adventure which is increasingly emphasized' – Jules Bertaut, *Le Père Goriot de Balzac* (Amiens: Edgar Malfère 1928), 121-2. '*Le Père Goriot* is thus put together from a multitude of ways of inserting the same unhappy story [i.e., of Goriot] into the novel' – René Quinsat, *Le Père Goriot de Balzac*, Poche Critique (Paris: Hachette 1971), 43; 'the work as such, of which Goriot incontestably forms the center' – Guy Michaud, *L'Œuvre et ses techniques* (Paris: Nizet 1957), 144.

2 Surer, 'Quelques cadres d'étude pour *Le Père Goriot*,' *Information Littéraire* 3 (1951): 197. For examples of others who share this opinion, see 'In spite of the title, Rastignac is doubtless the principal hero' – Pierre Barbéris, *Le Monde de Balzac* (Paris: Arthaud 1973), 87; 'The central character in the book is, of course, Rastignac; and the novel is essentially the story of his introduction to society – a *Bildungsroman*, in fact' – P.J. Yarrow, '*Le Père Goriot* Re-considered,' *Essays in Criticism* 7 (1957): 364; '[Rastignac,] le héros du *Père Goriot*' – B. Reizov, 'Rastignac et son problème,' *Europe* 447–8 (1966): 223; 'Rastignac . . . is absolutely central' – Anthony R. Pugh, 'The Complexity of *Le Père Goriot*,' *L'Esprit créateur* 7 (1967): 33; Pugh earlier took a similar stance in his 'Recurring Characters in *Le Père Goriot*,' *Modern Language Review* 57 (1962): 518; 'The true subject of the work is the initiation of a young man, Eugène de Rastignac, to the profound, awful corruption with which . . . life is made' – André Le Breton, *Balzac, l'homme et l'œuvre* (1905; rpt Paris: Boivin 1923), 242; George E. Downing later agrees: 'Le Breton was right in pointing out that the true subject of *Le Père Goriot* is "the initiation of a young man, Eugène de Rastignac" ' – 'A Famous Boarding House: *Le Père Goriot*,' in E. Preston Dargan, et al., *Studies in Balzac's Realism* (Chicago: University of Chicago Press 1932), 149; 'the central character, Eugène Rastignac' – C. Hobart Edgren, 'On Balzac's *Père Goriot*,' *Notes and Queries* 4 (Sept. 1957): 394; '*Le Père Goriot* is the story of Rastignac rather than that of Father Goriot' – Dominique Aury, *Lecture pour tous* (Paris: Gallimard 1958), 156-7; 'It is Rastignac's precarious and sinuous journey through these various

worlds which provides the unifying element in the novel's structure' –
Peter W. Lock, ed., *Le Père Goriot* (New York: St. Martin's Press 1968),
xxiii; Lock here repeats the point he had made in his earlier study,
Balzac: Le Père Goriot (London: Edward Arnold 1967), 36; '[T]he
structural imperfections would be much more serious, were we not to
consider Eugène the pivot of the action' – Donald Adamson, '*Le Père
Goriot*: Notes Towards a Reassessment,' *Symposium* 19 (1965): 106;
'There are four centers of dramatic interest in *le Père Goriot*: Goriot,
Rastignac, Vautrin, Mme de Beauséant. . . . and all four collaborate on
the unique subject of the book, which is the formation of Rastignac' –
Maurice Bardèche, *Balzac, romancier: La Formation de l'art du roman chez
Balzac jusqu'à la publication du* Père Goriot *(1820–1835)* (1940; rpt.
Genève: Slatkine 1967), 528; Nicole Mozet also views him as the 'Sub-
ject,' at least, 'judging from the whole of the tale' – 'La Description de
la Maison-Vauquer,' *L'Année Balzacienne* 1972: 107–9; Peter Brooks
focuses on Rastignac investigating the mysteries of his society – *The
Melodramatic Imagination: Balzac, Henry James, Melodrama, and the Mode of
Excess* (New Haven: Yale University Press 1976), 128–44; and, as one
final example, '*Le Père Goriot* . . . concentrate[s] on a brief period of
intense crisis in the development of the principal character, the resolution of which equips him to re-enter society with a new awareness of his
potential rôle. Rastignac's education is completed in three months' – R.
Butler, 'The Realist Novel as "Roman d'éducation": Ideological Debate
and Social Action in *Le Père Goriot* and *Germinal*,' *Nineteenth-Century
French Studies* 12 (1983–4): 68.

3   A point which has been made with varying sympathy by critics such as
Bardèche, *Lecture de Balzac*, 102; Mario Roques, *Etudes de littérature
française* (Genève: Droz 1949), 112; Pierre Barrière, *Honoré de Balzac
et la tradition classique* (Paris: Hachette 1928), 211; Pugh, 'Complexity of
Père Goriot' 28–30; Rolland Chollet, ed., 'Préface,' *Le Père Goriot, suivi
de Gobseck, La Fille aux yeux d'or* (Lausanne: Rencontre 1967), 14; Quinsat, *Goriot de Balzac*, 60; Pierre Barbéris, Le Père Goriot *de Balzac:
Ecriture, structures, significations* (Paris: Larousse 1972), 20–1; Catherine
H. Savage, 'The Romantic *Père Goriot*,' *Studies in Romanticism* 5 (1966):
112. James Smith Allen's position is closest to my own in that although
he emphasizes the importance of three main characters – 'In Goriot
[Balzac] portrays the social victim, in Vautrin the social rebel, and in
Rastignac the ambitious young man in society' (114) – he understands
that Balzac is primarily concerned with 'the historical context of nineteenth-century France: the loss of the tradition and privilege of the Old

Regime as perceived by his contemporaries, the new middle-class hierarchy and the role of money in determining its structure, and the pervasive fear of revolt by the many displaced social elements that resulted' (114–15) – 'Obedience, Struggle, and Revolt: The Historical Vision of Balzac's *Father Goriot*,' *Clio: A Journal of Literature, History, and the Philosophy of History* 16.2 (Winter 1987): 103–19.

4 Honoré de Balzac, 'Lettres sur la littérature, le théâtre et les arts, I' (*La Revue Parisienne*, 15 juillet 1840), HH XXIV.89.

5 'Introduction' to Stevick's edition of *The Theory of the Novel* (New York: Free Press 1967), 4.

6 Michel de Montaigne, *Œuvres complètes*, Bibliothèque de la Pléiade (Paris: Gallimard 1962), 425.

7 Though 'paternity' had not been treated as I do here prior to 1982, when I published the original version of this study – 'Image Structure in *Le Père Goriot*,' *French Forum* 7 (1982): 224–34 – it had by no means been ignored as an important theme. See, for example, Armand de Pontmartin, *Causeries du samedi. Deuxième série des "Causeries littéraires"* (Paris: Michel Lévy 1875), 77; Albert Thibaudet, *Histoire de la littérature français de 1789 à nos jours* (Paris: Stock 1935), 221; Jean-A. Ducourneau, 'Balzac et la paternité,' *Europe* 429–30 (1965): 190–202; O. Bonard, *La Peinture dans la création balzacienne; Invention et vision picturales de* la Maison du chat-qui-pelote *au* Père Goriot (Genève: Droz 1969), 174–5; Quinsat, *Goriot de Balzac*, 46; Brooks, *Melodramatic Imagination*, 142–4; Christopher Prendergast, *Balzac: Fiction and Melodrama* (London: Edward Arnold 1978), 176–81; and, more recently, Nilli Diengott, 'Goriot vs. Vautrin: A Problem in the Reconstruction of *Le Père Goriot*'s System of Values,' *Nineteenth-Century French Studies* 15.1–2 (1986–7): 70–6; Janet L. Beizer, *Family Plots: Balzac's Narrative Generations* (New Haven: Yale University Press, 1986), 103–39, especially 121–3.

8 Lorin A. Uffenbeck, 'Balzac a-t-il connu Goriot?' *L'Année Balzacienne* 1970: 175–81.

9 Conner, 'On Balzac's Goriot,' *Symposium* 8 (1954): 71.

10 The wallpaper where the mythological scene appears also prefigures Rastignac's voyage through the Parisian world. See, in this regard, Fischler, 'Rastignac-T élémaque,' 840–8. Given the fact that it presents the banquet Calypso gave Ulysses' son, one might also connect it to Joseph H. Bourque's study of eating: 'Latent Symbol and Balzac's *Le Père Goriot*,' *Symposium* 32 (1978): 277–88.

11 III.61, 82, 137, 139, 201, 203, 204.

12 III.137, 142, 145, 202.
13 Kermode, 'Novel and Narrative,' in *The Theory of the Novel: New Essays*, ed. John Halperin (New York: Oxford University Press 1974), 155.
14 See Marie-Jeanne Durry's discussion, in *Guillaume Apollinaire: Alcools*, II (Paris: SEDES 1964), 204–5.
15 Quoted from Frank's *The Widening Gyre: Crisis and Mastery in Modern Literature* (Bloomington: Indiana University Press 1968), 8–9.
16 Olson, *Tragedy and the Theory of Drama* (Detroit: Wayne State University Press 1961), 46.
17 See my *Novel Configurations*, 56–71.
18 See my extended discussion in *Novel Configurations*, especially 57–62. Pierre Larthomas has some pertinent remarks of a more general nature in his excellent study of the image, 'angel' – 'Sur une image de Balzac,' *L'Année Balzacienne* 1973: 301–26.
19 *Lettres à Madame Hanska*, 15 juillet [1839], I.651.
20 Cf. for example, 'Balzac was always drawn to high flying adventuresses: Marie de Verneuil, Lady Dudley seduce him. Diane de Maufrigneuse has his untempered indulgence' – Arlette Michel, *Le Mariage et l'amour dans l'œuvre romanesque d'Honoré de Balzac* (Lille: Atelier Reproduction des Thèses, Université de Lille III 1976), II.1058. 'The reader's awakened sympathies prevent too harsh a view of Diane's duplicity in her seduction of d'Arthez. Somewhat defiantly, one takes her side, unaware that that is what the author wants. . . . One *wants* Diane to prevail in her undeclared contest for supremacy, to conquer, to love and be loved, in spite of her past and of her lies' – Diana Festa-McCormick, 'Linguistic Deception in Balzac's "Princesse de Cadignan," ' *Nineteenth-Century French Studies* 14 (Spring-Summer 1986): 219. 'Daniel d'Arthez, who more often than not is the spokesman for Balzac's ideas as well as the paragon of his ideals' – Gretchen R. Besser, *Balzac's Concept of Genius: The Theme of Superiority in the* Comédie humaine (Geneva: Droz 1969), 227. Claude-Edmonde Magny goes on at some length in pointing to the resemblances between d'Arthez and Balzac – FR VIII.237 –41.
21 Armine Kotin Mortimer's important 'Problems of Closure in Balzac's Stories,' *French Forum* 10 (1985): 20-39, points to the significance of this addition, though the inferences she draws from these terminal lines differ markedly from my own. For her, 'after Mme d'Espard's dinner, Daniel cannot hold to Diane's innocence, nor can he reveal his knowledge, and this is *his* secret. . . . This means that the closure must include the complete knowledge of his secrets, not hers' (31). I shall argue that the story remains from start to finish centered on Diane's secrets.

22 Jean-Loup Bourget, 'Balzac et le néo-classicism: A propos des *Secrets de la princesse de Cadignan,*' *Romanic Review* 66 (1975): 273–4, limits his discussion to her resemblance to Renaissance or classical statues of the goddess.

23 Alexander Fischler, 'Duplication and "Comédie Morale" in Balzac's *Les Secrets de la princesse de Cadignan,*' *Studies in Romanticism* 24 (1985): 260–1.

24 Frappier-Mazur, *L'Expression métaphorique dans* La Comédie humaine (Paris: Klincksieck 1976), 128.

25 Fortassier, *Les Mondains de* La Comédie humaine: *Etude historique et psychologique* (Paris: Klincksieck 1974), 316.

26 I quote Voltaire from the Littré under the rubric '*Esprit.*' The Robert dictionary suggests that '*les gens d'esprit*' manifest a certain 'piquant vivacity of wit [*esprit*]' or an 'ingeniousness in the way of conceiving and exposing something.'

27 Besser, *Genius*, 22. Larthomas shares this view: 'A tragic conclusion, it seems, since the author wrote about his hero: ..."his publications have become excessively rare." A victim of happiness and false angelism, the writer in d'Arthez perishes' – 'Sur une image de Balzac,' 315.

28 VI.1004. In the manuscript, he defended her ('*défendue*'). By the first publication in *La Presse*, the text reads '*vengée*' (VI.1534, n.*d* to IV.1004).

CHAPTER THREE: Unifying Units

1 Pierre Citron, ed., 'Introduction,' *Splendeurs et misères des courtisanes* (Paris: Garnier-Flammarion 1968), 23.

2 Jean Pommier, *L'Invention et l'écriture dans* La Torpille *d'Honoré de Balzac* (Genève: Droz 1957), 19.

3 A. Adam, ed., *Splendeurs et misères des courtisanes* (Paris: Garnier 1964), x. Criticism along this line began very early. In 1844, for example, one review of *Splendeurs* turned into a condemnation of Balzac's entire oeuvre: 'In fact, M. de Balzac's books are distinctive in that they end before their characters have finished their roles and left the stage. One is quite surprised to arrive at the end of the novel at the moment when the action is the most intense, when matters are the most confused, when interest is at the highest level. For the novels to be exactly like serials, they only need the words: *To be continued*' – reprinted by René Guise, 'Balzac et le *Bulletin de Censure,*' *L'Année Balzacienne* 1983: 283.

4 C. Affron, *Patterns of Failure in* La Comédie humaine (New Haven: Yale University Press, 1966), 110.

5 V.724. For others this reading is equally clear. See, for example, Marguerite Drevon and Jeannine Guichardet, 'Fameux sexorama,' *Année Balzacienne* 1972: 271; Philippe Berthier, 'Balzac du côté de Sodome,' *Année Balzacienne* 1979: 154.

6 Prendergast, *Balzac: Fiction and Melodrama*, 84.

7 For example, VI.482, 587, 589, 644–5, 789, 813, 820, 907.

8 Prendergast's analysis, while going to the heart of Balzac's commentary on the corruption of both the institutions of justice and politics, admirably demonstrates that 'Vautrin does not change. . . . [T]he violence and brutality of Vautrin are exactly what the society requires' – *Balzac: Fiction and Melodrama*, 88–9. See, also in this regard, Berthier, 'Sodome,' 175.

9 W.H. Van der Gun, *La Courtisane romantique et son rôle dans* La Comédie humaine (Assen: Van Gorcum 1963), 6.

10 Antoine Adam makes the point in his edition of *Splendeurs et misères des courtisanes*, though he is by no means blinded to the novel's many weaknesses – xxv–ix. See also in this regard Bernard N. Schilling, *The Hero as Failure: Balzac and the Rubempré Cycle* (Chicago: University of Chicago Press 1968): 194–8. It seems to me, however, that Prendergast's *Balzac: Fiction and Melodrama* convincingly demonstrates 'Balzac's ability imaginatively to adapt the conventions of contemporary popular fiction to the aims of significant art' (89). In regard to masks and their relation to theatre, illusion, and disguise on the stage of Balzac's society, see Martha Niess Moss, 'The Masks of Men and Women in Balzac's *Comédie humaine.*' *French Review* 50 (1977): 446–53.

11 Pierre Grimal, *Dictionnaire de la mythologie grecque et romaine* (Paris: PUF 1969), 56

12 Bardèche, *Lecture de Balzac*, 159.

13 Adam, *Splendeurs*, 739.

14 Jean-Louis Bory, ed., 'Préface,' *La Rabouilleuse* by Balzac (Paris: Français Réunis 1970), vi.

15 Pierre Citron, ed., 'Introduction,' *La Femme de trente ans* de Balzac (Paris: Garnier-Flammarion 1965); Maurice Allem, ed., 'Introduction,' *La Femme de trente ans* de Balzac (Paris: Garnier 1962), xvi; Bernard Gagnebin and René Guise in the 'Introduction' of the Pléiade edition, II.1029.

16 Nathan, 'Zoologies parisiennes,' *La Femme au XIXe siècle*, ed. R. Bellet (Lyon: Presses Université de Lyon 1978), 193. While, for reasons that

will become increasingly clear, 'monsters' and 'monstrousness' seem to me to provide the best access to 'La Fille aux yeux d'or,' Doris Y. Kadish's fine study of 'hybrids' is thought provoking and should be considered – 'Hybrids in Balzac's *La Fille aux yeux d'or*,' *Nineteenth-Century French Studies* 16 (1988): 270–8.

17 Jean Chevalier and Alain Gheerbrant, *Dictionnaire des symboles: Mythes, rêves, coutumes, gestes, formes, figures, couleurs, nombres* (Paris: Robert Laffont 1969), 156.

18 Diel, *Le Symbolisme dans la mythologie grecque* (Paris: Payot 1952), 62–3.

19 Felman, 'Rereading Femininity,' *Yale French Studies* 62 (1981): 37.

20 A *concha* is also a 'shell' in Spanish, what the French would call a *coquille*. It is worth noting that when Henri is finally ushered into the voluptuous bedroom where Paquita awaits him, 'he was surprized by its appearance of a shell, similar to the one in which Venus was born' (V.1089).

21 Echidne was also the sister of the Gorgons. Was the locating of Concha's birthplace in Georgia a result of the author's perhaps unconscious pun: 'the old Georgian' (V.1109)? Certainly, Balzac associated Georgia with slavery – see, for example, X.433. Geneviève Delattre suggests Paquita's mother 'is gambling. . . . She also incarnates gold and pleasure, that is, desire oriented uniquely towards a passion for material things' – 'De "Séraphîta" à "La Fille aux yeux d'or," ' *L'Année Balzacienne* 1970: 219.

22 Festa-McCormick, 'Balzac's *Girl with the Golden Eyes*: Parisian Masks, Not Faces,' *The City as Catalyst: A Study of Ten Novels* (Rutherford: Fairleigh Dickenson University Press 1979), 23.

23 Moïse Le Yaouanc, 'Le Plaisir dans les récits balzaciens,' *L'Année Balzacienne* 1972: 300. However, not all would agree that Lord Dudley is bisexual. Félicien Marceau insists that the matter remains unclear – *Balzac et son monde* (Paris: Gallimard 1970), 541.

24 See, for example, Pierre Michel, 'Discours romanesque, discours érotique, discours mythique dans "La Fille aux yeux d'or," ' *La Femme au XIXe siècle*, ed. Bellet, 179–87; Jean-Yves Debreuille, 'Horizontalité et verticalité: Inscriptions idéologiques dans "La Fille aux yeux d'or," ' ibid., 158–60; Leyla Perrone-Moisés, 'Le Récit euphémique,' *Poétique* 17 (1974): 27–38; Felman, 'Rereading,' 27–36. Le Yaouanc even wonders whether Henri may have previously indulged in homosexuality: 'It is possible. He was the beloved and grateful student of the priest, Maronis, a personage presented as vicious. The same term will be applied to Jacques Collin' ('Plaisir,' 300).

25 See, for example, Festa-McCormick, *City*, 24, 27; Debreuille, 'Horizon-talité,' 158–9.

26 J. Wayne Conner noted years ago that Mariquita is a diminutive nick-name for Maria and has no linguistic connection with Margarita. While he considered the possibility that it might be a mistake, he correctly refused to dismiss the thought that it could be intentional – 'La Com-position de la "Fille aux yeux d'or," ' *Revue d'Histoire Littéraire* 56 (1956): 535–47. Most other critics, however, have followed in Henri's path: for example, Delattre, 'De Séraphîta,' 224; O'Connor, *Balzac's Soluble Fish*, 174; P.–G. Castex, ed., 'Introduction,' 'La Fille aux yeux d'or,' *Histoire des Treize* de Balzac (Paris: Garnier 1956), 362; Adeline R. Tintner, 'James and Balzac: *The Bostonians* and "La Fille aux yeux d'or," ' *Comparative Literature* 29 (1977): 244; Beizer, *Family Plots*, 67.

27 Serge Gaubert, '"La Fille aux yeux d'or": Un Texte-Charade,' *La Femme au XIXe siècle*, ed. Bellet, 172. Gaubert goes on to note that Henri's pseudonym – Adolphe de Gouges – is also suggestive: '*Gouges* signifies woman or girl' (177 n.4). Although Adolphe reminds Gaubert of the Greek *adelphos* (brother), the normal derivation from *adel-wulf-* (noble wolf) – Albert Dauzat, *Dictionnaire étymologique des noms de famille et prénoms de France* (Paris: Larousse 1951), 3 – is a more likely meaning. Readers might also think of Constant's very successful *Adolphe*, which tells the story of another young man who, after seducing and compro-mising another's mistress, loses interest. Olympe de Gouges, who proclaimed the rights of women, is perhaps an appropriate, though ironic, allusion.

28 Delattre suggests that Henri and his sister combine to make an andro-gyne ('De "Séraphîta," ' 201). Lucienne Frappier-Mazur, however, notes that while their common love for Paquita might seem to unite them, in fact, it reflects their polarization – 'Balzac et l'androgyne,' *L'Année Balzacienne* 1973: 256–7. Certainly, Balzac began preparing the theme as early as 'Ferragus': 'Is not the treatise of *yes* and *no* one of the most beautiful works of diplomacy, philosophy, logography, ethics, which remains to be done? But would not an androgynous genius be required to accomplish this diabolical work? Consequently, it will never be attempted' (V.835).

29 The danger of multiplying brief fragments was discussed in recent years by A. Robbe-Grillet: 'It is possible that *L'Eden et après* owed its success to the somewhat excessive length of certain elements in the diegesis, or narrative content, which allowed the spectator to eliminate what puzzled him or upset him in order to retain only what could have had or

appeared to have a normal functioning. I think that the length of the fragments is extremely important, for at the opposite end you have the experiments of certain groups – the *Tel Quel* group [that is, especially, Philippe Sollers], for example – in which the ideological fragments are so small that in the time that they last one does not recognize them. One then falls into the other danger of completely escaping from the world as if one were outside of society, outside of ideology, as if the revolution were already accomplished' – 'Order and Disorder in Film and Fiction,' tr. Bruce Morrissette, *Critical Inquiry* 4 (1977): 16.

30 At least, so it seems – cf. VI.661.

31 See, for snakes (for example, V.1054, 1056, 1083), masks (Festa-McCormick, *City*, 21), gold (Felman, 'Rereading,' 38), fire (Juliette Frølich, 'Une Phrase / un récit: Le Jeu du feu dans "La Fille aux yeux d'or" de Balzac,' *Revue Romane* 14 [1979]: 59–73); or words like 'curious' or 'monstrous' (Tintner, 'James and Balzac,' 251–2).

CHAPTER FOUR: Conjoining the Disjoined

1 Ingram, *Representative Short Story Cycles of the Twentieth Century: Studies in a Literary Genre* (The Hague: Mouton 1971), 138.

2 Mozet, 'Introduction,' in the Pleiade edition, III.658. Elsewhere Mozet calls it 'a text so dislocated as to be nonsensical and contradictory' – 'Les Prolétaires dans "La Fille aux yeux d'or," ' *L'Année balzacienne* 1974: 92. Lucienne Frappier-Mazur terms it 'disparate and poorly motivated. The accommodations are scarcely concealed, inconsistencies crying for attention remain which could easily have been corrected, and there is no dearth of contradictions' – 'Lecture d'un texte illisible: *Autre étude de femme* et le modèle de la conversation,' *MLN* 98 (1983): 713. There is much to be said in defense of these conclusions. Still, although my purposes here are to seek the principles that might explain why, however unsuccessfully, Balzac brought the stories together, I do share Armine Kotin Mortimer's appreciation for certain aspects of *Autre étude de femme*: '*La Grande Bretèche* unites in its closure elements from all the rest of the *nouvelle*. Balzac was right to add it to his disjointed masonry, for it fills in the holes and carries the illustration of the theme to its highest and most somber point, the maximum degree of proof – 'Problems of Closure in Balzac's Stories,' *French Forum* 10 (1985): 21–7; the quotation is taken from page 26. Likewise, I am persuaded by Ross Chambers, who insists on the importance of the implicit social pact in

gossip, a pact that is established and broken in *Autre étude de femme* – 'Gossip and the Novel: Knowing Narrative and Narrative Knowing in Balzac, Mme de Lafayette and Proust,' *Australian Journal of French Studies* 33 (1986): 212–21.

3 The articles are cited in n.2, above.

4 In 'La Fille aux yeux d'or,' when he suspects Paquita of infidelity, such diminishment is of course impossible, since the slave-girl is already at the lowest rung of society. Because of his youthful experience with Charlotte, however, he understands that Paquita must be absolutely committed to him or *he* will be diminished.

5 See the discussion of *Gobseck* in my *Novel Configurations*, 51–71.

6 For critics who emphasize the fragmentary nature of *Jésus-Christ en Flandre*, see, for example, Jean Pommier, ed., 'Introduction,' *L'Eglise: Honoré de Balzac: Edition critique* (Paris: Droz 1947): vii–xix; Pierre-Georges Castex, *Nouvelles et contes de Balzac (Etudes philosophiques)*, 'Les Cours de Sorbonne' (Paris: Centre de Documentation Universitaire 1961): 19–26; Michel de Ghelderode, quoted by André Vandegans, '*Jésus-Christ en Flandre*, Erasme et Ghelderode,' *L'Année Balzacienne* 1978: 44–5.

7 Vandegans, '*Jésus-Christ*,' 27–48.

8 Roland A. Champagne is the only critic to sense any progression in the work. While I was not convinced by his inferring an important opposition between Protestants and Catholics from the textual mention of the historical fact that Middelburg was later to gain importance in the annals of protestantism, his intuition of a triadic '"deep structure" ... which is similar to the Biblical organization of Old Testament, New Testament, and Apocalypse' proves a useful analogy – 'The Architectural Pattern of a Literary Artifact: A Lacanian Reading of Balzac's *Jésus-Christ en Flandre*,' *Studies in Short Fiction* 15 (1978): 49–54.

9 X.1371, 326, n.2.

10 Matt. 3.17; 17.5 (NIV).

11 Balzac surely preferred the explanation published under the name of Félix Davin: '*Jésus-Christ en Flandre* is the demonstration of the power of the faith, considered as idea' (X.1215).

12 Joan Dargan argues at length in her *Balzac and the Drama of Perspective: The Narrator in Selected Works of* La Comédie humaine (Lexington: French Forum 1985) that *Histoire des Treize* constitutes 'experimentation with fragmented perspective and chronology' (13). She is particularly drawn to Balzac's refusal to limit his vision to one perspective, to his acceptance, rather, of several narrators who are more or less well

integrated into a single narration and who openly flout 'the law of chronology' (15). I do not disagree with Professor Dargan. I would say, however, that the 'obvious and concerted shifting of the narrator's point of view' (14) is typical of not just Balzac's but those of most nineteenth-century narrators. Above and distinct from these inconsistent narrational perspectives, I believe one can identify another character, whom I have called the *auteur*.

13 Through his spokesman, Davin – I.1169.

14 V.789. Alain Henri and Hilde Olrik, for example, discuss the 'heterogeneousness' of the work, calling it a 'hybrid product in which *disparate* products come into obvious conflict' – 'Le Texte alternatif: Les Antagonismes du récit dans l'*Histoire de Treize* de Balzac,' *Revue des Sciences Humaines* 175 (1979): 77–97. Joan Dargan's original position (in her dissertation) that '[e]ach novel in the *Histoire des Treize* is a self-contained unit with a separately conceived, and independently elaborated, narrative form,' has been modified somewhat in her more recent *Drama of Perspective*: 'Only Balzac's vision of Paris can be said to unify the novels' (67); 'One need not know *Ferragus* before reading *La Duchesse de Langeais* or *La Fille aux yeux d'or*, but it reveals no less than they the preoccupations of the artist who wrote them' (86). I shall refer to one of O'Connor's insights. We agree that '[e]ach novel in the set must be seen, when considered by itself, as constituting a form of incompleteness, the attribute of completeness belonging, rather, to the three novels taken together and it is therefore not the individual novel but the set itself which now appears to us to provide the limiting form' – *Balzac's Soluble Fish*, 212. O'Connor and I disagree, however, on the thrust of the whole, and I shall attempt to supplement his comments on the vehicles and process that bring the three 'episodes' into one 'story.'

15 Such, at least, is an indication in a manuscript passage of 'La Duchesse de Langeais' that Balzac deleted – V.1109, n.1.

16 Barbéris, *Le Monde de Balzac*, 117.

17 Cf. O'Connor, *Balzac's Soluble Fish*, esp. 138–43, 158–63, 176–81. See, as well, Mileham, *Conspiracy Novel*, 44–61.

18 See, V.1031, 1523, n.a.

19 For example , V.986–7, 1028, 1081.

20 V.802, 882, 981, 1065, which, of course, does not exhaust the references.

21 I.1147; repeated with little change in his other essay, X.1205. See, for considerations of the significance of setting in 'Ferragus,' especially – Henri Mitterand, 'Le Lieu et le sens: L'Espace parisien dans *Ferragus*,

de Balzac,' *Le Discours du roman* (Paris: FUF 1980), 189–212;
Festa-McCormick, 'Paris as the Gray Eminence,' 33–43.

22 Tzvetan Todorov, 'The Fantastic in Fiction,' tr. Vivienne Mylne, *Twentieth Century Studies* 3 (1970): 88.

CHAPTER FIVE: Unframing Frames

1 E.H. Gombrich, *The Sense of Order: A Study in the Psychology of Decorative Art* (Ithaca: Cornell University Press 1979), 75. Roland Barthes expands the thought: 'Every literary description is a *view*. You would say that the enunciator, before describing, sets himself at the window, not so much to be able to see well but to establish what he sees by means of the frame itself: the opening creates the spectacle. Describing is then placing the empty frame that realistic authors always transport with them . . . in front of a collection or a continuum of objects' – *S/Z*, 61.

2 Caws, *Reading Frames in Modern Fiction* (Princeton: Princeton University Press 1985), 3.

3 Ross Chambers, '*Sarrasine* and the Impact of Art,' *French Forum* 5 (1980): 218–38.

4 Bixiou, as mentioned below, may be an exception.

5 Armine Kotin [Mortimer], '*La Maison Nucingen*, ou le récit financier,' *Romanic Review* 69 (1978): 60–71. Although Balzac's text uses the term *aventure à tiroirs*, to describe something different from the tale Bixiou tells, its usage functions effectively to begin a characterization of Bixiou's extraordinarily complex creation (VI.367).

6 Barthes, *S/Z*, 24.

7 Mortimer, 'Le récit financier,' 64.

8 Jean-Loup Bourget, 'Ni du roman, ni du théâtre: *La Maison Nucingen*,' *Poétique* 32 (1977): 461–5, studies the narrator's strange perspicacity in detail.

9 For Roger J.B. Clark, then, Nucingen is a good example of Balzac's superior man, for he is 'lucid, able to direct his will and dominate his passion'.– 'Vers une édition critique de *La Maison Nucingen*: Genèse et épreuves,' *Balzac and the Nineteenth Century (Studies Presented to Herbert J. Hunt)*, ed. Donald G. Carlton, Jean Gaudon, and Anthony R. Pugh (Leicester: Leicester University Press 1972), 96.

10 I think of course of Gide's 'an intersection – a meeting place of problems' (cf. his *Journal*, vol. I, 17 juin 1923). Ruth Amossy and Elisheva Rosen term it a 'place of convergence' – 'Du banquet au roman "réa-

liste": *La Maison Nucingen,' Le Roman de Balzac: Recherches critiques, méthodes, lectures,* ed. Roland Le Huenen and Paul Perron (Montreal: Didier 1980), 162.

11 Slatka, 'Sémiologie et grammaire du nom propre dans *Un Prince de la Bohème,' Balzac: L'Invention du roman,* ed. Claude Duchet et Jacques Neefs (Paris: Belfond 1982), 255.

12 Pugh, 'Note sur l'épilogue de *Un Prince de la Bohème,' L'Année Balzacienne* 1967: 360.

13 D'Aulnoy, *Serpentin vert: Conte nouveau, tiré des fées* (Tours: Placé 1835), 3. I am grateful to Amy Vanderlyn DeGraff, author of *The Tower and the Well: A Psychological Interpretation of the Fairy Tales of Madame d'Aulnoy* (Birmingham: Summa 1984), for sharing her knowledge of Mme d'Aulnoy with me.

14 'Le Chef-d' uvre inconnu' is, of course, important for other reasons as well – it is a masterpiece in the short-story genre, and, as numerous critics have pointed out, it poses interesting problems in respect to the author's esthetics. For a summary of the controversy, see Jerrold Lanes, 'Art Criticism and the Authorship of the *Chef-d'œuvre inconnu*: A Preliminary Study,' *The Artist and the Writer in France: Essays in Honor of Jean Seznec,* ed. Francis Haskell, Anthony Levi, and Robert Shackleton (London: Oxford University Press 1974), 86–99.

15 Frenhofer's name is, as so often, suggestive. Wayne Conner – 'Balzac's Frenhofer,' *MLN* 69 (1954): 335–8 – believes that Fren- may constitute a play on the marquis de Veren, whom Mabuse was serving at the time he imitated, with paint and paper, the damask cloth he had been given and had sold to squander on drink. For Conner, the second element, -hof-, may mark Balzac's debt to E.T.A. Hoffmann and his story 'Der Baron von B.' I do not dispute these suggestions, though it seems to me at least as likely that Balzac was thinking of the ash tree (*frêne,* in French), which symbolizes life and has the additional virtue of suggesting the magic world of Germanic legends – Ernst and Johanna Lehner, *Folklore and Symbolism of Flowers, Plants and Trees* (New York: Tudor 1960), 20–1.

16 See Claude E. Bernard, 'La Problématique de l'échange dans "Le Chef-d' uvre inconnu" d'Honoré de Balzac,' *L'Année Balzacienne* 1984: 201–13.

17 X.431. For reasons given ch. 1, n.17, I have used the Pléiade edition. In a few instances like the present, however, this particular edition differs importantly from other widely accepted texts. Under these circumstances, some explanations are in order. Although most editors and

most editions follow the lessons of the so-called Furne *corrigé* (and in most cases they are right to do so), René Guise, the Pléiade's editor for the 'Le Chef-d' uvre inconnu,' chooses on the whole, rather, to accept the text published in *Le Provincial à Paris* of 1847. He convincingly justifies his decision (X.1407–9). Among the most interesting variants affected are those instances where in earlier versions Frenhofer's Catherine is referred to as a courtesan and termed 'la Belle-Noiseuse.' In *Le Provincial à Paris* text, each of these passages was suppressed, thereby, as Guise points out, eliminating a contradiction between Catherine's character and the love that Frenhofer has for her.

18 X.75. I quote this from *La Peau de chagrin*, since, as Balzac pointed out, '*Massimilla Doni, Gambara, Le Chef-d'œuvre inconnu* . . . are works that continue, in a way, *La Peau de chagrin*, by showing the disorder that thought in its most developed state produces in the soul of an artist' (II.271).

19 Bernard, 'L'Echange,' 205.

20 István Fodor, 'Les Chefs-d' uvre inconnus de Balzac,' *Acta Litteraria Academiae Scientiarum Hungaricae* (Budapest) 17 (1975): 464.

21 Cf. Maurice Bardèche, 'Notice,' HH IX.11, who insists that 'people cannot understand it if it is not reclassified and mentally put with the *Etudes philosophiques* where it was originally put.' André Lorant believes that the story rests 'on this axiom which overrides the *Etudes philosophiques*': 'Life decreases in direct proportion to the power of desires or the dissipation of ideas' – 'Introduction,' Pléiade, VI.1009. For Henri Evans, 'Facino Cane' is a 'hybrid.' He notes that only the introduction and conclusion occur in Paris, while the main action takes place in Venice. For him also, 'Balzac had good reasons for placing it in the *Etudes philosophiques*, since it includes a definition, applied to itself, of the psychic powers which constitute the general theme of these *Etudes*' – 'Notes,' FR II.xxvi-vii.

22 Béguin, 'Préface,' FR II.852.

23 See comment by Anne-Marie Meininger, VIII.1648-9, n.3. Léon Gozlan gives a delightful account of Balzac's choosing Marcas's name: 'Marcas! . . . don't you find that it has a sinister significance? Doesn't it seem to you that the man bearing it ought to be martyred! Although strange and wild, this name has nonetheless the right to go down to posterity. . . . But doesn't it seem unfinished? I wouldn't want to take it upon myself to suggest that names exercise no influence on destiny, but between the men's names and the events of their lives there are secret and inexplicable harmonies or visible discords, which are surprising. . . .

Don't you see an air of frustration in the construction of the Z? . . . .
Marcas was named Zéphirin. Saint Zepherin is very revered in Brittany.
Marcas was a Breton' – *Balzac en pantoufles* (Paris: Lemercier 1926),
111–21; I quote from 120–1.

CHAPTER SIX: Configuring the Whole

1 György Lukács, *Balzac et le réalisme français* (Paris: Maspero 1967), 60.
2 Barbéris, *Le Monde de Balzac*, 411–12.
3 X.281; cf. II.966.
4 For example, X.177, 229, 230, 287. See also André Vanoncini, 'La
   Dissémination de l'objet fantastique,' *Balzac et La Peau de chagrin*, ed.
   Claude Duchet (Paris: Société d'Edition d'Enseignement Supérieur
   1979), 62–3.
5 For example, Letter to Mme de Castries, quoted by Forest, *L'Esthétique*,
   33; through his spokesmen Chasles: X.1188–9, and Davin: X.1216.
6 Emile J. Talbot, 'Pleasure / Time or Egoism / Love: Rereading *La Peau
   de chagrin*,' *Nineteenth-Century French Studies* 11 (1982): 75. The entire
   article is printed 72–82.
7 In an early note, probably suggesting the work to come, Balzac wrote:
   'The invention of a skin which represents life, oriental tale' (HH
   XXIV.669). Subsequently, Philarète Chasles suggests that Balzac's
   original conception had not changed: '*La Peau de chagrin* is the expression of human life' (X.1189); as does Félix Davin: '*La Peau de chagrin* is
   the formula of life' (X.1216).
8 Samuel Weber is then correct to insist on the parallels between the
   novel's introductory casino and the subsequent antique establishment:
   'Everything in the store,' Weber points out, ' . . . is covered with gold.
   Here, as in the *salon de jeu* money destroys a certain life in its immedia-
   cy and its individuality, and yet, paradoxically, appears itself as eternal
   life: incarnated first in the passion of gambling and here in the inde-
   structible power of the antique dealer' – *Unwrapping Balzac: A Reading
   of* La Peau de chagrin (Toronto: University of Toronto Press 1979), 39.
9 James Smith Allen says, for example, '*The Human Comedy* is among the
   best sources available for a social history of France from 1815 to 1848'
   – 'Obedience,' 103.
10 For example, Bardèche, *Balzac, romancier* and *Lecture de Balzac*; Philippe
   Bertault, *Balzac et la religion* (Paris: Boivin 1942); Ernst Robert Curtius,
   Balzac (1923; tr. Paris: Grasset 1933); Bernard Guyon, *La Pensée*

politique et sociale de Balzac (Paris: Armand Colin 1947); Per Nykrog, *La Pensée de Balzac dans* La Comédie humaine: *Esquisse de quelques concepts-clé* (Copenhagen: Munksgaard 1965); Gaëton Picon, *Balzac par lui-même* (Paris: Seuil 1956), and *L'Usage de la lecture* (Paris: Mercure de France 1961). II.9–97; Prendergast, *Balzac: Fiction and Melodrama.*

11 I am using Gaëton Picon's summary of 'the three essential tendencies of Balzacian criticism': Balzac as an observer, as a philosopher, and as a poet – *L'Usage de la lecture*, II.13.

12 HH XXIV.214. In his scrapbook, which he titled 'Pensées, sujets, fragmens,' he wrote, for example, 'Logic, sentiment, hidden under appropriate images... all literature is there' (HH XXIV.699).

13 Gaius Suetonius Tranquillus, 'Julius Caesar,' *The Twelve Caesars*, tr. Robert Graves (Harmondsworth: Penguin 1957), 45, 81.

14 For a more developed study of *Ursule Mirouët*, see my 'Ursule Through the Glass Lightly,' scheduled to appear in the October 1991 issue of *French Review.*

15 *Lettres à Mme Hanska*, 21 avril 1842, II.73.

16 I have generally taken the dates of works' settings from Fernand Lotte's index, as revised by Pierre Citron and Anne-Marie Meininger (vol. XII of the Pléiade edition I am using). Doing so does not solve all the problems. Here, for example, in the passage I quote below, the index gives the year as 1824 under 'Rastignac.' Under 'Emilie de Fontaine,' however, the date for the episode seems to be 1821. The FR edition puts *Le Bal de Sceaux* under 1819. 1825 appears, in fact, to be correct for the main events. Early in the story and several years before the titular ball, during the winter after the Coronation of Charles X (I.124), which took place in 1820, M. de Fontaine redoubles his efforts to encourage Emilie to accept one of her suitors. He comes to talk to her specifically about several possibilities near the end of the following Lent (I.125), thus in 1821, and it was during this conversation that Emilie makes the remark I quote. 'Etude de femme' (which I discuss below) poses similar problems. Under 'Rastignac,' the index offers the information that the story took place in 1828 (FR uses the same date). The text of the story, however, gives several contrary indications: 'Eugène blushed. One has to be older than twenty-five not to blush on being reproached for being faithful...' (II.179). Balzac said Rastignac was born in 1799 (II.265), which mean he was twenty-nine rather than twenty-five years old in 1828. In addition, though while the letters were being misaddressed, Rastignac and Bianchon chatted about the Morée expedition, which took place in 1828 (II.174 and n.3), Rastignac's interest in Mme de Listomère began at a performance of *William Tell*,

which was staged 3 August 1829 (II.173 and n.1). In short, the dates, whether I take them from the Pléiade edition or calculate them myself, are approximate. Difficulties with Balzac's chronology are well known. Here and elsewhere, when Balzac's characters are considered, Pugh's *Balzac's Recurring Characters* is essential and invaluable.

Index

UNIVERSITY OF TORONTO

ROMANCE SERIES